THE IMPORTANCE OF BEING BRANDED

An Irish Perspective

John Fanning

The Liffey Press

Published by
The Liffey Press
Ashbrook House, 10 Main Street
Raheny, Dublin 5, Ireland
www.theliffeypress.com

© 2006 John Fanning

A catalogue record of this book is
available from the British Library.

ISBNs: 1-904148-93-X (paperback)
1-905785-00-3 (hardback)

Printed in Ireland by Colour Books Ltd.

CONTENTS

PART ONE
THE HISTORY AND DEVELOPMENT OF BRANDING

PART TWO
HOW TO BUILD A STRONG BRAND

PART THREE
BRANDING IN IRELAND: FOUR CRITICAL ISSUES

PART FOUR
THE FUTURE OF BRANDING: WHAT NEXT?

ABOUT THE AUTHOR

John Fanning is Chairman of McConnells Advertising, Adjunct Professor of Marketing at Trinity College Dublin and a non-executive director of *The Irish Times*. For many years he was Managing Director of McConnells Advertising, Ireland's largest marketing communications business, where he was responsible for the planning and marketing communications of some of Ireland's leading brands. He has written numerous articles and papers for *Marketing*, the *Irish Marketing Review*, the European Market Research Society Annual Conference, and elsewhere.

ACKNOWLEDGEMENTS

The origins of this book stretch back at least over the 25 years since I first wrote a paper on branding for the Irish Marketing Society Annual Conference in 1980. Some of the chapters in it are based on themes which formed the basis of conference papers and articles since then and I would like to thank the organisers and editors concerned for encouraging me to make some theoretical sense of my day-to-day work.

Special thanks are due to Aidan O'Driscoll, long-term editor of the *Irish Marketing Review* who has published a number of my papers on branding and marketing communications in general. Editing such publications in small countries is a thankless task but they perform an invaluable role in allowing people to take the first tentative steps to airing their views in public and allow Irish voices to be heard against the cacophony of publications from bigger, more powerful countries.

Working with some of the most famous Irish and International brands in McConnells Advertising during that time forms the backdrop to most of what I have to say on the subject. I would like to thank these businesses for allowing me the privilege of working with their brands; and my colleagues in McConnells for all the debates, arguments and stimulating discussions as we agonised over brand positions and strategies. It would take another book to record all of these names but special thanks are due to Greg Jones, who was Deputy Managing Director for most of the time and who read all of the original papers and articles and in the process saved me the embarrassment of gross errors of judgement, taste and grammar, not to mention potential libel. Thanks are also due to three special people, Pat Forrester, Sandra Ronayne and Karen Meagan, who had to struggle with my impenetrable writing until I could safely be entrusted with a laptop.

The gap between the marketing communications business and the business academic world is disgracefully wide and I would like to acknowledge Professor Jim Quinn, who himself managed successfully to cross the divide, for encouraging me to narrow the gap. Paul Tansey's support at critical stages when my enthusiasm for the whole process was beginning to flag was also much appreciated.

I would like to thank David Givens, managing director of The Liffey Press, who was prepared to take a chance on a first book; and his thorough and professional editor, Brian Langan, whose incisive editorial interventions were critical in its preparation.

Final thanks to my wife Kaye, and children, David and Martha, for their forbearance in the face of more than usual contrariness over a long gestation period.

For Kaye

Introduction

Once upon a time in the mid-1970s I was the account executive on the Golden Vale account in McConnells Advertising. The agency had only acquired the account a few years earlier after a lengthy and very competitive pitch process. But within a few years the traditional honeymoon period where the client marketing team and the agency team are deeply in love with each other was well and truly over. The problems arose not on the packaged cheese brands, which had been the main focus of the pitch, but on Golden Maverick, a brand which competed in the milk replacer market and was sold exclusively to farmers. For a variety of technical reasons to do with the arcane world of the then Common Agricultural Policy of the then European Economic Community, the milk replacer market suddenly became very profitable. It was more advantageous for farmers to feed their calves milk replacer than fresh milk. It was a very competitive market which included all the leading co-ops, none of whom had yet succumbed to the blandishments of stockbrokers or investment bankers, and a number of pharmaceutical companies.

Conventional advertising wisdom at the time in this sector dictated that the secret of success in trying to communicate with Irish farmers, a notoriously difficult target market, was to convince them that the product was pure, easy to mix and utterly reliable. As a result, every brand vied with every other brand to present a scientific, rationally based campaign which inevitably meant that most of the ads in the category were fronted by actors dressed up as earnest scientist types wandering around a laboratory extolling the virtues of their brand. Golden Vale, not unreasonably, wanted something a little more imaginative but that was as far as the brief went. These were the days before the wonders of account planning had permeated the sleepy corridors of Irish advertising and although I was supposed to combine a planning role with my account executive duties — having been exposed a few years earlier in London to the exciting revolution then being fomented in Boase Massimi and Pollitt — I was not sufficiently experienced to delve into the mind of the Irish farmer.

After a number of failed presentations we were given to understand, in the most roundabout of ways, that we were on our last chance. As always on these occasions, panic gripped the agency. Although only five or six people were directly involved in the milk replacer side of the account, everyone was aware that there was a problem. Everyone you met had a "sorry for your trouble" look on their face as they muttered words of encouragement — "good luck next week".

Then we had the unexpected breakthrough. The art director on the account, Terry Pattison, was downtown one lunch time and wandered into a bookshop where he spotted a new lavishly illustrated series of books just published by Time-Life on the history of the Wild West. Because of the problem preoccupying his mind he turned to the first in the series, *The Cowboys*, and looked up the word "maverick" in the index. There it was on page 51:

> . . . in Texas there were two or three mavericks — unbranded calves — for every branded one. The word maverick itself carried a warning. It came from Sam Maverick, a cattleman on the San Antonio River who neglected his branding and discovered, only after a year of ranching on this rich, well-watered ground that he had been forced out

of business by avaricious neighbours and outright rustlers
who had made off with his unmarked stock.[1]

The art director immediately knew he was on to something and
within a few days we had a completely new campaign based on the
ever-potent theme of the Wild West. The launch commercial introduced the new theme and we had a whole range of point-of-sale
leaflets, farmer's promotions, trade incentives and advertising
support material. All the material featured the western theme and
a special symbol based, appropriately enough, on a branding iron.
We even prepared a special wrap-around cover for 200 copies of
the Time-Life book that featured the origin of the story for promotional gifts for key buyers. The printed cover featured a detailed
account of the thinking behind the campaign. Although the term
"Integrated Marketing Communications" was a few decades away
we had in effect created a completely integrated campaign including a range of non-traditional media; *plus ça change*!

Before the fateful trip to Charleville to present the campaign,
there was the inevitable hitch. The brand manager at Golden Vale
used to phone regularly, demanding details of our progress. When
I was finally able to tell him that we had a new approach in which
we had every confidence, he insisted that I give him an advance
outline of the campaign. Although a very inexperienced account
executive at the time, I had an instinctive feeling that it would not
be a good idea to attempt to present the concept over the phone.
But as anyone in this position will testify, might is always right and
I was given no choice but to divulge some of the thinking behind
the new concept. If I had any reservations beforehand, halfway
through the conversation I knew I was in deep trouble. "Is that all?
You're comparing us with a bunch of cowboys? You can't come
down with that!" was the sarcastic response from Charleville. He
threatened to cancel the meeting there and then but I was pretty
sure that, because there were so many people attending, he

---

[1] *The Cowboys*, Time-Life Books, 1973.

wouldn't have the power. In the event there was no further word from the client but it was a rattled and fairly apprehensive agency team that prepared for the fateful journey to Golden Vale.

A more senior account executive who was not involved in the account but had been keeping a watchful eye on the progress wished us well, saying as we departed that we'd have no trouble. "How can you be so sure?" I asked. "Sure, haven't you loads of stuff." "Is that how it works?" I asked, a little disillusioned. To be fair to her, she had a point. The client was overwhelmed with the amount of detail and the way we had worked the core theme into so many promotional areas. To some extent they correctly attributed that to our confidence in the power of the core concept and its ability to go the distance.

And go the distance it did. During the next fifteen years we made a whole series of commercials all based on a variation of the core Western theme. It was a theme that had endless possibilities and gave great scope to copywriters. Perhaps the most memorable was the second commercial, a shameless rip-off of the Sergio Leone spaghetti westerns, when we were at the height of our confidence. It featured the actor Ronan Wilmot, subsequently the long-running star of the Lucozade ads, playing Clint Eastwood. The voice-over can be quoted verbatim by a whole generation who grew up in the late 1970s and early 1980s:

> I hear tell this here's Maverick country, and if there's one thing that riles me more than a man kicking my mule it's an hombre who don't appreciate Golden Maverick; it's the best milk replacer money can buy — the brand you can really trust.

On the printed page this may seem a little bland to the jaded palates of twenty-first-century sophisticates; but to the 1970s account team in McConnells it was positively Shakespearean.

The campaign was a huge success. Maverick became the dominant brand leader in the milk replacer market, commanding a premium price over all other brands. Although the market is not as heavily competitive today, the brand is still advertised at regular intervals and the western theme is still going strong over a quarter of a century later.

Following the initial presentation in Charleville, the sceptical brand manager had grudgingly congratulated us, adding that we were bloody lucky that the marketing director was a big western fan. An obvious moral of the whole story is to research the film preferences of prospective client marketing directors but there are also some more serious lessons to be learned from this little case history. During the initial phase of basking in the success of the campaign we felt that we had cracked the ultimate marketing problem — after all, if you could persuade Irish farmers to pay a premium price for what is essentially a commodity product, the world was presumably your oyster. We did, however, carry out regular market research among farmers to assess their reactions to Maverick and its competitors and to investigate their reasons for buying the brand. In one of the discussions a farmer inadvertently came up with one of the most profound insights into the nature and process of branding: "I reckon that if Golden Vale are prepared to spend all that money on those fancy commercials on RTÉ then they couldn't afford to take any chances with the product; it must be top class stuff." This was a critical insight. At one very important level branding is a guarantee of quality. In typical Irish farmer fashion he had given a somewhat backhanded but nevertheless critical testament to the quality of Maverick. But the ads were also hugely popular with the target audience so the campaign added a layer of emotional warmth to a fairly mundane product and provided a powerful quality guarantee.

The campaign ensured that Maverick was well turned out, in fact better turned out than any other brand — and has a better story to tell. To some extent that remains the essence of branding.

* * *

It is now over thirty years since the start of the Maverick campaign and since then branding has moved from the marketing department to the boardroom, into the home and onto the streets. Even children below the age of ten are brand-conscious and exert their "pester power" to ensure they are fashionably attired.[2] This book will explain how the branding phenomenon has become so powerful and discuss where it might be heading in the immediate future. Using a variety of Irish case histories, it will show how important it is for Irish business to come to terms with the subject and how Irish brands can compete with the homogenising and colonising power of global brands.

---

[2] Friedman, V., "Kids Jump on the Brand Wagon", *Financial Times Weekend*, 18–19 February 2006.

PART ONE

THE HISTORY AND DEVELOPMENT OF BRANDING

"or maybe it's the name you buy and not the thing itself."
— Ciaran Carson, "The Irish for No"

"A good name is better than riches."
— Cervantes, *Don Quixote*

"Once reserved for cattle, sheep and criminals, branding in its contemporary sense is still about ownership but it has become a complex set of beliefs and images that represent the dialogue between the branded product and the essence of that product."
Wall Street Journal, 23 October 2000

Early Irish butter wrappers, including the first Kerrygold wrapper from 1962 (courtesy of the Cork Butter Museum).

1

BRANDS AND BRANDING:
AN OVERVIEW

What is a Brand?

The classic definition of a brand was made in one of the first academic papers on the subject published in 1955 by the *Harvard Business Review*:

> . . . a brand is more than a label employed to differentiate among the manufacturers of a product. It is a complex symbol that represents a variety of ideas and attributes. It tells the consumer many things, not only about the way it sounds (and its literal meaning if it has one) but more important via the body of associations it has built up and acquired as a public object over a period of time. The net result is a public image, a character or personality that may be more important for the overall status (and sales) of the brand than many technical facts about the product.[1]

This definition introduced the idea that a brand represents more than just the physical attributes of the product in question. Some commentators took the idea of the brand as a personality a stage further and suggested by way of explanation that people choose their brands in the same way as they choose their friends:

---

[1] Gardner B.V. and Levy S.J., "The Product and the Brand", *Harvard Business Review*, March/April 1955.

People do not usually choose their friends solely because of specific skills or physical attributes, although such things can be very important. They usually choose them because in addition to the skills and physical characteristics (or maybe in spite of them) they simply like them as people. It is the total person that is chosen as a friend, not a compendium of vices and virtues. The choice and use of brands is just the same.[2]

We Buy With Our Hearts As Well As Our Heads

The essence of branding is the recognition that all purchases involve a combination of rational and emotional considerations, and that when purchasing, consumers judge not only the functional or physical characteristics of a product or service but also its emotional characteristics. In other words, people make decisions with their hearts as well as their heads. When Stephen King first wrote about brands over thirty years ago this was a difficult concept for many people to grasp. Most models of consumer behaviour assumed that the consumer acted rationally at all times and always sought to maximise the economic value of any transaction. Now that advances in neuroscience have taught us more about how we make decisions we know that thoughts are never separate from emotions and emotions are never separate from thoughts:

> . . . emotions constitute an integral part of even the most rational decision-making — whenever thinking conflicts with emotions, emotions win.[3]

---

[2] King, S., *Developing New Brands,* Pitman, 1973.

[3] Franzen, G. and Bouwman, M., "The Mental World of Brands", WARC (World Advertising Research Centre) (UK), 2001.

Branding Applies to Everything

In a much-quoted comment on branding in the 1960s, Professor Ted Levitt argued that the principles of branding apply equally to all goods and services and not just to consumer goods:

> Whether the product is cold rolled steel or hot cross buns, whether accountancy or delicacies, competitive effectiveness increasingly demands that the successful seller offer his prospect and his consumer more than the generic product itself. He must surround his generic product with a cluster of value satisfactions that differentiate his total offering from his competitors. He must provide a total proposition the content of which exceeds what comes out at the end of the assembly line.[4]

Apart from pointing out the need for all products and services to be viewed from a branding perspective, this definition is useful because it focuses attention on a critical aspect of branding: the need to differentiate from competitors. This imperative has become even more important today when technical or physical differences between most brands in most markets are minimal.

In recent years the concept has been applied to just about everything that moves:

> . . . soon branding was being applied to not only products but to the companies that supplied them too, then it became apparent that just about everything that competes for attention such as political parties, football clubs, charities, museums and universities can be regarded as brands. Eventually people started to think of themselves and each other as brands.[5]

---

[4] Levitt, T., "Marketing Success through Differentiation: Of Anything", *Harvard Business Review,* January/February 1980.

[5] Tomkins, R., *Financial Times,* 8 September 2003.

The Brand Manager is Never in Total Control

Brands are often described as being created in the minds of consumers and therefore owned by consumers rather than by the businesses that technically control them. This is a difficult concept to grasp but it contains an important insight about brands: that because they are bundles of ideas, associations, images and impressions in consumers' minds, we can never be in complete control of how consumers actually pick up this information.

> We build an image as birds build nests — from scraps and straws we chance upon, and we imbue everything about that brand, however trivial, with meaning and significance. We infer all the time — we try to make consistent sense of things because minds dislike inconsistency and dissonance. People build brands in their heads whether or not the owners of that brand intend them to.[6]

The increasing use of the internet has added to the lack of control businesses are able to assert over their brands. Some brands, such as Shell, have been forced to make radical changes in their operations and their brand communications because of the actions of consumer activists communicating through the internet. More advances from the emerging world of neuroscience point to the reality of brands today:

> The history of the brand is hard-wired to the brain. We need to resist the efforts of brand managers to change the world of the brand without understanding how the world was built and which parts are essential to retain.[7]

---

[6] Bullmore, J., *Behind the Scenes in Advertising*, NTC Publications, 1991.

[7] Gordon, W., "Brands on the Brain: New Scientific Discoveries to Support New Brand Thinking", chapter in *Brand New Brand Thinking*, Baskin, M. and Earls, M. (eds.), Kogan Page, 2002.

Brands are Profitable

Most people are prepared to pay a premium price for well-managed brands and they are prepared to buy again and again over time: "brands are machines for delivering quality earnings at high margins".[8] It was statements like this that started to prompt the more widespread business interest in brands that we have seen over the last few decades. There have been a number of studies analysing the profitability and share price performance of companies in the same market sectors where the company with the better-known and better-managed brands significantly outperform their competitors, and this has had a huge impact on the growth of interest in the subject.

Although there is always the suspicion that a company with well-managed brands will be better managed in every aspect of its operations, the fact remains that branding is now well and truly on the radar of business leaders. When C&C were seeking a public placing in 2002, the literature sent out to potential investors featured a headline which proclaimed the company as "The Brand-masters". That concept would have been incomprehensible to financial opinion leaders a few years earlier:

> You won't find it in the balance sheet; it's not listed in a 10k or in a proxy. If you ask the wizards of Wall St exactly how it figures into a company's network be prepared for some mighty blank stares — but more and more companies are now beginning to realise that when managed correctly a good name can be their most valuable asset.[9]

Brands Exist Whether They are Consciously Managed or Not

When brands are not consciously managed they can be "unconsciously" managed well or badly. The latter usually fail. A good ex-

---

[8] Broadbent, T., *Advertising Works, Vol. 11*, IPA (London), 2000.
[9] *Fortune,* 10 February 1992.

ample of the former is the Irish poetry publisher Gallery Press. Within its admittedly small target market — buyers of new Irish poetry — Gallery's image is superb and they have succeeded in achieving the two main goals of all well-managed brands: a premium price and repeat purchases. Their only form of marketing communications, apart from their website and a small mailing list of regular purchasers, is the design of their covers, which usually feature an illustration of a painting from a contemporary Irish artist, and an introductory reading event for an invited audience. They publish around a dozenbooks a year, mostly at a premium price (approximately €20 for a slim volume of around eighty pages). Each book is beautifully produced in terms of design, quality of paper and typeface, and although distinctive in their own way there is a common design theme. There is a sense of good taste and attention to detail. A Gallery book is instantly recognisable to its target group as a Gallery book. As a result, the average poetry buyer, who in the normal course of events might buy two or three, is tempted to buy five or six different titles, because of the stylish branding and the quality guarantee that the Gallery name imparts.

There is another important lesson here about branding: poetry buyers will assume that a poet they have never read, or perhaps never heard of, could be worth reading simply because they have been published by Gallery. After all, if the publisher pays such meticulous attention to detail in terms of design, materials and printing, one can assume that the same standards would apply to the choice of poets to be published. This represents the power of the brand.

Brands are Becoming More Ubiquitous

Although the concept of branding can now be used in any walk of life, the increasing dominance of global clothing brands in the late twentieth century (for example, Armani, Versace, Manolo

Blahnik) was largely responsible for the introduction of the term into everyday discourse:

> Branded goods represent the hope of transforming us and our lives from something drab and ordinary into something exciting and extraordinary. Moreover they represent the power to transport us to a wonderful world of fantasy in which our lives are joyful, satisfying and fun — our primary source of hope has shifted from religion to art and science and finally to consumption.[10]

Quotations along these lines are now a regular feature of the literature of branding, and at times it can appear that some commentators are losing the run of themselves:

> Brands in this world are the new antidotes, taking over as role models from discredited institutions like governments, parents or doctors. Post-modern brand authority is fluid, flexible and instantly changeable and speaks only on the level of the individual's desires. The brand does not talk about the world beyond its relationship with you; indeed it lets you take on all the responsibility for your choices.[11]

Some of these comments are a little over the top but they convey the ubiquity of the subject and the way it has infiltrated the everyday world. A very small minority of brands do attract cult-like status — Harley-Davidson, Apple and BMW are examples — but the majority of brands are not accorded undue deference and the majority of consumers have a more balanced attitude to life. However, brands are being consciously used by more people to define their place in the world and there is some truth in the following quote:

---

[10] Belk, R., "On Aura, Illusion, Escape and Hope in Apocalyptic Consumption", chapter in *Marketing Apocalypse,* Brown, S., Bell, J. and Carson, D. (eds.), Routledge, 1996.

[11] Castell, S., *Market Research Society,* December 2002.

> . . . solving the consumers' problems of being and express-
> ing values may come to be the marketing opportunity of the
> 21st century.[12]

Good Branding is All About Being Well Turned Out and Having a Good Story

It could be argued that generations of Irish Mammies have been exemplary brand managers, training and guiding successive waves of little boys and girls into the world who were well turned out and able to give a good account of themselves. Theory sometimes lags well behind good practice in branding and it has taken a long time for the academy to catch up with Irish Mammies, but the link between good branding and storytelling is now the height of academic fashion. From the beginning of time human beings have created stories, myths and legends. Stories are part of what we are and represent a critical element in what it means to be human:

> As human beings stories have always formed a crucial part of our ongoing evolution. And in a Western market economy that is increasingly driven by our emotions and our pursuit of "the good life" our need for them seems to get stronger and stronger — we navigate our world using symbols and visual expressions that signal our personality and our values, and strong brands are one of the means by which we do this.[13]

Strong brands are all characterised by well-defined stories and the more recently established successful brands were created by entrepreneurs who are highly conscious of the power of storytelling. One of the most successful Irish brands of the last decade has been Ryanair, a brand based on the universally familiar story of David

---

[12] Marsden, P., "Marketing Values: Rising to the No Logo Challenge", *Admap,* January 2002.

[13] Jensen, R., *The Dream Society*, McGraw-Hill, 1999.

and Goliath. One of the most successful recent product launches in the UK is Innocent, whose smoothie brand captured 20 per cent of the market within five years and who continually tell witty stories on their packs. Finally, Starbuck's Scott Bedbury, speaking of one of the most successful new American brands, re-iterated the importance of storytelling:

> A brand is a metaphorical story that's evolving all the time. This connects with something very deep — a fundamental human appreciation of mythology.[14]

All societies try to resolve contradictions through stories and myths and sometimes these are described and written about in great art, but as Patrick Kavanagh wisely pointed out in his poem "Epic"[15] when contemplating how on earth he could make art out of local clashes between the Duffys and Maguires over a field:

> I inclined
> to lose my faith in Ballyrush and Gortin
> Till Homer's ghost came whispering to my mind
> He said I made the Iliad from such
> A local row. Gods make their own importance.

The long running "row" between Persil and Aerial begins to take on a whole new significance when viewed from this perspective.

Brands Resist Simple Formulas and Precise Measurement

As long as brands remained the preserve of marketing departments and marketing communications the issue of measurement was treated in a fairly cavalier fashion. People who work in these areas were never renowned for their mathematical precision. But once branding became a mainstream management topic the need for more discipline became apparent. Accountancy firms were suspi-

---

[14] Jensen, Ibid.
[15] Kavanagh, P., *Come Dance with Kitty Strobling*, Longmans, 1960.

cious from the beginning and tried to ignore it but management consultancies, sensing a new business opportunity, devised all kinds of cunning measurement plans which in spite of a certain elegance when explained in PowerPoint presentations failed to make an impact in the real world. Global market research companies were more successful and had better relationships with marketing departments and some of their measures are widely used, but although they satisfy the deep-rooted need for legitimacy in numbers there are doubts as to how legitimate the numbers really are:

> We should abandon the search for the Single Criterion — the feeling that quantification is the ultimate source of unerring accuracy and oracular wisdom and that the evaluation process is "nothing but" the one or two figures that result.[16]

Brands Must be Vigilant — Because Consumers Are

Although consumers are buying more high-profile brands than ever before, and are consciously using them to make statements about themselves, they are also more "marketing communications literate" than ever before and will penalise brands that attempt to pull the wool over their eyes or that fail to live up to their promises.

The more that brands adopt positioning statements that seek to transcend the confines of their own market and claim universal attributes, the more likely it is they will be brought down to earth if any of their actions appear to transgress their lofty ambitions. For example, Nike have been forced to fight a rearguard action in recent years following revelations about conditions in factories in developing countries where their goods are outsourced

But even if the company behind the brand has an impeccable record in its dealings with employees, the local community, the environment and society at large, it must still guard against exag-

---

[16] Tesgal, A., "The Science of Brands: Alchemy, Advertising and Accounting", Market Research Society Conference Papers (UK) 2003.

gerated and grandiose claims. There is now a real danger that brands are being tempted to a level of hyperbole in their marketing communications that the public find either laughable or incomprehensible, and that we are now in danger of creating flatulent brands — all hot air — or Malteser brands — sweet and sugary on the outside but mostly hot air in the middle.[17] It may be time for a little humility:

> Brand humility is about having the confidence to regulate one's brand to a sort of "second place" — recognising that what our brands do is simply play their role, make things work or taste nice. Ultimately brand humility is recognition of the fact that we will be judged (by consumers) by what our brands actually deliver, not by what they proclaim.[18]

Brands will continue to fulfil a role for most people but in an increasingly interconnected world overblown claims will rapidly come back to haunt brand managers who must never allow themselves to worry about "being googled":

> Communities are the counter balance to brand dominance in this century — by examining what word-of-mouth, when enhanced by the powerful digital echoes of mobile phone communities and other network communications can do we see that communities have been an undefined or underestimated barrier to recent marketing successes.[19]

---

[17] Mitchell, A., "The Emperor's New Clothes", *Market Leader,* Issue 15, 2001.

[18] Lidstone, R., "The Need for Brand Humility", Market Research Society Conference, 2005.

[19] Ahonen, T.T. and Moore, A., "Communities Dominate Brands: Business and Marketing Challenges for the 21st Century" *Futuretext* (UK) 2005.

2

WHY BRANDS?

When we live with something for a very long time we have a tendency to assume that it has always been around. So it is with brands, at least to some extent. Brands in some shape or form have been around forever but it is only in the twentieth century that we began to refer to them as such, and it is only since the late 1980s that branding has become a critical issue in business. Prior to that, branding was regarded as being the preserve of marketing departments in fast-moving consumer goods companies, typified by two giant businesses, Procter & Gamble and Unilever. Their 100 years' war in the detergent market defined branding for many people. But in the late 1980s a number of high-profile takeovers catapulted branding to the top of the wider business agenda. It was a time characterised by tooth-and-claw capitalism, an era of corporate raiders and asset stripping, with Margaret Thatcher belligerently dominant in the UK and Ronald Reagan pursuing an equally single-minded agenda in the US. It was a time immortalised in the film *Wall Street* by the line "Greed is Good".

One of the most swashbuckling corporate raiders was the Hanson Trust run by the eponymous Lord Hanson. In 1986, it took over the Imperial Tobacco Group, a long-time pillar of the British business establishment that had more latterly become a little less confident as the anti-smoking movement gathered strength. In what was to become a pattern in takeovers of this type, the victor was judged by financial analysts to have paid over the odds but

was significantly vindicated by the massive earnings generated by the brands it had bought. Two years later another corporate raider, Goodman Fielder Wattie, made an opportunistic bid for Rank Hovis McDougal, a company that owned a range of well-known bakery brands whose asset value was effectively ignored in its balance sheet. If the attempted takeover of RHM in 1988 alerted the financial community to the value of brands, it was the takeover of the venerable British confectionery manufacturer Rowntree Mackintosh by Nestlé in the same year that caught the public imagination.

The impetus for all of these bids was not so much the traditional reasoning behind hostile takeovers, where a dynamic, determined group of managers feel that they could manage the assets of another company much better than the existing management; rather, the raiders had spotted an accounting anomaly whereby the value of their brands was not included in the balance sheets of these companies. There were long-established accountancy reasons for this (the subject of brand valuation will be examined later), but the fact that the real value of brands was rarely represented in the share price of consumer goods companies meant that the share price was undervalued, often by a significant extent, and this enabled the raider to offer a price that was substantially greater than the quoted share price.

The accountancy practice row over valuation rumbled on – and to some extent is still rumbling on to this day — but the potential earning power of brands was left in no doubt. After the Rowntree takeover the entire business world began to re-examine its assets in a new branded light, and the concept of brands dominated not only the boardrooms but every other room as well.

During the 1980s businesses also realised that branding was not only relevant to fast-moving consumer goods companies; business-to-business markets were also affected by the branding issue. The famous catchphrase "No one was ever fired for recommending IBM" was suddenly viewed in a new light. It referred to the fact that

IBM was the biggest operator in the market, and although that was undoubtedly a factor involved in any purchasing decision, it was now recognised that it was also testament to the enormous power of the IBM brand. Suddenly companies began to consider themselves as brands. Retailers had no difficulty adopting this concept, which coincided with the expansion of their own brand offerings

Banks, however, remained one of the last bastions of traditional practice and had resisted (and in some cases are still resisting) the concept of marketing for longer than most. For a long time they turned up their noses at the idea of being thought of as brands. However, even they finally began to see the light and the 1990s saw the launch of some highly ambitious branding campaigns by the leading clearing banks around the world.

> At some point in the 20th century brands became all pervasive, the maintenance of brand image and value became the driving force for producers and brand owners and even global brand names began to dominate local markets.[1]

By the end of the 1990s even places, politicians and religious orders were joining the brandwagon. The very idea of countries being referred to as brands was anathema to many, but consideration of Ireland as a brand had been the starting point for the highly successful *Young Europeans* campaign for the IDA in the 1980s. By the 1990s a number of countries and regions began to carry out formal market research in order to establish their brand image with a view to managing that image more systematically. (The Irish brand image will be discussed in more depth in Chapter 11.) It therefore was no surprise when the city of Manchester appointed a brand manager, who argued:

---

[1] Pavitt, J., "In Goods We Trust", chapter in *Brand New*, ed. Pavitt J., V&A Publications, 2000.

In a world of modern communications where people can live and work almost anywhere a city needs to develop its brand image to reflect its culture and vibe.[2]

Politicians, always attracted to anything that would make them more electable, were eager to climb aboard and they too began to research their brand image, thus annoying the press who felt that their traditional right to be the sole interpreters of the public pulse and political popularity was being usurped by brand consultants and market research. In the process they managed some initial revenge by trying to discredit the ubiquitous "focus groups".

Eventually, in America (inevitably) the concept of branding was applied to individual people, who were advised that they themselves could be regarded and therefore managed as brands and so another series of ephemeral, badly written personal self-help books began to litter the bookshops:

In today's world you're distinct — or extinct, I win, thrive, triumph by becoming — Brand You! The fundamental unit in today's economy is the individual, a.k.a. You! Jobs are performed by temporary networks that disband when the project is done. So to succeed you have to think of yourself as a freelance contractor, Brand You![3]

The revolution was now complete. Branding had conquered the world. However, in spite of the millions of column inches, countless academic papers and bucket loads of books, the concept remained elusive and it was obvious that many people who spoke confidently about the subject were not always sure what they were talking about. Those who considered it carefully found it more difficult to clarify and define than it appeared on the surface. In or-

---

[2] *Financial Times,* 5 October 2004.

[3] Peters, T., "The Brand Called You", *Fast Company*, issue 10, August/September, 1997.

der to come to a better understanding of brands and branding it is necessary to consider the origins of the concept.

The Origins of Brands and Branding

From the beginning of time people have mentally formed bundles of impressions, associations and images of other people, places and, inevitably, goods of all kinds. In today's commercial language these "bundles" would be referred to as "brand images". The first direct mentions of branding occur in the nineteenth century when commercially traded packaged goods were introduced, but conscious attempts to create favourable impressions and to be aware of the importance of one's reputation in securing future business date from much earlier, at least since the Middle Ages.

Somewhere between the ninth and twelfth centuries in Damascus, the splendidly named Ja'far b. Ali ad-Dimishqi wrote a book with the not-so-splendid title *Book of Knowledge and the Beauties of Commerce and Cognisance of Good and Bad Merchandise and of Falsification*.[4] It was presumably one of the first written warnings of *caveat emptor* and implied that there were trusted and not-so-trusted brands at this time. By 1266, bakers were required by English law to put their mark on every loaf of bread, "To the end that any bread be faultie it might bee then knowne in whom the fault is".[5] Craft guilds in continental Europe in the Middle Ages required their members to put a special identifiable mark on their produce. In fact, the word "brand" derives from the old Norse word *brunin* — to burn. This ties in with the practice of identifying cattle in the American West by literally burning a symbol with a branding iron.

In the Middle Ages most of the goods that people bought were from local manufacturers — the butcher, the baker, the candlestick

---

4 Zeldin, T., *An Intimate History of Humanity*, Vintage, 1998.

5 Baker, S. and Mouncy, P., "The Market Researcher's Manifesto", *International Journal of Market Research*, Vol. 45, Issue 1, 2003.

maker — who would all have been personally known to the purchaser. They would therefore be able to judge the character and quality of the goods by what they knew about the people who made them.

Everything came down to identification, trust and integrity. The great Italian merchant families of the fifteenth century — the Buonsignori of Siena, Ricciardi of Lucca and the Frescobaldi of Florence — were acutely conscious of the need for protecting their reputations if their businesses were to thrive.[6] Brands therefore first and foremost have always represented a guarantee of quality. Trust, reputation and integrity were always important attributes and from the beginning people who made goods of all kinds and who took a pride in the quality of their products went to considerable lengths to safeguard their reputation and their good name in order to protect the future of their business.

The guarantee of quality has become even more important in modern times. The modern history of branding began in the second half of the nineteenth century when developments in transportation, especially the growth of the railways in Britain and the US, enabled the distribution of consumer goods from the new manufacturing plants to a mass audience for the first time. Goods had always been traded, mainly by sea but in much smaller quantities than we now take for granted. The early civilisations of Egypt and Mesopotamia grew out of the trade routes along the Nile, the Tigris and the Euphrates rivers. But rail revolutionised trade, so much so that an extraordinary number of household brand names date from the mid- to late nineteenth century. Joseph Campbell began making his condensed soup in 1860; Henry Heinz started his ketchup company in 1871; and William Colgate founded his toothpaste company in 1873. William Wrigley started making soap in 1891 and gave away free chewing gum with every bar, only to

---

[6] Anholt, S., *Brand New Justice: The Upside of Global Branding*, Butterworth Heinemann, 2003.

discover that the free offer was more popular than the soap, so he quickly changed business. The most famous brand of all, Coca Cola, was founded in 1892; the magnificently named King Camp Gillette started making safety razors in 1901; and William Kellogg set up his Battle Creek Toasted Cornflake Company in 1906.

In Ireland, where brewing and distilling were one of the few large-scale manufacturing industries, many of the famous brand names that are still thriving today date back to the eighteenth century or earlier: Smithwick's in 1710, Guinness in 1759, Jameson in 1780, Power's in 1791 and of course not forgetting the oldest distillery in the world, Bushmills, which was founded in 1608.

A critical characteristic of the early manufacturing pioneers was a fierce pride in their products and an obsession with quality. They were acutely aware of the fact that, unlike their manufacturing predecessors who could only distribute locally and were therefore known to most of their customers, they knew very few of their customers personally and were extremely anxious to tell them about their products and reassure them about their quality. Luckily, another new technological revolution was on the way — mass circulation newspapers — which were all too eager to facilitate the manufacturers in communicating with their customers.

Prior to the launch of mass manufacturer-branded goods, people bought commodity goods from their local retailer and it was the retailer's name that effectively represented the brand. It was the retailer's reputation for quality and innovation that determined whether and what people bought. An early twentieth-century advertisement for a Dublin retailer, Humphreys of Ranelagh, who are still operating as a licensed premises, shows a range of different teas, all sold under the retailer's name, which makes the modern multiples' own-label strategies seem a little less revolutionary (see illustration below).

Ironically in the late nineteenth century a Northern English retailer, Ronan Knox, who was dissatisfied with the quality of the goods on offer from his suppliers wrote to the *Lancashire Grocer* announcing his intention to begin manufacturing for himself: "The products of so many manufacturers are so low or varying for our shops so we are obliged to make our own brands." The retailer was William Lever, he began manufacturing in Port Sunlight, and the rest is history.

Quality Guarantee: The First *Raison d'Être* of Branding

The more people moved to urban societies and lost track or contact with the people who made the goods they bought, the more they needed some kind of quality guarantee. Branded goods fulfilled that role.

Brands that satisfied consumers came to be trusted and valued not only for their quality but for their consistency; they were perceived to be completely reliable. They were also well presented and packaged and although people have been warned from time immemorial not to judge the book by the cover, there is more logic to this practice than is commonly assumed (as the Irish farmers quoted in the introduction were quick to comprehend). Today the assumption is more likely to be that someone who goes to great lengths in terms of the design and appearance of the cover would also go to the same lengths to ensure the quality of the book inside. There will of course be exceptions but they are the ones that prove the rule.

Therefore, the first and still the most important reason why people buy brands is because they're well known and well presented through design, advertising or other forms of marketing communication. Well-packaged brands are invariably a guarantee of quality and as a result in most markets people are prepared to pay a premium price for the quality and reassurance.

Convenience: The Second *Raison d'Être* of Branding

The second reason for the power of branding is convenience. It has been calculated that the average English home at the end of the nineteenth century contained approximately 500 goods. The equivalent figure today would be in the region of 3,500. A typical Tesco store now stocks 30,000 items. It is obvious that no one in their right mind could possibly evaluate the characteristics of all of the different items on display in today's retail outlets before making a purchase. The cornucopia of choice is so enormous that in some coffee shops in Dublin nowadays you could be presented with a choice of seven different types of coffee, five different toppings, four different milks, four different types of sugar, three different cup sizes, three different strengths and up to eight different syrups. Mathematically that means around 6,000 different combinations, which means it would take sixteen years, at a rate of one a day, to exhaust every different one.

Clearly, in order to survive in the modern world with some vestige of sanity intact we need shortcuts in making choices, and branding provides just such a shortcut. In most product categories that we choose from we therefore tend to have a small repertoire of tried and trusted brands which go a long way to making shopping and daily life tolerable. Familiar brands help us to cope with the clutter and chaotic range of choice that face the modern consumer.

Social Cachet: The Third *Raison d'Être* of Branding

The first two reasons that explain the importance of branding in choosing goods and services — quality and convenience — are internal. They are mechanisms that help people to navigate their way in today's complex urban society. The third reason — social cachet — is external. It takes into the account the fact that people are now more conscious of the power of the goods and services they buy in making statements about themselves, even to the extent of defining their personalities to the outside world:

> Brands simplify our lives — the most complex role of brands is the symbolic one — they are often used as a signal or measure of personality. You might assess others on first meeting, by the car they drive or the clothes they wore; we do the same interpretive job on our own sense of self. We go through life trying to find answers to existential questions — what does it mean to be young, what does it mean to be a mother, to be respected, to be professional. Increasingly we use brands to answer these questions. When we consume a product or service we do not just consume it on a physical

level; we also consume it on a symbolic level. Outwardly to communicate to others the kind of person we are, inwardly to bolster our sense of self.[7]

Like the other two reasons why people are prepared to pay over the odds for well-managed brands, the importance of social cachet has grown as societies have become more urban, complex and fragmented. When everyone lived together in small rural communities, society was more stratified and people's lives were mainly determined by the families they were born into. Everyone knew everyone else and they also knew their family histories and their status in the community. In the latter part of the twentieth century the pattern changed; more people were free to adopt whatever persona they wanted and even to change persona if they so wished. There was an inevitable sense of liberation but as always there was a price to be paid as people were overwhelmed with a bewildering range of options.

Brands act as enablers by making it easier for people to construct whatever identity they wish to adopt at any given time. It is sometimes assumed that this role only applies to consumer durables and more expensive goods, but it has also been argued that it is equally relevant to everyday brands in everyday categories, the kind that get tucked away inside cupboards, in bathrooms and kitchens and garages. The point is that there is more to the link between brands and personal identity than badge values. It's not just a question of "What does this brand say about me to others?" Just as important is "What does this brand say about me to me?"[8]

---

[7] Barwise, P., Dunham, A. and Ritson, M., "Ties That Bind Brands, Consumers and Businesses", chapter in *Brand New*, ed. Pavitt, J., V&A Publications, 2000.

[8] Edwards, H. and Day, D., *Creating Passion Brands*, Kogan Page, 2005.

3

THE THREE AGES OF BRANDING

Thinking in threes seems to be a universal practice, as at least one marketing commentator has noted:

> . . . regardless of the extent of one's agreement or disagreement with commentators who consider thinking in threes to be imbued with deep symbolic-cum-cabbalistic power — and doubtless bad luck, which also runs in threes, attaches itself to anyone who scoffs at such mysticism — it is undeniable that trinitarianism is widespread in the theory and practice of marketing.[1]

Not wanting to be left out of the trinitarian movement, I've arbitrarily divided the last 120 years into three stages of developments in branding. There is considerable overlapping in that some brands have always practised what I will refer to as "third age" branding and there are many successful brands today that are prime examples of "first age" branding. The division into three ages, however arbitrary, does allow us to consider how branding has evolved.

---

[1] Brown, S., "Trinitarianism, The Eternal Evangel and The Three Eras Schema", chapter in *Marketing Apocalypse*, Brown, S., Bell, J. and Carson, D., Routledge, London, 1996.

The First Age of Branding: The Functional Age

The first age dates from the 1880s to somewhere in the 1960s. It could be described as the Functional Age where, to use the discourse of the detergent market, the dominant message was:

"My brand washes whiter"

Mass consumer goods began to be available all over the developed world for the first time at the beginning of the twentieth century. Although a wide range of products became available, most of these goods had one thing in common: they represented considerable time saving for the housewives they were primarily aimed at. Ready-to-eat cereals were less time-consuming to serve to the family than porridge; tinned soup was less time-consuming than having to prepare and cook all the ingredients; and, for men, safety razors were not only safer than the traditional alternative, they were also faster. Because the products were new, and freed housewives in particular from much of the drudgery of the past, people were interested in the details of how they performed their functions, so there was genuine interest in reading advertisements, which contained an inordinate amount of information by today's standards. Newspapers were the dominant medium in the first half of the twentieth century and were ideal for communicating product details.

The so-called nuclear family was a relatively new phenomenon, with husband, wife and children living in their own house. Before this time, extended families living in overcrowded conditions in rural communities was the norm. Housewifely skills were much commented on in the new social conditions of the early twentieth century. Feeding their families nutritious meals was important, but cleanliness was widely considered to be "next to godliness". Many of the new consumer goods had to perform the delicate balancing act of suggesting that they would eliminate drudgery without in any way impinging on the role of the hard-working housewife.

A famous case history from the early days of motivational research will put this in context. Motivational research, now referred to as qualitative research, or "qual" to the verbally challenged, entered the marketing arena in the late 1940s. The leading practitioners all had middle-European sounding names, claimed an Austrian connection and sported a "Dr" prefix. They were heavily immersed in Freudian psychology and many of their conclusions had unlikely sexual overtones. In this particular example of their work in the US market, matching groups of housewives were shown two shopping lists. The lists were identical except that one included coffee beans and the other instant coffee, an innovation recently introduced into the market. Both groups of respondents were asked to describe the type of housewife who would have such a shopping list. The first was described in exemplary terms, a pillar of society, a credit to her family and an all-round "good egg". The second was regarded as a slut.

The heyday of the First Age was in the 1950s in the US when TV became a reality in nearly all households. Its most famous practitioner was the legendry Madison Avenue chairman of the Ted Bates agency, Rosser Reeves. He coined the term "Unique Selling Proposition" to represent the agency's philosophy. There are three rules for a USP: "First you need a definite proposition: buy this product and you get this specific benefit. Then, second, it must be a unique proposition, one which the opposition *cannot* or *does not* offer. Third, the proposition must sell."

However, as often happens when a particular view seems all-pervasive, the seeds of destruction began to emerge. A new kid on the Madison Avenue block believed that bombarding people until they submitted to the power of the USP would ultimately be self-defeating as audiences became better educated and more experienced in dealing with commercial messages. Bill Bernbach introduced more visually sophisticated advertising with stylish, witty, finely crafted copy. His "Think Small" ad for Volkswagen was to become one of the most admired advertisements of all time and

Bernbach himself is the most revered creative director in advertising. Characteristically, Rosser wasn't all that impressed and was reputed to have remarked, "Do you want fancy pictures, fine words, or do you want the goddamn sales to rise?"[2]

The first age of branding lasted until mid-century when markets were becoming more competitive and the initial gloss of the new consumer goods was beginning to wear off.

The Second Age of Branding: The Emotional Age

Following the Second World War there was a profound sociological change in Western society as women began to enter the workforce in large numbers. During the war, women had been drafted into areas of the workforce that had hitherto been the exclusive preserve of men. When they proved equally capable, there was no reason for the situation not to continue in peace time. This coincided with the first stirrings of what came to be known as the "Women's Liberation Movement" and the combined effects had a profound impact on the purchasing of mass consumer goods. Sociological change usually does have this effect but businesses are notoriously reluctant to study the wider aspects of social change going on around them, in spite of the fact that the most successful businesses are those that consciously or unconsciously respond best to those changes. The changes that took place ushered in the second age of branding sometime during the 1950s. The obsession with functional benefits and pseudo-scientific explanations for minor technical improvements gave way to softer, less frenetic, more entertaining brand communication. The dominant economist of the era, J.K. Galbraith, mercilessly poked fun at the typical advertisements of the First Age:

> Even minor features of unimportant commodities are
> enlarged upon with a solemnity which would not be

---

[2] Martin Mayer, *Madison Avenue*, The Bodley Head, 1958.

unbecoming in an announcement of the combined return of Christ and all of the apostles — more important services such as the importance of whiter laundry are treated with proportionately greater gravity.[3]

But we had now arrived at the Emotional Age and the new medium of television was the ideal transmitter of marketing communications designed to provide brands with more rounded personalities. Maintaining the detergent analogy, the second age could be summarised as follows:

"My brand washes whiter than theirs and leaves you with a nice warm feeling"

It was the beginning of the golden age of the TV commercial, and of the advertising agencies who embraced the new medium with enthusiasm and creativity. Some time later, in the 1960s, the new age of branding was rationalised and put into context by a few of the leading thinkers from advertising agencies. In the area of branding, theory tends to lag behind practice and until recently theory tended to emanate from practitioners rather than from "the academy". The foremost of the agency commentators was Stephen King, a director of the London office of one of the US-owned global agency networks, J. Walter Thompson, now part of the UK-based WPP Holding Group. In a series of articles and books, King identified the main characteristics of the emotional age of branding:

> A product is something that is made in a factory; a brand is something that is bought by a consumer. A product can be copied by a competitor; a brand is unique. A product will be quickly outdated; a successful brand is timeless. People do not choose their friends because of specific skills and physical attributes, although such things can be very important, they usually choose them because in addition to the skills and physical characteristics – or maybe in spite of

---

[3] Galbraith, J.K., *The New Industrial Estate*, Hamish Hamilton, 1967.

them – they simply like them as people. It is the total person that is chosen as a friend, not a compendium of virtues and vices; the choice and use of brands is just the same.[4]

The JWT agency was the biggest in the London market at the time and they created many classic emotionally based campaigns for brands they made famous: Andrex, with the iconic puppy signifying strength and reliability; Kellogg's Rice Krispies featuring Snap, Crackle and Pop; and Kit-Kat with its long-running "Have a Break" vignettes. It is a testimony to the power of emotional branding and the creativity of these campaigns that all three brands are not only still brand leaders in their respective categories but are essentially running the same campaigns.

The new television medium was ideal for a more soft-focus message where viewers were relaxed into a closer relationship with the advertised brand through pleasant visual imagery and music rather than being beaten into submission with rational arguments. Instead of rational or functional arguments, brand managers sought to develop their brands' emotional potential in an attempt to create a more rounded personality. Not everyone at board level was convinced of the need for soft-focus messages, so managers were forced into making a case for this type of marketing communication. It is hardly a coincidence, therefore, that the theory of branding dates from this period.

A classic example of emotional branding in Ireland was the late 1960s' television campaign for Carroll's No 1, the leading cigarette brand in what was at the time one of the most fiercely contested of all consumer markets. Until then, Carroll's had concentrated their marketing communications on persuading the smoking public that their tipped cigarettes delivered the same satisfaction as the plain cigarettes that had dominated the market in the first half of the century. Their advertisements were dominated by stories about how carefully chosen the tobacco was at tobacco auctions and

---

4 King, S., *Developing New Brands*, Pitman, London, 1973.

ended with the copyline, "Plain smokers like you prefer the taste of Carroll's No 1". The new campaign didn't show any tobacco but used beautifully photographed tourist-type images of rural and scenic Ireland featuring plenty of running water from idyllically positioned brooks and mountain streams. Healthy-looking smokers dotted the landscape and a gently cheerful soundtrack accompanied the action which drew to a close with an image of three packs of Carroll's No 1 carefully balanced on top of each other with the legend, "Carroll's Stand on Quality". The campaign was hugely popular and not only succeeded in developing a warm personality for the brand but also wrapped a very green Irish tint around it. Carroll's No 1 became the quintessential Irish brand in the market, a position which played a significant role in prolonging its life when the pressure on this market sector from mild cigarettes began to mount.

Another brand with a well-developed emotional side to its personality was Persil, the long-time brand leader in the Irish detergent market. Detergent advertising had traditionally featured hard-selling arguments, often beating people over the head with scientifically based "advances" guaranteed to make your clothes cleaner and whiter than anyone else's. Persil adopted a completely different approach; their advertisements usually featured happy families in beautiful settings with a good-looking (but not glamorous) Mum lovingly tending the needs of two or three impossibly cute little children while they waited for Dad to come home from work. These campaigns developed a caring, sharing family image for the brand and people were very clear about the nature of the brand personality.

There is an interesting brand lesson in this market, because the other leading brand, Ariel, adopted a completely different personality, eschewing any concessions to emotional warmth as it continued to convince housewives that it did really remove "deep down dirt". The different personalities of the two brands was so well established that, in the early 1990s, when housewives were asked in group discussions which RTÉ personalities matched the two brands, respondents had no difficulty in matching Persil with Marian Finucane and Ariel with Pat Kenny. The lesson here is that having a strong distinctive personality is the most important issue for a successful brand. Two brands in the same market can have completely different personalities as long as they stand for something that is relevant and desirable for that market.

The second age of branding produced some of the most memorable and enduring brands, creating vast revenue for the businesses that owned them. But people and businesses change and brand communication is always in a state of flux as managers try to come to terms with new situations and seek competitive advantage through innovation and disruption of the status quo. By the 1990s it was apparent that we were entering into a new age of branding — the third age. These changes are never seamless; there is always a considerable amount of overlap. Many successful brands continue to pursue the functional branding route, as the relentless onslaught of Power City's advertising exemplifies. There were also many examples of the new third age branding before the 1990s. In fact, one of the most iconic commercials of the late 1960s, and a highly emotional one at that, could be seen in retrospect as a harbinger of the third age. At that time the most famous brand in the world, Coca Cola, brought a group of young teenagers from different countries on to the top of a mountain to sing in harmony. It is worth considering the lyrics:

> I'd like to buy the world a home
> and furnish it with love
> grow apple trees and honey bees
> and snow white turtle doves
> I'd like to teach the world to sing
> in perfect harmony
> I'd like to buy the world a Coke
> And keep it company.

The most effective brand communications often manage to reflect the social conditions, preoccupations and mores of the time and although these lyrics would sound odd today they represented a powerful evocation of the mood of optimism about the essential goodness of mankind that characterised the late 1960s.

The Third Age of Branding: The Conceptual/Intellectual/ Philosophical Age

The third age of branding dates from the 1990s as a number of forces combined to make brand owners take measures to keep their brands fresh and relevant to a new generation of consumers. Brought up on a diet of pop videos and a constant barrage of marketing communication messages, their palettes for brand communication were jaded long before they had enough disposable income to make their own purchasing decisions. In addition they were the first generation of "marketing literate" consumers, having absorbed the rudiments of marketing theories and strategy from the educational system and the media. Finding a way "under their radar" demanded new brand communication strategies.

Another factor was the inevitable onward march of competition. It is always tempting to assume that one's own time in business is vastly more competitive than any time in the past, and although this is not necessarily the case, what is true is that as innovations in any area are adopted by most of the leading products or services in a market sector, there is natural pressure to generate new initiatives to gain a competitive advantage. By the 1990s most leading brands in most markets had absorbed the main elements of branding theory and were committed to developing rounded personalities for their brands, so it was time for the more ambitious ones to make a fresh move. Continuing with the detergent analogy this move went in the direction of attaching higher order values to brands:

"My brand washes whiter than theirs and gives you a nice warm feeling and fits in with your values and beliefs."

A key factor in propelling the third age of branding to centre-stage was the fact that by the turn of the century most products in most market sectors performed their basic function very well — *everything* washed whiter; all cars now started in the mornings — and new product or service features were immediately imitated by competitors. Brands therefore needed new bait to attract customers. On a more fanciful level there was a surprising degree of support for the notion that brands with higher-order values were being sought after by the public because of the decline in traditional sources of authority — the church, politicians and other sources of long-established power; in other words, the rise of the individual:

> Adrift in a world with a paucity of traditional institutions that develop, spread and nourish values people began to latch on to popular icons of any kind hoping to derive from them the comfort structure and inspiration that school, church, country and family had always provided — brands are now gunning for a share of the lives of consumers, their values, their beliefs, their politics and, yes, their souls.[5]

Although these kinds of comments show that brand commentators are not immune from hyperbole, the fact that similar sentiments were shared by so many writers on the subject during the last decade is evidence of the extraordinary level of attention that was being given to the branding phenomenon. There may be some confusion here about what exactly is replacing religion in people's lives, and perhaps these commentators are confusing the ritual of visiting shopping centres and shopping in general with brands in particular. But there is no doubt that the 1980s and 1990s witnessed a shift from "society" to "market" and from "person" to "consumer".

---

[5] Khan, H., "How Fit is Fittest", ESOMAR Annual Conference Papers, 1996.

Not for the first time an artist may be way ahead of the marketing or sociological commentator and back in 1968 Arthur Miller put it like this:

> The car, the furniture, the wife, the children — everything has to be disposable because you see the main thing today is — shopping. Years ago a person who was unhappy, didn't know what to do with himself, he'd go to church, start a revolution — something. Today you're unhappy? Can't figure it out? What's the salvation? Go shopping.[6]

One aspect of this phenomenon which has not received much attention is the changing nature of what goods and services are being referred to under the brand umbrella. For most of the twentieth century when people talked about brands they were usually talking about fast-moving consumer goods, the kind that could be bought in supermarkets. The inexorable rise of interest in the subject which took place in the 1990s, moving from the marketing department to the boardroom, meant that more and more businesses beyond fast-moving consumer goods began to realise that their goods and services could also be regarded as brands.

If we go back for a moment to the three reasons why people are prepared to pay a premium for well-branded goods and services, the first two — quality and convenience — apply to all brands. However, the third — social cachet — is less relevant to fast-moving consumer goods but very relevant to the product areas that attracted attention from brand commentators in recent years; for example, clothing and electronic gadgets. At the same time, while these categories of goods were the subject of increased attention the more traditional fast-moving consumer goods were under severe pressure from the growing concentration of retailer power.

---

[6] Miller, A., *The Price (a Play)*, Viking, New York, 1968.

The third age of branding is a much more diffused development than the first two periods and it may be useful to categorise it under four sub-headings.

1. The Philosophical Approach

The first and probably the most important is the **philosophical** approach. Using this strategy, brands attempt to appropriate philosophies which transcend the physical properties of the market they operate within:

> *"My brand washes whiter than theirs and gives you a nice warm feeling and represents an idea you would be proud to be associated with."*

Two of the best-known examples of this approach are Nike and Apple. Nike is one of the most successful examples of branding in the last twenty years. It is a marketing legend which has had some of the most iconic advertising campaigns of the period, advertisements that have attracted the kind of literary criticism that the majority of novelists could only dream about:

> Nike ads come in two forms; one is of an irreverent winking attitude towards everything that smacks of commodity culture, the other is where Nike constructs itself as the vehicle of an ethos that integrates themes of personal transcendence, achievement and authenticity — it has been observed in the US that the religious mood in the mid-90s shifted away from a theology of fixed beliefs towards an experiential quest attuned to body, mind and self — Nike advertising sometimes envisages sport as a form of secular salvation or redemption.[7]

Nike epitomises a philosophy of personal achievement as exemplified by its ubiquitous slogan, "Just Do It".

---

[7] Goldman, R. and Patson, S., *Nike Culture,* Sage Publications, 1998.

Apple seeks to appropriate an equally ambitious philosophy, "we believe that people with passion can change the world for the better". In one of its most famous TV commercials, which shows images of well-known innovators, this philosophy is clearly spelt out:

> Here's to the crazy ones, the misfits, the rebels, the troublemakers, the round pegs in the square holes, the ones who see things differently; they are not fond of rules and they have no respect for the status quo. You can quote them, disagree with them, glorify or vilify them. About the only thing you can't do is ignore them; because they change things, they push the human race forward and while some may see them as the crazy ones we see genius because the people who are crazy enough to think they can change the world are the ones who do — Think Different.

This approach is not advisable for all brands and there are dangers in seeking to occupy such high ground, as Nike found out to their cost when some dubious working practices were uncovered in the Third World countries where their sub-contracted production takes place. To their credit, however, they survived the controversy by addressing the issues involved. Another potential danger in adopting this approach is that brands are not, as brand managers sometimes appear to think, disembodied abstractions divorced from the product itself. Both the products and the organisations that make them must be seen to be aligned with the philosophical values being espoused in their marketing communications, and in addition those products must perform to an exceptional degree. Both Apple and Nike conform to these conditions.

2. The Intellectual Approach

A second type of third age branding could be called the **intellectual** approach. This was heavily influenced by one of the most important management books of the 1990s, Garry Hamel and C.K.

Prahalad's *Competing for the Future*.[8] One of the main ideas put forward in this book was that the best way for a company to control its own destiny was to control the destiny of the industry in which it operated. This premise was heavily influenced by the blurring of boundaries between previously discrete industry sectors: "it is a view of strategy that recognises that companies not only compete within the boundaries of existing industries; they compete to shape the structure of future industries". This approach represented the following viewpoint:

> *"My brand washes whiter than theirs,*
> *and gives you a nice warm feeling*
> *and represents the future of this market."*

The famous campaign for Orange in the UK mobile phone market is one of the best examples of this brand strategy in operation. The brand was launched in 1994 into a market dominated for the previous ten years by the two brand leaders, Cellnet and Vodafone. Orange had no natural advantages; it wasn't the cheapest and it didn't have the best coverage. Extensive research prior to the launch showed that although people were enthusiastic about the benefits of mobile telephony, they were frustrated with the technical limitations that existed at the time and bored with product details. The Orange strategy was to ignore the existing realities of the market and look to the future. Their brand vision was outlined as follows:

> There will come a time when all people will have their own personal number that goes with them wherever they are so that there are no barriers to communication — a wirefree future so that you can call people, not places, and where everyone will benefit from the advances in technology.[9]

---

[8] Hamel, G. and Prahalad, C.K., *Competing for the Future*, Harvard Business School Press, 1994.

[9] Vallance, C., "How Two Years of Advertising Created Twelve Years of Value" in *Advertising Works 9*, NTC Publications, 1997.

This "vision" was encapsulated in the slogan, "The future's bright, the future's Orange", and the campaign was a spectacular success, featuring futuristic scenes of a wirefree world and generating additional revenue of £300 million for an advertising expenditure of just over £26 million. When the company went public in 1996 and the advertising theme continued to portray the same vision, an award-winning case study was able to demonstrate that as a direct result of the advertising, market capitalisation had increased by £3 billion.[10]

There are numerous examples of companies trying to portray themselves as the future of the market but none more successful than that of Orange. To some extent, the IDA's "Young Europeans" campaign represents an earlier example of this strategy. The campaign suggested that the future of the market for transnational mobile investment would be more concerned with the quality and commitment of the workforce rather than the tax breaks or incentive grants that were available.

3. The Experiential Approach

A third form of third age branding could be called the **experiential** approach. This became very popular in the 1990s as an increasingly jaded and world-weary public demanded new more intense experiences from a wide range of markets. Today's consumers take product quality for granted; what they want is "product communications and marketing campaigns that dazzle their senses, touch their hearts and stimulate their minds".[11] This time the promise could be expressed as follows:

> *"My brand washes whiter than yours*
> *and gives you a nice warm feeling*
> *and gives you a deeper more intense experience."*

---

[10] Izbicki, D. and Saunders, C., "Orange — The FTSE's bright, the FTSE's Orange" in *Advertising Works 10,* NTC Publications, 1999.

[11] Schmitt, B., *Experiential Marketing*, The Free Press, 1999.

One of the most famous examples of this approach was Haagen Dazs. Prior to the launch of their sexy campaign, ice-cream was regarded as a family-type product category with an emphasis on treats for the kids. Some brands were launched on a more sophisticated product platform as an up-market dinner party desert alternative, but Haagen Dazs went much further with its portrayal of ice-cream as an accompaniment to foreplay. Gordon's Gin created a similar experiential effect in an attempt to communicate the "refreshing" qualities of gin. Their campaign showed people diving into a glass of gin and tonic to experience the refreshing qualities of the drink.

A number of important books have been written on the subject of experiential marketing and all stress the need to consider all five senses — sight, sound, taste, smell and touch — when planning marketing communications campaigns. Martin Lindstrom's book *Brand Sense*[12] includes examples, like the automobile industry creating a "new car smell" by using aerosol canisters to spray new cars with this smell as they are leaving the assembly line. The book also includes the case study of Singapore Airlines, who used sensory branding techniques in the 1990s when they introduced Stefan Floridian waters, an aroma that had been specifically designed as part of the overall airline experience. It formed the scent in the flight attendant's perfume, was blended into the hot towel served before take-off and generally permeated the entire fleet of Singapore Airlines planes.

Retailers have been excellent exponents of intense brand experiences and have obvious advantages over traditional manufacturers in this respect. Superquinn has always represented a particularly Irish service experience, with the founder and until recently chief executive Feargal Quinn regularly in evidence around the stores, sometimes even helping out with the checkouts. Some of their stores also ensure that the aroma of freshly baked bread is

---

[12] Lindstrom, M., *Brand Sense*, Kogan Page, 2005.

particularly in evidence close to the entrances. Bewley's coffee shops in Dublin also offered a unique experience over and above the beverages and food served on the premises. In recent years in order to compensate for their lack of a specific space where their own products can be experienced, some manufacturers have created their own spaces, with the Guinness Storehouse being the most ambitious Irish example (see Chapter 5).

4. The Spiritual Approach

The fourth and final form of third age branding could be called the **spiritual** approach. Although there are some examples of this approach in Europe, it is a form of branding that is most likely to be found in America. It is also associated with a move towards a more ethical approach to business and there are some commentators who believe that brands that ignore the public's requirements for a more ethical approach will not survive in the twenty-first century. The brand promise could be expressed as follows:

> *"My brand washes whiter than theirs,*
> *and gives you a nice warm feeling*
> *and will make you feel a better person."*

Once again there has been a mini-publishing boom in books and articles around this area of branding, which is often referred to as "cause-related marketing". This has been defined as "a strategic positioning tool which links a company or brand to a relevant charity or cause in a partnership for mutual benefit".[13] Tesco Ireland's "Computers for Schools" promotion is one of the best-known examples in Ireland. There are also a number of well-known UK examples including Andrex, whose advertising features a golden labrador and who have linked up with Guide Dogs for the Blind, but while these promotions were designed to add a cause-related element to the brand positioning they were not an integral

---

[13] Pringle, H. and Thompson, M., *Brand Spirit*, Wiley, 1999.

part of the positioning. Tesco's core brand story remained "every little helps" and the philosophy behind the proposition was that it was the hundred and one things that Tesco did to make the shopping experience better that made their level of service superior to their competitors.

A number of brands put spiritual branding at the core of their positioning. Body Shop is an obvious example but the most interesting case studies of this type of branding come from the United States. It has been mischievously suggested that the reason for this is the number of chief executives in that market who were radical hippies in their earlier years is greater there than in other markets:

> Business was abolishing war, business was bringing together the races. Business was building a multi-cultural society; business thinkers and industry leaders shared a deep concern for the environment and enjoyed intimate friendship with whales, dolphins, orphans and peoples of the Third World. Brands were the intangible magic that separated the good corporations from the bad; brands were democracy itself.[14]

A good example was General Motors' Saturn brand which was portrayed as a new concept in car manufacturing as well as positioning. One commercial for the brand in the 1990s didn't show any cars at all but featured a run-down area in New York with a group of people building a playground. The voiceover explained everything:

> When we first came here we saw that there were three swings, six horses, one slide and one set of monkey bars for a hundred and twenty children. We looked around and realised these kids need a heck of a lot more. What do you suppose would happen if everyone decided to put just a weekend's worth of effort into their community? Building,

---

[14] Frank, T., *One Market Under God*, Doubleday, 2000.

renovating, whatever; things might just begin to change, which is why on one weekend in June a group of Saturn retailers, owners, and team members got together and built twelve playgrounds in the New York area, and while in the grand scheme of things that may not seem like much, it's a start.

If America has seen the most visible examples of spiritual branding it is the Danish futurologist Rolf Jensen who has stated the case most concisely:

> Most recently we are witnessing the emergence of the Third Wave in branding in which the promise has been extended into hitherto uncharted territory, namely the ethical or spiritual dimension of the brand — nowadays it seems it is no longer enough for consumers to know what a product or service does, or what imagery it bestows upon the purchaser, now they need to understand what the brand they buy believes in.[15]

There are three possible reasons for the interest in this area of branding: Maslowisation, Globalisation and Ecologisation.

The first derives from the sociologist Abraham Maslow who published his now-famous hierarchy in the 1940s,[16] which showed that human needs at the bottom of the triangle were physiological ones — hunger, shelter and so on — and then proceeded upwards through safety needs, social needs, personal esteem and ended with personal enlightenment. The shape of the triangle was meant to signify that there were many more people in the bottom segments. A decade earlier, one of the most influential economists of the twentieth century, John Maynard Keynes, writing in the depths of the great economic depression, made the remarkable prediction that within a hundred years "the problems of economic necessity will be relieved for an increasing number of classes and

---

[15] Jensen, R., *The Dream Society,* McGraw-Hill, 1999.
[16] Maslow, A., *Motivation & Personality*, Harper, 1954.

groups of people" and went on to suggest that they would then be left with the problem of how to live wisely and well. We are now three-quarters way through Keynes's hundred-year period and in much of the western world his prediction is coming true. For that reason, we could now invert Mr Maslow's hierarchy and see that there may now be a significant number of people who could afford the luxury of choosing brands whose causes they are most comfortable with.

Increasing globalisation could intensify this trend. People won't want to give up the economic benefits that globalisation brings in its wake but they will also be increasingly conscious of the potential downsides. Thomas Friedman, the *New York Times* columnist and a strong supporter of free trade, has warned that people need to develop some defences against excessive globalisation and ensure that they are not "so overwhelmed by it that it turns their culture into a global mush and their environment into a global mash".[17] Sentiments like these are likely to find an increasing audience especially in smaller countries like Ireland and could also lead to a more receptive audience for more spiritually based brands.

A third factor which could lead to an increase in the spiritual dimension of branding is the growing concern for the environment. This is the one chink in the armour of even the most committed free market fundamentalist. No matter how strongly a business believes that maximising shareholder revenues is their only legitimate goal, the likely public and media backlash against any perceived enviromental wrongdoing is now too great a risk for any company to take. But once the overriding priority for maximising profits has been breached, there will inevitably be pressure to consider the wider responsibilities of a business.

---

[17] Friedman, T. *The Lexus and the Olive Tree*, Harper& Collins, UK, 1999.

Conclusion

The four possible directions for brand positioning in the third age of branding are not mutually exclusive; intellectual and philosophical positionings do not preclude experiential or spiritual elements. This analysis is meant to help brand managers by presenting different options that should be taken into account when considering the most desirable and distinctive stance for a brand, whether it is a product brand, a service brand or the branding of a total business.

The point has been made earlier that many brands can thrive in the twenty-first century by continuing to adopt second age or even first age branding; it all depends on the conditions of the particular market and the competitive situation. The retail market is an example where first age branding still predominates because the majority of retailers can never stray too far from a factual price-based message.

But there will also be brands that will want to move on from the third age of branding to gain a competitive advantage by breaking new ground and following the path less travelled. The final section of the book, "The Future of Branding", will take a look at possible new directions.

PART TWO

HOW TO BUILD
A STRONG BRAND

"Branding is now recognised as a central and essential component of business success. Branding is no longer considered cosmetic."

— Alec Raltey, Landor Associates

"Strong brands do not just happen; they are built over time through a deliberate management process involving strategic decisions and corresponding actions"

— Karman Kashani, "Mastering Management",
Financial Times, 18 December 2000

"Branding may be thought of as the process of creating the totality of meaning which consumers attribute to a brand — the unique and relevant bundle of values that are internalised and combined with past experience and/or current perceptions of the brand itself."

— Gordon & Langmaid, 1986

Jacob's, one of the first Irish consumer brands, was founded by two Waterford brothers, William and John Jacob, in 1851.

4

BUILDING STRONG BRANDS (1): THE STRATEGY

The "brand planning cycle", which originally came from the account planning discipline in advertising agencies, is probably the best place to start the process of devising a strategy for building a stronger brand. It involves answering the following series of questions and is usually portrayed in circular form because the process of brand-building is a continuous one. Once you have devised one strategy and implemented it you will have to monitor the brand's subsequent performance and then devise another strategy to maintain progress or, if necessary, change direction.

Figure 1: The Brand Planning Cycle

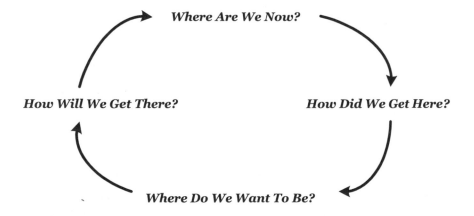

We will discuss each step of the cycle in turn, beginning with the critical examination of where the brand is now.

Where Are We Now?

Detailed knowledge of a brand's current position is the essential first step in preparing a plan for the future and we therefore need answers to all of these questions:

- Definition of the market

- Awareness levels for all brands in the market — spontaneous and prompted

- Market share data for all brands

- Demographic breakdown for all brands

- Behavioural breakdown for all brands

- Attitudinal breakdown for all brands

- Definition of attributes which affect purchasing behaviour

- Rating of brands for these attributes.

There are a wide range of market research techniques that can be used to provide answers to all of these questions but it might be useful to consider each of them in turn.

Defining the Market

This may seem very obvious but many brand owners make the mistake of defining the market in their own terms, often from a production or historic perspective, and lose sight of the fact that consumers may for their own good or not-so-good reasons see things differently. Given the nature of branding — the fact that brands are simply collections of perceptions in people's minds — it should be obvious that it is the consumer's view on what consti-tutes a market that counts. For example, when measuring market share in the beer market, Guinness, now Diageo, used to include only stouts, ales and lagers. But following a very successful adver-tising campaign in the 1990s, Bulmer's cider began to increase sales and it was obvious that some of this increase was at the expense of stouts, ales and lagers. It was equally obvious that many consumers, especially younger men who are responsible for a significant proportion of total sales, regarded cider as just another "pint" to be included in their repertoire. Guinness eventually decided to include cider in their brand share measurement data, the market began to look a little different, and their planning and new product development strategies were improved.

A small programme of qualitative research should be sufficient to enable consumers to define the parameters of any market, but if the conventional questioning techniques fail to produce an agreed definition of a particular market there are a number of more elaborate methods of uncovering the sometimes complex ways that people categorise different goods and services. One such method is the oddly named Kelly's Repertory Grid,[1] which like many market research techniques originated from clinical psychology. It is based on personal construct theory and entails defining a universe of interest, for example a market, and describing the elements or entities that are part of this universe. For our purposes it would mean printing out the names of every conceivable brand name that could be included in a particular market, shuffling the resulting pack of cards, dealing out three at a time and asking people to say why two of the three are the same and different from the third. Keep shuffling the cards, dealing them out in threes and asking the questions until every possible combination is exhausted and the resulting answers should enable you to define the brands that constitute the market.

Defining what brands constitute a market is critical but it is also much more difficult than it was in the past for two reasons. First, there has been a vast proliferation of choice. Not all that long ago, there were only three beers on tap in most Irish pubs: Guinness, Smithwick's and Harp. Now there are dozens. The second reason is that the boundaries between many markets have

---

[1] Kelly, G.A., *The Psychology of Personal Constructs*, Routledge, 1955.

crumbled as people increase their repertoires, expand their purchases and demand new experiences. Even in the professional services markets boundaries are being dismantled. Some of the leading accountancy firms are now offering legal advice and some of the leading law firms are offering financial advice. So should a law firm contemplating a brand management strategy, as many are now actively considering, include accountancy firms within their competitive framework? Should wine be included within the competitive framework for beers, given the increasing amount of wine being consumed by beer drinkers? And are Kellogg's in competition with bacon and eggs, porridge and fruit? To some extent the answer to all of these questions has to be "yes", but we need to be realistic. If wine really is a competitor to beer then the way for Diageo to respond is to build up its own wine sales and concentrate on making sure that all its beer brands are pursuing the optimal strategy to increase their share of the beer market. Brands with a dominant position in a relatively well-defined sector of a wider overall market — for example, Kellogg's in the ready-to-eat cereal sector of the breakfast market — will always have one part of their marketing communications emphasising the benefits of the category in the total breakfast market.

Once the market has been defined we then need to estimate its size and whether it is expanding, declining or static. Nowadays reasonably accurate information about the size of most markets by volume and value is readily available from trade and industry sources, and if the information has been collected for a number of years we will know whether the market is expanding, contracting or static. But if all else fails, specially commissioned market research surveys will give an accurate estimate of market size. You will, of course, have to collect the data for a few years before trends will be obvious. The answers to all of these questions will be important in determining the final brand plan.

Awareness Levels for All Brands in the Market

The increasing proliferation of choice in most markets has made it more difficult for brands to maintain awareness levels among consumers. It has also made awareness an increasingly important first step in purchasing. Maintaining awareness is becoming more difficult as more choices jostle for the public's attention; if people have never heard of a brand they are hardly likely to buy it. Jeremy Bullmore tells the story of Posh Spice, whose first public utterance reputedly was that she wanted to be more famous than Persil Automatic. In spite of the curious nature of this ambition, Bullmore gives her full marks for prescience:

> If her earlier ambition to be more famous than Persil Automatic seemed to you surprising, or even laughable it shouldn't have done. It was very astute of young Posh Spice to choose not Robbie Williams, nor Madonna as her benchmark of fame but the country's best-known washing powder, because just about the only thing that successful brands have in common is a kind of fame.[2]

Measuring awareness is easy; just add a simple question to any of the nationally representative omnibus surveys that the leading market research companies carry out on a monthly or weekly basis. Awareness is usually measured in two ways: spontaneous and prompted. With the former, respondents are asked to say which brand names they can remember from a particular product category. A follow-up question presents respondents with a complete list of all the brands in the market and respondents are again asked to say which they have heard of, thus providing a prompted awareness score. Because of the increasing importance of awareness, some businesses are now attaching value to being the first brand mentioned when people are asked to name all the brands they can think of in any market.

---

[2] Bullmore J., *More Bullmore*, WARC, 2003.

Market Share Data for All Brands

It is likely that one of the main objectives when producing a strategic plan will be to increase market share, so we need to know what our current market share is in relation to competitive brands. This is usually a fairly straightforward process. In many markets brand share data is publicly available because it is collected by official industry bodies. Below is the brand share data for the Irish motor market for 2004 as collected by the Society of the Irish Motor Industry.

Table 1: Irish Car Market 2004–05[3]

	Passenger Cars 2004	Passenger Cars 2005	% of Market Share
Toyota	20,183	24,260	14.1
Ford	16,973	20,413	11.9
VW	15,185	14,653	8.5
Nissan	12,530	13,755	8.0
Renault	11,461	10,969	6.4
GM (Opel)	10,801	12,239	7.1
Peugeot	8,417	9,128	5.3
Hyundai	5,857	6,928	4.0
BMW	4,819	5,623	3.3
Skoda	3,307	5,248	3.1
Mercedes	4,707	4,875	2.8
Audi	3,500	4,587	2.7
Mazda	4,591	4,137	2.4
Citroen	3,339	4,055	2.4
Seat	3,369	3,212	1.9

---

[3] Data supplied from the Society of Irish Motor Industries, Dublin, 2005.

Although not all markets are covered in this way almost every market has some kind of trade magazine and they usually have a good idea of the up-to-date market share position. If the information is not freely available the market research companies omnibus surveys will always be able to provide the necessary data.

Demographic Breakdown for All Brands

Market share data is important but we will always need the information broken down by the main demographic variables — age, sex, socio-economic class and region. This information is usually not publicly available so you will have to commission a survey of your own or better still attach the necessary questions to one of the omnibus surveys. One of the few markets where it is freely available is the newspaper market because the information is required by the advertising agencies to help them allocate their advertising budgets. Surveys paid for by the industry are carried out on a continuous basis and the results are widely available. Table 2 overleaf shows the latest demographic breakdowns for the main newspapers.[4]

This table shows the importance of detailed demographic data. The circulation figures are obviously vital but the breakdowns show that there are critical distinctions between the newspapers, which are only revealed by the age and social class data. For example, although the *Irish Independent* is the biggest selling daily, the profile of the *Star* is much younger and *The Irish Times* more middle class.

---

[4] Data supplied from the Joint National Readership Survey (JNRS).

Table 2: Demographic Breakdown of Newspaper Readership (2005)

Title	ABC Circulation (Jan-Jun 2005)	Readership Universe x 000's				Social Groups Universe x 000's			Age Groups Universe x 000's		
		All adults	Men	Women	HWives	ABC1	C2DE	F1F2	15-34	35-54	55+
Mornings											
Irish Independent	164,202	17.8%	19.0%	16.6%	16.2%	22.7%	11.5%	30.1%	13.5%	19.6%	22.0%
Irish Times	117,543	10.3%	10.0%	10.5%	11.0%	20.5%	3.8%	1.6%	9.0%	11.4%	10.8%
The Examiner	57,331	7.5%	17.9%	7.1%	8.1%	8.1%	6.1%	12.2%	5.3%	8.0%	10.1%
Irish Daily Star	108,221	13.1%	14.9%	11.3%	10.6%	8.6%	17.4%	8.7%	16.8%	12.5%	8.1%
Evenings											
Evening Herald	93,830	9.6%	9.3%	9.9%	9.0%	8.6%	12.0%	1.6%	10.4%	9.5%	8.7%
Sundays											
Ireland on Sunday	139,170	14.4%	13.2%	15.6%	14.2%	13.1%	15.7%	13.1%	13.2%	16.9%	12.9%
Irish Daily Star Sunday	50,587	5.5%	5.9%	5.0%	4.1%	3.6%	7.2%	4.2%	8.0%	4.7%	2.6%
Sunday Business Post	51,823	5.4%	6.1%	4.8%	5.3%	9.6%	2.7%	2.9%	4.6%	6.5%	5.3%
Sunday Independent	291,036	32.4%	31.6%	33.1%	32.0%	40.3%	23.4%	46.2%	26.2%	32.3%	41.9%
Sunday Tribune	71,187	7.2%	6.9%	7.6%	7.5%	11.5%	4.4%	4.8%	6.0%	8.8%	7.2%
Sunday World	273,667	24.8%	25.9%	23.8%	22.8%	15.8%	31.1%	29.2%	28.4%	24.4%	20.0%

Behavioural Breakdown for All Brands

In addition to demographic breakdowns we also need to know as much as possible about how people behave in different ways in the market. For example, if we were examining the petrol market and had obtained demographic breakdowns for all motorists, we could reasonably assume that all motorists would have considerable variations in their annual mileage and that it would be important to further divide the market into behavioural categories. Once again a simple question attached to an omnibus survey will determine estimated annual mileage and we can then define heavy, medium and light users. We might define heavy as over 20,000 miles per annum, medium as 10,000 to 20,000 miles and light as less than 10,000 miles.

It is important to have this kind of breakdown for all markets because when we come to defining the target group for any marketing communication proposals we will see that, almost without exception, there is a Pareto effect in every market, in that around 20 per cent of customers will be responsible for around 80 per cent of the revenue.

Attitudinal Breakdown of All Brands

This type of classification is much less common but tends to enjoy brief flourishes of fashion from time to time. Doubts are always being expressed about the relevance of socio-economic class as a discriminatory system. However, it has stood the test of time and can still explain variations in behaviour in many markets, the newspaper market being a case in point.

In the 1960s numerous attempts were made to classify buyers in different markets into broad psychological types, for example extrovert–introvert, conservative–radical, tough-minded–tender-minded. But the results of this analysis proved disappointing and rarely provided any real insights into buying behaviour, so this particular management fad went out of fashion. During the 1980s there was a move away from generalised attitudinal categories towards attitudinal types based on behaviour related to the market sector under review. Companies in the drinks market were especially keen on exercises of this type and brand managers had great fun attaching cute little names to the categories — "promiscuous Pat", "nervous Nora", "steady Sarah" and, inevitably, "louche Louise". This trend proved a little more durable but there were fundamental flaws in the approach — the descriptions were too arbitrary and although the classifications often provided useful planning insights they were too restrictive. When the concept of Need-States became more widely known this type of classification went out of favour. The Need-States concept, originally associated with the well-known UK market researcher Wendy Gordon,[5] rejected the notion of assigning definitive psychological labels by suggesting that people exhibit multiple psychological characteristics depending on circumstances and their state of mind at any given time. It is therefore important to establish people's attitudes to consumption in different places, at different times and in different moods.

However, it is always a mistake to fall into the most common of all traps in the marketing communication business, which is the tendency to dismiss out of hand previous theories and practical approaches in favour of whatever happens to be the current flavour of the month. There are many markets where the definition of typologies based on attitudinal characteristics related to the market in question can be extremely useful. Here's an example from the home décor market which appears to make sense and should contribute to better planning. The market has been divided into six attitudinal types:[6]

---

[5] Gordon, W., "Meeting the Challenge of Retailer Brands", *Admap*, March 1994.

[6] Robinson, J., "Beyond the Traditional Socio-Demographics", paper at the "Re-Thinking the Consumer" conference *Admap*/WARC, London, 17 January 2001.

- *Home is my Castle*: "I don't like anything abstract; I haven't got time for that; the crystal and porcelain we bought ourselves."

- *Not Really Interesteds*: "We're not really mad on decorating; we do it when it needs doing; it's nice to feel comfortable rather than sitting and thinking, 'oh, that needs decorating'."

- *Just Normals*: "The idea of floorboards horrifies me. I would never never have wooden floorboards."

- *Self-expressives*: "My style is colourful — happy, cheerful, quite way out; some people say, 'how do you have the nerve to have it like this?' but it's just me."

- *Child-bound*: "With kids everything has to be washable, and of course there's the safety aspect."

- *Modern and Co-ordinated*: "I like to go to exhibitions to see what's new; I got rid of all my ornaments, my daughter took them to a car-boot sale."

Although some of these clusters will undoubtedly be highly correlated with age and socio-economic class, there is also likely to be so much overlap that the six clusters will be a useful starting point for brand planning in their own right. The above study was carried out for IKEA in the UK.

There have been numerous studies of this type carried out in the food sector and the following is an example carried out among teenagers in Ireland:[7]

- *Microwavers*: 27 per cent of all 12–18 year olds with a distinctively high pattern of cooking for themselves and also for using microwaves.

---

[7] "Youthscope:Youth Attitudes and Opinions", IAPI, Dublin, 1999.

- *Modern Munchers*: 20 per cent of young people who eat out to an above-average degree are interested in "exotic" cuisine and healthy foods but who are also intensive snackers and fast food eaters.

- *Slimmers*: 19 per cent of young people primarily interested in low fat and healthy products; they are also interested in exotic foods but are the lowest users of fast food outlets.

- *Health Nuts*: 18 per cent of young people into healthy foods but not necessarily low fat ones.

- *Fast Foodies*: 17 per cent of young people primarily distinguished by their high incidence of fast-food restaurants and take-away shops, they are not experimental and have a low interest in health foods of any kind.

Once we go beyond demographic and behavioural classifications the best way to assess whether there are any further insights to be gained from a more detailed attitudinal investigation is to carry out a qualitative study of the market, an exercise that will in any case be required for the next section. In the newspaper market a study of this type would probably reveal that an above average interest in politics and current affairs is a factor that could determine people's choice of newspaper, and although it might have some correlation with socioeconomic class it would not provide the total explanation.

Definition of the Attributes which Affect Purchasing Behaviour

This is one of the most critical areas for investigation in any market and the type of qualitative market research exercise outlined above is the most efficient method of obtaining this information. Although there are a number of attributes common to many markets, for example "quality" and "value for money", there will always be attributes that are specific to each individual market. A qualitative research programme of around twenty individual in-depth interviews and eight group discussions with as representa-tive as possible a range of respondents should be enough to pro-vide the necessary information. The type of information we are looking for here include: what people feel is important about products or services in the market; how they choose between the different offerings; how they feel about the category; why they buy in this market in the first place; what levels of satisfaction they are looking for; where they get their opinions about this market; and how they segment the market into different categories.

The following is a list of attributes which emerged from an ex-ercise of this type in the Irish petrol market:

- Good service

- Safe environment

- Friendly service

- Attractive forecourt

- Quality brand

- Value for money

- Well-stocked retail outlet

- Up and coming brand

- Good facilities

- Expensive.

Sometimes a number of negative attributes are included — for ex-ample, "expensive" above — to see if this provides more sensitive information.

Inevitably some research companies and consultants have at-tempted to assign mathematical values to all the attributes that are deemed important in a given market and then claimed to be able to define precisely how individual brands need to be rated for each attribute to maximise their position in the market. It is doubtful there is any great merit in exercises of this type because the whole area is simply not amenable to mathematical precision. It should be fairly obvious from the qualitative study which attributes are more important than others and this is about as much as we can expect from exercises of this type.

Brand Attribute Ratings

The next step is to rate all of the brands in the market for each attribute. Quantitative research among a representative sample of the population will be required to do this, and again the omnibus surveys are the most efficient method of carrying out this exercise, which is relatively straightforward.

Additional Information

Every market is different and there will be important aspects of individual markets that we will also need to investigate before we can start to draw up brand plans for the future. If advertising or other forms of marketing communications are a significant factor in the market, as they would be in the drinks market, we would need to find out how people regard the advertising for the different brands in the market. Distribution could also be a factor, as not all brands in any market are universally available, but in general most of the factors that are relevant should emerge in the preliminary research.

If all the foregoing information has been collected we should be in a position to proceed to the next phase of the planning cycle.

How Did We Get Here?

This is an area that is often completely neglected, especially by younger brand managers who appear to have accepted, hook, line and sinker Henry Ford's dictum that history is bunk. On the contrary, it can be argued that it is impossible to understand a brand's current position without a thorough knowledge of how it came to be there in the first place.

Although not every business will have good historical records, it is surprising how much useful information so many businesses have that they rarely use. Sales data over the years is the first port of call, and this can shed much light on why a brand is in the situation it is in today. It is also surprising how many market research reports companies have, some of whose pages when turned over look suspiciously like they have never been opened before. Company employees, especially retirees, are another source of potentially valuable information.

One of the most common misconceptions in the marketing profession is the assumption that a single brilliant brand insight or marketing communication initiative can transform the fortunes of a brand overnight. There are a number of well-known case histories which support this assumption but they tend to be the exception rather than the rule. Most established brand images are more or less hard-wired and re-wiring is complicated, time-consuming and not always successful. Understanding the history of how we have come to where we are is the best defence against over-optimistic or wrong-headed plans for the future.

The Irish banking market provides an interesting example of how an understanding of history is a prerequisite for being able to interpret the brand image of the two major banks. Allied Irish Bank and Bank of Ireland dominate the Irish market and each have approximately a 40 per cent market share. If you carry out all of the exercises recommended above — defining the attributes that are important in this market and rating both brands for each attribute — there will be very little variation in the resulting scores. On the surface it would appear as if they have identical brand images. This is hardly surprising given that they have almost the same number of branches, identical products and staff numbers. But intensive qualitative research questioning will show that there are subtle variations in their respective images, with Bank of Ireland being seen as somewhat more conservative and AIB being seen as more pioneering and adventurous. I believe that part of the reason for this lies in the different histories of the two banks. Both were formed as a result of the merger of three smaller banks in the 1960s. AIB is an amalgamation of the Munster & Leinster, the Provincial and the Hibernian, while Bank of Ireland is the result of an amalgamation of the National, the Royal and the Bank of Ireland. Of the three banks that formed AIB in 1966, the Provincial had its headquarters in London up to 1953 and the Royal was restricted mainly to Dublin. The Munster & Leinster, with deep roots in the Munster area, had a different ethos to all of the other Irish banks: "Although its Cork support consisted both of Catholic and Protestant businessmen, it was able consistently to present a distinctive image, one of its Directors in 1890 even claiming that it was the only 'Irish' bank."[8] Over a century later, traces of this attitude are still evident.

The wider financial services market has been described as the most resistant of all markets to branding and marketing, and it is notoriously difficult for conventional market research to differentiate significantly between the brand images of the different banks. Extra sensitive probing of customers in the Irish market, however, will invariably come up with subtle distinctions between the two leading banks which are based in the cultures of their historical backgrounds. Henry Ford was wrong: history is not bunk; it can often provide critical insights into hitherto impenetrable markets.

Before moving on to the next phase of the planning cycle it may be useful to consider another element which is not part of the conventional planning process but which can add to the effectiveness and creativity of brand management planning capabilities in smaller markets like Ireland: the scope for benefiting from the experiences in other geographical markets.

---

[8] "Root and Branch: Allied Irish Banks — Yesterday, Today, Tomorrow", published by AIB, December 1979.

Can We Learn Anything from Other Markets?

If young brand managers suffer from the delusion that the world only began when they were born, the rest of us suffer from the delusion that we are the centre of the universe. This is equally short-sighted. Ireland may have taken her place among the nations of the world, economically at least, but we have to face up the fact that, with the possible exception of the music business, we are rarely in the forefront of developments in most markets. This may not be good for the soul but it gives us the advantage of being able to watch out for emerging trends from around the world that might be replicated in our own market. It is important therefore for anyone responsible for brand management in Ireland to monitor worldwide trends and to keep up-to-date with the latest new product or service initiatives. Modern communications have made this task much easier, but it is a mistake to rely on the internet alone — you need to be able to touch, smell and feel what's happening.

Most businesses have annual trade fairs, exhibitions, conferences or some king of jamboree where the latest developments are on display in one place and leading sector thinkers are lecturing, expounding or just *there* — so you need to be there too. The food business is well catered for with the giant food fairs in Sial, outside Paris and Anuga, near Cologne, every alternate year. The Irish dairy industry was always well represented at these fairs and it was at one of them in the 1970s that a Golden Vale marketing executive spotted the emergence of packaged cheese slices and came back to launch Easi-Singles, the first brand in the category in the Irish market and the brand leader in the category to this day. In preparing brand plans, therefore, we should take into account emerging consumer trends and new products and services from around the world.

Where Do We Want to Get to?

This is the easiest "box" to fill in and to some extent it depends on how ambitious we are or want to be. Usually we will want to increase brand share, so most people will complete this section by introducing some kind of growth target. For example, if our brand has a current market share of ten per cent, we might set a target of twelve per cent for the coming year. A two per cent increase in market share may seem modest enough but in fact it represents a sales increase of twenty per cent which for most markets would be extremely ambitious. Although sales targets cannot be ignored, brand plans are sometimes confined to setting targets for how we want the brand image to be strengthened. For example, if our brand image ratings are falling behind on any of the following attributes — "value for money", "high quality", "for people like me", or "progressive" — we might want to set targets for an improvement in these ratings and plan our future marketing communications programme accordingly.

The question of setting targets raises a very important issue about the relationship between marketing strategy and overall business strategy. The performance of marketing departments has come under the spotlight in recent years with allegations of being too concerned with the minutiae of advertising and other marketing communication techniques at the expense of wider business strategy. Marketing departments can be obsessed by fiddling while businesses are burning. The more ambitious the brand targets, the more likely it is that the business as a whole will have to become involved. In spite of the undoubted power of marketing communications initiatives to transform the fortunes of a business, most real transformations are as a result of new product developments, new delivery channels or new financial initiatives. When marketing emerged as a more or less formal discipline in the middle of the twentieth century its original pioneers were very conscious of the need for marketing as a philosophy to pervade the whole business. In the best-run businesses this is the case but in too many companies the marketing function has become somewhat detached from the real centre of power:

Marketing management appear to believe that their function is unique, that it is the only area of modern business
for which no period of intelligent specialist training is required. It is a field for amateurs. With such a self-view it is
hardly surprising that the value of the marketing department is under attack from other business professions.[9]

Therefore when setting brand targets the overall strategy of the
business must be taken into account and if targets can only be met
by making changes which involve other departments this must be
faced up to.

How Can We Get There?

Defining the communications strategy for achieving our targets is
the most creative area of brand management and it is now acknowledged that decisions in this area involve the same degree of
creative commitment as the creative work itself. In some cases the
communications strategy will be obvious. If a brand has very low
awareness or has very low scores for an attribute that is a critical
factor in purchasing decisions in the market then it is relatively
easy to devise the communications brief. In cases like these the
strategy comes directly from the data we have assembled from the
earlier stages of the planning process. However, it is increasingly
less likely that the next stage will be so straightforward:

> No matter how difficult or unprecedented the problem, a
> breakthrough to the best possible solution can come only
> from a combination of rational analysis, based on the real na-
> ture of things, and imaginative reintegration of all the differ-
> ent items into a new pattern, using nonlinear brain power.[10]

---

[9] Doyle, P., "Brand Equity and the Marketing Professional", *Market Leader*, Issue
1, Summer 1998.

[10] Ohmae, K., *The Mind of the Strategist*, Penguin Books, 1983.

In the first and second ages of branding it was more likely that the data would reveal the strategy but with most brands in most markets now offering acceptable standards of quality and delivery, successful brands are forced into the more unstable, uncertain and unpredictable world of the third age, forcing strategists to look for insights to position brands in a desirable and distinctive way. It is no surprise therefore that the question of creative insight generation has become the current holy grail of the marketing communications business, spawning a variety of silly titles — "Head of Consumer Insights" — and the inevitable raft of consultancies.

There are numerous definitions of "insight" but a useful distinction should be made between those which involve "flashes of inspiration, or penetrating discoveries that lead to specific opportunities" and those which are more concerned with "having a deep embedded knowledge about the customers and the market around us that helps structure thinking and sound decision making".[11] For the purposes of brand management, the best insights usually involve leveraging an aspect of the product or service with a requirement of consumers in the relevant market.

An example of how this works in practice would be the following insight for Kellogg's All Bran: "When my insides aren't feeling right it really affects my attitude and the way I feel outside." This example is also illustrative of a subtle shift that has taken place over the last twenty years in the relationship between brand managers and account managers in communications agencies and the creative teams who are responsible for creating the finished material. There was a time when the brief to the creative teams was fairly loose, a time fondly remembered by an older generation of managers who would instruct the creative team to "gimme an ad". Not so any more; now the managers are forced into being creative themselves by coming up with "insights" (see Chapter 6).

---

[11] Wills, S. and Williams, P., "Insight as a Strategic Asset", Market Research Society (UK) Conference Papers, 2004.

The Brand Planning Cycle in Action

The following three case histories illustrate some of the ways in which brand strategy problems can be tackled.

Case Study 1: IDA

The Industrial Development Authority was established by the first inter-party government in 1949 to "advise and assist the government in the identification of industrial development on the best possible basis". In the beginning it was mainly a planning and research organisation at a time when there was very little industrial development in a primarily agricultural country. However, the establishment of the Common Market in 1957 between the six founding member countries, and the publication a year later in Ireland of the seminal economic planning paper *Economic Development*, changed forever the economic landscape of Ireland. It was recognised that the country could not afford to isolate itself any longer from the growing move towards trade liberalisation, and in 1961 the newly confident political establishment in Dublin applied for membership of the Common Market, which is now the EU. Although we did not achieve membership until 1973, the die had been cast, a more outward economic strategy was pursued and the IDA was charged with attracting foreign investment into Ireland.

McConnells Advertising was given the task of producing an advertising campaign for the main markets where the IDA hoped to recruit business to locate in Ireland, namely the US, Germany and the UK. The first campaigns in the late 1960s concentrated on communicating the range of financial incentives available from the Irish government to persuade overseas firms to re-locate in Ireland. These were classic functionally based campaigns that were successful in raising the profile of a country which was widely regarded as an economic backwater. But by the early 1970s a number of other locations were starting to follow the Irish example, especially in the critical US market, and the agency was directed to come up with a new approach that would position Ireland as the most favourable location in Europe for US investment. Still heavily influenced by functionally based arguments, McConnells analysed the market from every available angle and eventually the IDA office in New York provided us with a vital set of statistics which we felt could provide the basis for a compelling campaign.

The US Dept of Commerce, which was a mine of information on the financial performance of American companies in overseas markets, discovered that the average return on investment for US companies in Ireland was 29 per cent, which was twice the average return on investment for all European countries. By the early 1970s, around 300 US businesses had already located in Ireland so the sample was fairly robust, but it didn't reveal that most of the businesses that had located in Ireland were in the newer economic sectors like electronics and healthcare where profit margins where higher than in more traditional industry sectors that had been established for much longer in the bigger European economies. In advertising you have to make the best of the hand you're dealt with and we gratefully milked the statistics for all they were worth.

The first campaign showed a smug-looking US businessman gazing out of an aircraft window accompanied by the headline, "I flew the Atlantic for 29 cents". The body copy went on to explain the return on investment statistics and the ad made a huge impact in the days before the idea of low fares airlines had occurred to anyone. The campaign was eventually pared down to a dramatic presentation of the 29 per cent figure. A caption at the end of each advertisement read: "the highest return on investment in the EEC". The campaign created a major impact among the target group and won a series of awards in the American business press.

By the end of the decade Europe was in serious economic difficulties following successive oil price rises and unemployment in all the major European economies was very high. Every other European location had witnessed the success of the IDA in attracting overseas businesses into Ireland and soon every European

country, and some individual regions, had their own little IDA offices in New York.

By this stage we were becoming more sophisticated in advertising planning and research was commissioned among middle
and senior level businessmen to determine attitudes towards investing in Ireland compared to other European locations. The results were disappointing in that they showed that the majority of
respondents were only vaguely aware that some economic progress had been achieved and continued to view Ireland through
Quiet Man-tinted glasses. The claim to be the most profitable
country in Europe, when considered in comparison to the alternative range of options that were now competing for attention, was
forcing the target market back to their comfortable view of Ireland
as a tranquil rural backwater. When we had the field more or less
to ourselves we were very successful but the results suggested that
in a more competitive environment we would suffer unless we
could create a more dynamic impact.

At the time that we were agonising over these findings we were
also experiencing our own "Road to Damascus" branding moment
with the Golden Maverick campaign (see Introduction) and we
suddenly began to realise that in the context of our campaign to
US business, Ireland itself was a brand. The country had a brand
image made up of a whole range of attitudes, associations, opinions and impressions taken from a variety of sources, some fairly
accurate, some wildly off the mark, but all contributing to a brand
image that was playing a crucial role in determining whether senior executives would decide to invest in Ireland as opposed to
some other location such as Scotland, which was by then our most
serious competitor. The idea of treating a country as a brand is
now commonplace but in the early 1980s it was revolutionary and
we had to be very careful in presentations to our client that we
were not demeaning the country in any way. For more on countries as brands, and Ireland in particular, see Chapter 11.

The revelation of Ireland as a brand enabled us to start looking for insights that could be used to position the country in a more advantageous light in the minds of the target audience. We took the classic definition of an advertising planning insight — "the leveraging of a truth about the product or service with a requirement of the target market" — and applied it to our situation. We had always made a point of keeping up to date with the latest management thinking in the US market, and we knew that management academics and consultants were urging businesses who were investing overseas not to base all their decisions on the amount of grants and other financial inducements on offer but to consider the wider business climate, especially the availability and suitability of staff. That became our "requirement of the target market" and we eventually came to the conclusion that the Irish people themselves were probably our most powerful asset. Senior US business people may have had their doubts about the sophistication of the industrial infrastructure, but Irish people were universally popular among the target market. Given how many of this market were themselves of Irish stock, this was hardly surprising.

Our first creative interpretation of this insight was probably too literal. We showed pictures of attractive young Irish people with the following headlines: "People are to Ireland as champagne is to France" and "People are to Ireland as oil is to Texas". We also attempted to brand the country with a more youthful self-confident image using the latest demographic data, which showed that fifty per cent of the population were under the age of twenty-five. We created a slogan, "The Young Europeans", together with a visual of a group of attractive young people, and this device appeared in all the advertisements. The campaign was launched in March 1983 but we weren't entirely happy with the main theme and the analogy with people in other countries seemed a bit forced. After repeated planning exercises designed to examine in more detail what the target market really wanted in a potential workforce and renewed studies of management literature in the

US, we came to the conclusion that education was the key factor. An educated workforce was the key to success in the more flexible knowledge worker era that was dawning and there was the added advantage that education and Ireland would be a credible combination in America. For the remainder of the decade, all advertisements featured education and the "Young Europeans" theme.

We became more confident as the campaign appeared to be having a major impact among the market and although it never appeared in Ireland it did create enormous interest and the line "The Young Europeans" was widely quoted. One of the most successful ads in the campaign featured a headline which became controversial at home in Ireland but was probably the most successful of all in the US, "Hire Them before They Hire You". This headline seemed to symbolise a new more self-confident and dynamic Ireland, not coming cap-in-hand looking for favours but boldly stating its case. There were numerous requests from Irish-American businessmen for copies of this advertisement. Perhaps the boldest of all the ads in the campaign was the one featuring the three schoolchildren on a lonely road in Connemara waiting for a school bus with the simple headline, "Knowledge is Power". In the august pages of *Business Week*, *Forbes* and *Fortune* it had little difficulty standing out from all other competitive advertisements.

IDA outdoor poster on the Bayshore Freeway, Palo Alto, California, 1981

Branding Lessons from the IDA Campaign

- Countries are brands. Therefore from a marketing perspective it is advisable to apply the tried and trusted consumer marketing principles of branding, whether we are trying to attract oversees investment or tourists.

- Don't throw out the baby with the bathwater. Sometimes the thinking behind a campaign can be spot-on but the creative execution may not be perfect. In this situation keep trying to improve the creative execution.

Case Study 2: Surf

In almost every country in the world Unilever are locked in mortal combat with Procter & Gamble for brand share in the detergent market. During the 1980s there was a frenzy of new product developments as both companies tried to gain market share advantage through technological improvements. However, research in the early 1990s indicated that some consumers were resisting the move to the new concentrated products, preferring to stay with conventional powders which were seen to provide better value for money.

Capitalising on this opportunity, P&G launched Daz Automatic, a conventional powder in the economy sector, in the early 1990s. Lever Ireland had an existing brand in this sector, Surf, but it had not received any marketing communications support for some time and was languishing at the bottom end of the market with a share of between one and two per cent. In 1992 it was decided to relaunch the brand on a value-for-money platform. The decision to compete in the value sector of the market was an obvious one because the brand had always been associated with this attribute. The real task therefore was to find a credible yet compelling position for the brand within the economy sector. Being an economy brand was not in itself enough to succeed. In this case the planning exercise looked in detail at the conventions, or what would now probably be referred to as the "semiotics", of detergent advertising and McConnells conducted a detailed examination of the history of the Surf brand.

One of the exercises in Adam Morgan's *Eating the Big Fish*[12] thesis is the "brand vault". This is the repository of stories, legends, myths and attributes from a brand's past which could be revived to form the basis of a new campaign. The analysis of detergent advertising showed that it was the advertising category most frequently singled out for criticism by consumers. This was not to suggest that advertising was not highly effective in selling detergents — it was — but individual campaigns were frequently intrusive and formula-driven. Celebrities from well-known TV programmes and soap operas were frequently employed as presenters and almost all detergent advertising in Ireland was imported from the UK.

The brand's history revealed the interesting fact that Surf's practical down-to-earth credentials were more soundly based than any of its competitors. In 1964 in Britain a Labour government under Harold Wilson was elected on a popular wave of discontent with "the Establishment" and a highly critical attitude to the so-called excesses of marketing, in particular packaging and advertising. Surf was launched by Unilever as a response to this criticism and marketing expenditure was kept to a minimum. Although the same level of political criticism was absent in Ireland it was felt that rather than communicating a lower price message we would build a more durable brand by building on the no-nonsense heritage. We would then be able to appeal to people who considered themselves practical and down-to-earth rather that merely wanting to save money. That would be an added, but unspoken, bonus.

For the new campaign we therefore settled on a target market of housewives who considered themselves practical and down-to-earth, who had a healthy scepticism about all the scientific claims of rival detergents and who wanted a product that would perform its function without having to pay over the odds.

---

[12] Morgan, A., *Eating The Big Fish*, John Wiley, 1999.

The creative solution was to choose a presenter who typified that attitude and Mary McEvoy, an actress who played just such a character in the most popular soap opera in Ireland, *Glenroe*, was ideal. She had the added bonus of being an Irish soap actress; in the past a variety of English stars had filled the role in detergent advertisements and there was evidence that consumers would respond positively to an Irish dimension in detergent advertising. It was essential that the scripts complemented Mary's directness, so the money-back guarantee on the pack was developed into a central selling point and the line, "and if you're not satisfied Lever Bros will give you your money back", became a national catchphrase as the campaign developed.

The first commercial went on air in February 1993 and there was an immediate sales response. By 1996 six commercials featuring Mary had been aired and Surf's brand share had increased from 1.3 per cent in 1992 to 8.25 in 1996. In the fiercely competitive detergent market this was a phenomenal achievement. A number of different Irish presenters have been used since then and the brand now has a market share of 12 per cent.

Branding Lessons from the Surf Campaign

- The brand vault can contain significant treasures. Marketing communications which are based on the real nature of a brand seem to fall on more receptive ears. It would appear that the public have very acute antennae for brand truths.

- Even in an era of third-age, higher-order or post-modern branding, where surreal production techniques were common, creative communication of functional benefits can still work.

- The positioning of the brand was crystal clear and the no-nonsense, practical, "I know what I want and I know my own mind" approach was maintained over a long period.

Case Study 3: Smithwick's

There was a time when the Irish beer market was a relatively simple affair. Most pubs had only three brands of draft beer, Guinness, a stout, Harp, a lager, and Smithwick's, an ale. In the 1970s Smithwick's had a brand share of around 30 per cent of the whole beer market. Although the brand has the longest pedigree of any contemporary beer in the market, dating from 1710, it was really only distributed nationally from the 1960s when it immediately benefited from the first signs of a renewed self-confidence among Irish people. In that much-maligned decade there was a prevailing mood of rebellion in the air and the new younger generation were increasingly impatient with existing shibboleths — de Valera, McQuaid and, to a lesser extent, Guinness. Smithwick's new bright look with none of the baggage of the past was the main beneficiary of the new mood and for a time it was the brand of choice of the younger generation. But the Smithwick's party didn't last all that long; Guinness re-invented itself with a hard-working campaign aimed at younger people and continental lagers with impeccable brewing credentials began to make their appearance. Smithwick's was suddenly caught between a newly resurgent Guinness, the most powerful Irish brand icon, and lagers from a sophisticated continent increasingly familiar to a more cosmopolitan generation. In a frighteningly short space of time, Smithwick's seemed to become very, very provincial.

A variety of marketing communication campaigns were run during the 1980s, some of them hugely popular with beer drinkers, but nothing succeeded in stopping the inexorable slide in brand share and in the early 1990s it slipped below 10 per cent of the beer market. Around this time a renewed attempt was made to resurrect the brand's fortunes.

A group of consultants was called in to facilitate an extended brainstorming session which took place in a hotel in the Dublin suburbs and lasted for three days. Teams from the Smithwick's marketing department and the advertising agency were ensconced in the hotel and there was even a ban on reading newspapers and watching TV in case we would lose concentration in our attempt to focus exclusively on the problems facing the brand. Consultants who specialise in these types of exercises are inclined towards the trivial, the pretentious and the downright ridiculous and these were no exception. Each day started at 7.00 am with *tai chi* exercises "to loosen up the mind", and the food was all macrobiotic. Needless to say, drink was frowned on, and needless to say, we ignored that little rule.

To be fair, however, we did come away with a heightened awareness of the brand's potential, which kept coming back to the Smithwick's drinker's loyalty to the brand. In this connection a follow-up exercise was to prove the most useful of all. This took place on a Saturday in a more central hotel where between sixty and seventy Smithwick's loyalists from all over the country were assembled in one of the large conference rooms. The marketing department and agency teams intermingled with the respondents and the sense of drama was heightened by masses of lights, cameras, microphones and wires as the entire proceedings were filmed. Respondents vied with each other to grab the microphone and tell their own "Smithwick's story".

As the day unfolded a remarkably coherent pattern emerged. A Smithwick's man — there were no women as the brand has the lowest percentage of female drinkers of any beer — was intensely loyal to the brand, in spite of the inevitable slagging he received from companions who drank stout or lager. They were also very conscious of the brand's declining fortunes and were bitterly critical of the company behind the brand for its neglect. The more they let off steam — and at times the atmosphere resembled a religious revival meeting — the more it became clear that the Smithwick's drinker saw himself as a beleaguered minority unfairly derided by the rest of the world but secure in the knowledge that the rest of the world was out of step and that he could see through the phoniness and pretensions of stout and lager drinkers. Smithwick's was an uncomplicated brand, beer was an uncomplicated category and they were uncomplicated people. A pint of beer was a social lubricant, not a deeply meaningful statement about themselves. It was some time before this idea took root to form the basis of a brand plan but it was clear that within all of the data we had collected there was the making of a potentially powerful positioning for the brand.

In 1995 an unapologetically single-minded strategy was adopted: to consolidate the existing brand loyalists and slow down the rate of decline. The brand proposition was based on the previous research insights, reflecting the quiet self-confidence of the drinker and their desire for a beer that was ideal for relaxed, easy drinking. The term "easy drinking" was to be understood in terms of both the product experience and the sociability of the drinking occasion. Thus we were again linking a product truth — the brand was easier to digest than stouts or lagers — with a requirement of the target audience — sociable drinking occasions with a group of friends in which the normal pub banter that characterises Irish drinking was a feature. Thus the "locals" campaign was born and it very quickly became the most popular beer advertising, even among drinkers who would never dream of choosing Smithwicks.

Over thirty "locals" commercials were made between 1995 and 2002, all featuring a core group of drinking mates and all filmed in a genuine local, Kavanagh's in Glasnevin, known affectionately to generations of Dubliners as "The Gravediggers". By 2000 the decline in the brand's sales had been halted and a slow increase in sales was recorded for the first time in over twenty years in 2001.

Branding Lessons from the Smithwick's Campaign

- Existing users of a brand can often provide the key to a more powerful positioning.

- More intense methods of market research can sometimes unlock insights into a brand that will remain hidden from conventional questioning techniques.

Conclusion

The Brand Planning Cycle can be very clear-cut; sometimes even a cursory look at a brand reveals an obvious direction and only one possible option for getting there. Most of the time, though, this is not the case, and often the question of where we want to be is not always that obvious. It is easy to set an objective of doubling sales or doubling brand share but other factors like profitability have to be taken into account and good brand management must maximise profitability at the expense of short-term sales or market share gains. But even profitability must be balanced by the long-term revenue potential of the brand and too often the demand for short-term profitability takes precedence over what might be a more prudent strategy for the long-term health of the brand.

The three case histories outlined in this chapter have important lessons for anyone involved in brand management. In all three a considerable amount of information about the current position of the brand — "where are we now?" — was assembled in advance. The solution in the case of Smithwick's was very much dependent on an acute understanding of the personality, mentality and motivations of existing users of the brand. There was also a high level of awareness in each instance of how the brand came to be in its current position — "how did we get there?" This information was the key to the adoption of the very successful strategy for Surf and was also mentioned in connection with the origins of AIB. Answering this question is probably the most neglected aspect of brand management because too few brand managers are prepared to listen to Polonius's final piece of advice: "above all to thine own self be true". The solution in the case of the IDA represents a classic instance of continuously interrogating all the data collected in the first two phases of the planning cycle with the objective of coming up with an "insight" which connects a truth about the product or service under review and a requirement or need of the target group. There are now a wide range of techniques for insight generation which are described in Chapter 6.

5

BUILDING STRONG BRANDS (2):
COMMUNICATING THE MESSAGE

Once the brand strategy is agreed, the next step is to communicate the agreed strategy to the target audience. The brand strategy can be regarded as the story we want people to know about our product or service. That story is made up of all the ideas, associations, impressions and opinions that the people we want to influence — the target group — have in their minds about our product or service. It is summed up by what the brand ultimately stands for in their minds, the core proposition. Some form of marketing communication channel will usually be used to achieve this objective. Not every brand has to use marketing communications; some exclusive brands can rely on discrete word-of-mouth and some brands have a deliberate policy of relying on the customer experience. The best-known example of the latter would be Marks & Spencer in the UK, who were able to trade off their considerable high-street retail presence. It is, however, interesting to note that they used advertising from the beginning in Ireland where they have a more limited presence and since their star has waned in the UK they have started to advertise, apparently with great success.

Until very recently, brand communication was synonymous with advertising and in the public mind it still is. But in recent years two factors in the business world have complicated this tidy little arrangement:

- The power of advertising is assumed to have weakened. Reports of its decline are greatly exaggerated, especially by practitioners of alternative methods of communication, but the fragmentation of the mass media means that it is not as easy to deliver huge audiences as it once was. For example, just ten years ago, over 40 per cent of Irish adults watched *The Late Late Show*. Today it is still one of the most popular programmes on TV but is only watched by around 16 per cent of all adults. More ominously, the technology is now in place which will enable viewers to bypass the ads completely. Part of the reason for the decline in individual audience figures is the proliferation of channels but we are also dealing with a more mobile, active population who are less likely to be sitting around at home in family groups. Another frequently mentioned reason for the supposed decline in the power of advertising is the ad-literacy of the public who are always assumed to be much more sophisticated than previous generations. However, we need to be careful not to patronise previous generations or assume that they were more naïve than they actually were.

- Other forms of marketing communications have become more sophisticated — for example, relationship marketing and sponsorship — and new channels based on the internet and the mobile phone are beginning to emerge.

Both of these developments have forced brand owners to look at the different communication methods in a more integrated way and the term , "marcoms" is now starting to become more widely used as a shorthand for marketing communications. But before looking at these methods in more detail it might be worthwhile taking a short digression, if only to prove yet again that "what goes around comes around".

A Digression

In the 1970s a new advertising agency called Marcom made an all-too-brief appearance in Dublin. It was effectively the re-launch of a long-established agency, Arrow Advertising, but the new company collapsed shortly afterwards. Arrow had a distinguished creative reputation and had been responsible for a series of high-profile advertisements during the early 1970s, including a memorable army recruitment campaign with a speeded-up music track of Beethoven's Fifth Symphony; and a campaign for the Irish language featuring a slogan which went into the vernacular: "It's part of what we are." The agency succumbed to hard times — the 1970s witnessed the great oil crises and were difficult for all businesses — and finally closed in 1983, leaving liabilities of £1.2 million, a substantial amount at the time.

The intention of renaming the agency as Marcom was to reflect the growing importance of non-advertising forms of marketing communications and in that sense it was ahead of its time. During the 1980s there was an increasing awareness of the potential role of public relations and sales promotion, but advertising was universally regarded as by far the most powerful and successful means of conveying marketing communications messages. Strangely enough, the term Marcom or Marcoms made little or no impression and even today the term is still not widely used outside academia where it is always referred to in connection with integrated marketing communications or more commonly IMC. The integration issue has been the subject of intense debate in the last few years but it is still the exception rather than the rule for anyone involved in the business to regard themselves as working in marketing communications. When asked, they will invariably describe themselves as working in a particular branch of marketing communications, e.g. advertising, public relations or sales promotion. This is not surprising given that the first definition of marketing communications is claimed to have been written as recently as the early 1990s:

> Integrated marketing communications is a concept of marketing communication planning that recognises the added value of a comprehensive plan that evaluates the strategic roles of a variety of communications disciplines; for example, advertising, direct response, sales promotion and public relations; and combines these disciplines to provide clarity, consistency and maximum communication impact.[1]

However, this definition is more about "integration" than about marketing communications itself, which is best described as the different methods business organisations use to tell their stories in the hope of influencing people to buy their products or services. In the past this was often referred to as "publicity".

Interestingly, the term "publicity" is rarely used nowadays but it has a long history. In the 1960s when Ireland was emerging from the post-independence economic nightmare of the 1930s, 1940s and 1950s, a new breed of business entrepreneurs began to appear, encouraged by the freedom promised by the Whittaker/Lemass reforms which opened up the country to economic development. One of the most prominent and successful was a Cavan-born car dealer, Con Smith, who built up a successful business empire, at the heart of which was the franchise for Renault cars. The French company was prepared to subsidise the costs of advertising in the Irish market and Con decided that he needed someone to oversee the process. There were hardly any marketing departments in Ireland at the time; a growing number of companies had sales managers but marketing was almost unknown. But all Con wanted was "publicity" for his cars, whose quirky continental design was proving too exotic for Irish tastes weaned from the be-

---

[1] Kitchen, P. and Schultz, D. "Integrated Marketing Communications: What it is and Why are Companies Working this Way", ESOMAR conference papers, 1997.

ginning of the automobile era on more humdrum Ford founda-
tions. He solved the problem in his own inimitable way by figuring
out that gaining "publicity" required creative flair — and where
better to find that than in the theatre. That was how Phil O'Kelly,
who had been Publicity Manager for the Abbey Theatre and the
Gaiety Theatre, came to be appointed to run Renault's advertising,
public relations and sales promotions for the Smith Group. The
advertising agency handling the Renault account at the time was
McConnells, a long-established Dublin agency who before moving
to their present offices in Charlemont Place had occupied a
prominent office in Pearse Street from the 1920s called, appropriately enough, Publicity House.

Publicity is not a word that would be heard in marketing circles today, with the possible exception of the term "free publicity".
Its original meaning has been subsumed into the individual forms
of marketing communications and in the past twenty years they
have all taken on very clear identities of their own.

Methods of Marketing Communication: More Ways than One to Tell a Story

There are a great many textbooks, including an excellent Irish
one,[2] which describe the different ways of telling the brand story.
The textbooks tend to treat them individually but it may be useful
to group them into different categories. The following are three,
admittedly arbitrary, categories — traditional, modern and post-
modern:

- **Traditional:** There is a reasonable level of agreement here,
  with most commentators regarding advertising, sales promotion, public relations and personal selling as the four main-
  stays of marketing communications.

---

[2] Medcalf, P., *Marketing Communications: An Irish Perspective*, Gill & Macmillan, 2004.

- **Modern:** This is not as neatly defined a group and it could be argued that relationship marketing, sponsorship and design, could just as easily be placed in the traditional category on the grounds that they have all been employed, in some shape or form, for most of the twentieth century. However, they all assumed much greater importance during the 1980s and 1990s and in the process became more professional and more systematically applied. Even design, long considered a passive vehicle by most businesses, became a powerful method of marketing communication in a more visually literate and design-conscious age.

- **Postmodern:** This refers to communication channels which owe their existence to recently available technology, such as the internet and the mobile phone, or to the blurring of distinctions between editorial content and marketing communications, which has revolutionised a rather haphazard communication vehicle known as product placement into a major sophisticated vehicle now referred to as *embedded marketing*.

Figure 2: Categories of Marketing Communications

TRADITIONAL	MODERN	POSTMODERN
Advertising	*Sponsorship*	*Multimedia*
TV		Internet
Radio	*Relationship*	Mobile phone
Press	*Marketing*	
Outdoor		*Embedded Marketing*
Cinema	*Design*	Product placement
Sales Promotion		
(including Point-of-Sale)		
PR		
Personal Selling		
(now includes call centres)		

There are three key differences between traditional media and new technology media:

1. Greater degree of permission required from the audience before they participate;

2. More interactivity between the audience and the marketing communications content;

3. More use of combinations of different forms of marketing communication.

The term "embedded marketing" is now being applied to the increasingly incestuous relationship between the entertainment business and marketing communications, exemplified by the phrase, "Madison and Vine",[3] referring to the New York thoroughfare associated with the advertising industry and Vine Street in Hollywood.

Integrated Marketing Communications

All of these developments have created a need for more professional integration of the different forms of marketing communications with the objective of producing the most effective and cost-efficient plan for telling the brand story:

> Integrated marketing communications started as a simple idea of juxtaposing promotional concepts so that every element spoke with one voice; it moved well beyond this to become an integrated philosophy which reaches out and touches every facet of the business which claims to be consumer orientated. There are a number of new 21st century factors driving the move to integrated marketing

---

[3] Donaton, S., *Madison & Vine*, McGraw Hill, 2004.

communication: digitalisation, intellectual property and information technology communications systems.[4]

Integrated marketing communications has been the cause of some controversy, not because anyone disagrees with the idea in principle, which makes eminent sense, but over who controls the overall brand strategy. When advertising was the main method of communication, there was no problem; the advertising agency agreed the strategy with the brand owner. In a more integrated world everybody wants to be in control. Public relations companies argue that because they are providing high-level strategic communications advice in a world where all business communications are being more carefully scrutinised, they should have the upper hand. Some media independents argue their case on the somewhat dubious grounds that 45 per cent of message takeout is attributable to content and most of the remaining 55 per cent to context — that is, the medium.[5] Sensing an opportunity for a quick profit, a myriad of consultancies, from the global general management behemoths to local one-man-bands have also started to edge into this area. In the last few years specialised marketing communications consultancies have made an appearance in the UK and US so the whole area is in a considerable state of flux with no indication at this stage as to who is likely to come out on top. The most likely outcome is that no one will; that different brand owners will adopt different strategies depending on the nature of their business and the degree to which they want to control the whole process themselves.

In spite of some predictions of their decline, the traditional advertising agencies should be ideally placed to continue to play a major role in brand communication in the future, but a certain lack of self-confidence in charging for strategic advice has left them vulnerable. However, they have vastly more experience in brand man-

---

[4] Kitchen, P.J. and Schultz, D.E., "The Status of IMC: A 21st Century Perspective", *Admap*, September 2000.

[5] Saunders, J., "Back to the Future (With a Difference)", *Admap*, May 2002.

agement than any of the other contenders and they have a more intuitive understanding of the nature of brands and branding.

Examples of New Integrated Marketing Communications

- **Club Energise:** This brand has been one of the most successful new product launches in the Irish market in the last five years and was aimed directly at one of the most powerful multinational brands in the Irish market, Lucozade. The most unusual feature of the launch was the innovative tie-in with the Gaelic Players Association whereby a percentage of each case sold was given to the GPA to foster the future of Gaelic games. Thus, instead of relying solely on the mass media to deliver the audience for the brand story, C&C gathered their own audience together in the first place. The brand has achieved around twenty per cent of the market.

- **Samsung**: The Korean consumer electronics manufacturer has been the fastest-growing brand in *Business Week's* "Top 100" Global Brands listings and is now positioned at number 20, having overtaken its longer established Japanese rival, Sony, in the process. Samsung spend much less of their resources on traditional media but are heavily involved in embedded marketing, having been one of the lead sponsors of films like *The Fantastic Four* in which a variety of their products play a role.[6]

- **BMW**: The motor manufacturer produced eight mini-films lasting about ten minutes each in 2001 and 2002 in the US under the collective title *The Hire*. Each film was under the control of a leading Hollywood director including John Frankenheimer and Ang Lee. They had complete control over the production, the only stipulation being that BMW cars must be featured. In a reversal of the traditional practice where production budgets are a small fraction of media budgets, in this

---

[6] "The Top 100", *Business Week*, 5 September 2005.

instance the production budget was $13.5 million and only $1.5 million was spent in media — mainly specialist film media — to inform the target audience that the films were available on the internet. The films were downloaded over 50 million times but more importantly double-digit sales increases were recorded in 2001, 2002 and 2003.[7]

- **Lynx**: A Unilever male deodorant brand with a history of innovative marketing communication. In 2004 the brand sponsored a live music concert in the Arctic Circle — the infrastructure was made of ice and an audience of 300 competition winners enjoyed a show featuring acts like Faithless and The Thrills. The show was filmed by Channel 4 in a one-hour special aimed at the target audience.[8]

- **Chanel No 5:** This brand was immortalised as Marilyn Monroe's answer to the question of what she wore in bed, but it had been losing its cachet during the 1980s and 1990s. In 2004 a new internet-based campaign was launched involving a three-minute commercial featuring Nicole Kidman which reputedly cost €27 million. The company's marketing department argued that all target groups were becoming more resistant to traditional forms of marketing communication but not everyone was convinced of the effectiveness of the new commercial. Prominent UK creative Trevor Beattie commented, "It sucks so hard it vacuumed my living room carpet."[9]

- **Burger King:** One of the most successful brand communications in the US in 2003 was a website called "Subservient Chicken", which was produced by Burger King. On the site a man dressed up as a chicken appeared with an invitation to

---

[7] Donaton, S., *Madison & Vine*, McGraw-Hill, 2004.

[8] Dawson, N. and Hull, M., "That's Brand Entertainment", *Admap*, February 2005.

[9] Tungate, M., *Fashion Brands: Branding Style from Armani to Zara*, Kogan Page, 2004.

type in whatever people wanted the chicken to do. Children of all ages responded in their millions and were pleasantly surprised by the range of activities that could be undertaken by the "Subservient Chicken". It was the most talked-about brand communication in the US that year.[10]

- **Innocent:** The brand leader in the UK smoothie market, which is now worth over £70 million. The brand has used a wide variety of innovative marketing communication methods, including the design of its headquarters building ("Fruit Towers"); its commercial vehicles covered in grass ("Hairy Green Vans"); to informal concerts in public parks in the UK ("Fruitstock"). Innocent has also produced a best-selling range of "small books" and all of its low-cost innovative marketing communication has created a huge word-of-mouth communication about the brand.

- **Guinness:** A key theme of the new marketing communications is an attempt to enable consumers to have a deeper experience of the brand than would be available from traditional marketing consumer communication methods. The Guinness Storehouse is an excellent example of a response to this trend. The brief was to use an ultra-modern facility to breathe life into the brand and reconnect with younger consumers: "It represents best practice in the experience economy — and a reimagination of how a company can connect with its core constituents. The Storehouse is located in an abandoned fermentation plant within the main Guinness brewing complex; a brick exterior gives way to a modern glass and steel interior that is illuminated by a dramatic combination of natural and artificial light. After paying an entry fee of about $10, visitors receive 'The Pebble', a palm-size Lucite token with a globule of Guinness stout inside. The pebble grants entry to the store-

---

[10] Collinge, M., "$elling the Futur£", *Esquire*, September 2005.

house, its displays, history, gift shop and once visitors rise slowly to the top floor the pebble acts as a drink ticket at the Gravity Bar, which boasts panoramic views of the city. A bartender scans the pebble, deactivating a metal strip inside, serves your pint and returns the pebble as a souvenir."[11]

- **Cully & Sully:** A new Irish food company, formed in 2004, making prepared food for the new cash-rich, time-poor Irish who have the money to pay for prepared meals, the time pressure to need this service and the sophisticated palettes to demand high-quality food. Marketing communications for the brand is two-pronged and arguably represents the best strategy for emerging Irish consumer brands: (a) design: distinctive, modern, laid-back and engaging; (b) website: high-level content, distinctive "cool" personality, is chatty, informal, sophisticated and "sticky".

Conclusions

Brand owners will have to be much more imaginative in telling their stories in future. They won't be able to rely as much on the mass media and may have to consider bringing audiences together themselves:

> The era of building brands mainly through mass media is over. The predominant thinking of the world's most successful brand builders these days is not so much the old game of reach and frequency, but rather finding ways to get consumers into their lives. The mass media won't disappear as a tool. But smart companies see the game today as making bold statements in design and wooing customers by integrating messages so closely into entertainment that the two are all but indistinguishable.[12]

---

[11] Kirsner, S., "Brand Marketing: 'Guinness'", *Fast Company*, Issue 58, May 2002.
[12] "The Top 100", Ibid.

6

INSIGHTS, INSIGHTS ANY OLD INSIGHTS: CREATIVE THINKING AND BRANDING

The world's leading management writers, academics, consultants and gurus don't always agree on very much as they plough their own very lucrative furrows but they are all aligned on the critical importance of innovation:

> Innovation is the central issue in economic prosperity (Michael Porter, Harvard Business School)

> Innovation, the vital spark of all human change improvement and progress (Theodore Levitt, Harvard Business School)

> Radical non-linear innovation is the only way to escape the ruthless hyper-competition that has been hammering down margins in industry after industry — non-linear innovation requires the capacity to escape the shackles of the present and imagine exciting innovative solutions to current needs (Gary Hamel, London Business School)

Innovation in branding can take many forms, from genuinely new product or service development, as opposed to superficial variants, to innovative new ways of positioning a brand. Brand managers in marketing departments usually concentrate on the latter as product and service development issues are the responsibility of other departments. Because this department is the one that should have the best understanding of consumers and be in possession of the available consumer research it makes sense to give it the responsibility for new product development; but the fact remains that the enormous focus on "insights" during the last decade has almost exclusively concentrated on new and innovative ways of positioning existing brands. Because of this there are now a wide range of case histories which demonstrate the power of new marketing communications insights to transform the fortunes of a brand.

The Need for More Transformational Ideas in Marketing Communications

There has been a significant shift in the way brand management and marketing communications were practised in the 1990s. This movement had been developing for the previous twenty years and had its origins in the birth of account planning in advertising agencies. The introduction of account planning began in London in the early 1970s and is usually attributed to two people: Stephen King of J. Walter Thompson and Stanley Pollitt of Boase Massimi and Pollitt. The latter believed that traditional market researchers were a little heavy handed when dealing with creative work.[1] The precise functions of account planning have always proved extremely difficult to explain and Jeremy Bullmore, a witty and erudite commentator on the advertising scene once wrote an essay entitled "What are account planners for, Daddy?"[2] which did not come to any definite conclusions but did contain the following endorsement: "At your most valuable you can illuminate and inspire — you can provide insight and intuitive hypothesis and you can clarify and crystallise." Account planners effectively took over the role of market researchers in advertising agencies but added another layer of expertise. The traditional market researcher investigated a market using either quantitative or qualitative methods, or

---

[1] Feldwick, P. (ed), *Pollitt on Planning*, Admap Publications, 2000.

[2] Bullmore, J., *Behind the Scenes in Advertising*, NTC Publications, 1991.

a mix of both, and then reported on the findings. The account planner not only reported on the findings but ventured into the creative arena by making recommendations about what to do next.

Not everyone that called themselves an account planner was capable of coming up with the creative insights that the position required and as a result the account planning function remained in some doubt for many years. But it is now firmly established and no self-respecting agency would dare enter a pitch for new business without including one in the team. To some extent the emergence of account planners represented a subtle shift in the balance of power in agencies from the creative department to account management. Prior to the introduction of account planning the main function of account management was to meet clients at a civilised hour in the morning, say around 10.30 am, discuss world affairs and sport, though not necessarily in that order, over a leisurely cup of coffee and gently guide them to a gin and tonic as near to midday as possible, and then sink slowly into the afternoon over an extended lunch while the creative teams produced the advertisements. This process meant that the creative teams not only created the ads but also, to some extent by default, created the strategy, even if it wasn't actually called that at the time. Sometimes this process worked very well and it certainly suited the participants. Many creative people were talented brand strategists but not all of them were and eventually the task of producing a communication strategy moved to account management and in particular to the account planning function.

We're All Creative Now!

For a variety of reasons, mainly the increasing level of competition in the marketplace, the characteristic sound in the world of brand management and marketing communications in the 1970s was the cry of "insights, insights, any old insights" and in a rare moment of serendipity at the same time a new revolutionary movement from

California was beginning to preach the message that we could all be "creative":

> The transformative technologies offer us a passage to creativity, healing, choices. The gift of insight, of making imaginative new connections, once the specialty of the lucky few, is there for anyone willing to persist, experiment, explore.[3]

The Esalen Institute in California's Big Sur area was the epicentre of humanistic psychology and the main inspiration for what became known as the human-potential movement. It was a forum for new ideas and was heavily influenced by Eastern philosophy and the concept of the different capacities of the left and right sides of the brain. The left side was associated with logic, reasoning, analysis, linear and digital thinking and numeracy while the right side of the brain was associated with music, rhythm, shape recognition, daydreaming and creativity in general. The Western education tradition tended to emphasise the left-hand side of the brain, often to the detriment of the right-hand side, with the result that our creative capacity is left underdeveloped. Post-modernism, with its emphasis on flux, fragmentation and flexibility, was closely aligned with the new focus on creativity and the acceptance of these ideas in wider management circles was greatly facilitated by the extraordinary success of the management bestseller written by two McKinsey consultants, *In Search of Excellence*.[4] This book argued strongly for a more creative and innovative approach to business and was critical of the overly rational model which had been in vogue for the previous half century. So it wasn't just the branding and marketing communications world that was being urged to become more creative; every corner of the business world was being urged to do the same.

---

[3] Ferguson, M., *The Age of Aquarius*, Paladin Books, 1983.

[4] Peters, T. and Waterman, R., *In Search of Excellence*, Harper & Row, 1982.

What Exactly is Creativity?

The new emphasis on creativity resulted in a renewed interest in the nature of creativity, a notoriously difficult subject to grasp. A leading twentieth-century intellectual who did try to come to terms with the subject was Arthur Koestler, whose dense and complicated tome, *The Act of Creation*,[5] achieved a certain cachet among those trying to understand how businesses could be helped to become more creative. Koestler's main contribution was the concept of "bisociation" which made a distinction between the routine skills of thinking on a single plane and the creative act which always involves thinking on more than one plane:

> The essence of discovery is that unlikely marriage of cabbages and kings, of previously unrelated frames of reference or universes of discourse, whose union will solve previously insoluble problems.[6]

This conclusion was very much in line with one of the most widely accepted definitions of insights in the marketing communications community as the leveraging of a product truth with a fundamental need or requirement of the target market. Koestler's other main contribution to the subject was the fact that the greatest barrier to creative solutions was that we are all conditioned to approach problems from the perspective of an existing set of rules which enabled us to deal with similar problems in the past. Almost by definition the existing rules have to be ignored or broken if a creative solution is to be found to a current problem.

But perhaps his most useful comment on the nature of creativity was to debunk the popular notion that solutions or great discoveries happen by chance, the "eureka moment" or the "bath, bed, bus" syndrome. He believed that fortune favoured the prepared mind or, to quote the famous remark usually attributed to Gary Player, "the

---

[5] Koestler, A., *The Act of Creation*, Penguin Books, 1973.
[6] Ibid.

more I practise the luckier I get". In spite of the implications of this advice, which I would interpret as becoming as expert as possible in whatever market you are involved with, the creativity industry blossomed during the late twentieth century as all kinds of weird and wonderful potions were hawked around the boardrooms of the business world. The philosophies of East and West were ransacked in an effort to provide suitably packaged products guaranteed to make even the most unimaginative executive into a wellspring of creativity. The East had an obvious allure; the art of Zen, which teaches that enlightenment is brought about by introspection and accessing the deeper mind, enjoyed a brief phase of popularity. There is no doubt that Western culture does tend to downgrade intuition in the mistaken belief that it is "not rational" and many of the techniques that became fashionable in the pursuit of better insights were designed to exercise the right-hand side of the brain which was largely underutilised by modern businesses.

Nothing was sacred in the search for the Holy Grail of better insights and even the Gods and Goddesses of ancient myths were brought to bear on the subject. The timeless myths that recur over and over again in man's history enable us to explore our innermost dreams and desires and can help us leap beyond the mundane realities of our everyday world. Greek mythology was a particularly fruitful source of brand archetypes — Hercules the hero brand, Odysseus the adventurer brand and Agamemnon the ruler brand.

Insight Generating Techniques

A wide variety of methods are available to help businesses to become more creative and produce better insights. The ones that are most commonly referred to are a range of specific techniques which can either be carried out within a business or with the aid of outside specialists and which are designed to generate insights in response to specific problems. These are discussed in Part One of what follows. But there are also a range of mental exercises which should be engaged in on a continuous basis by anyone involved in any area of brand management because ideas may occur at any time in response to the daily interaction with brands. These are discussed in Part Two.

PART ONE: TECHNIQUES FOR INSIGHT GENERATION

Brainstorming

The easiest to use and the most widely used, brainstorming is the granddaddy of all the insight-generating techniques. It is usually attributed to an advertising man, Alex Osborn, the "O" in BBDO. He argued that brainstorming increased both the quantity and the quality of ideas generated by groups of people. Underpinning the concept is the belief that most real breakthroughs sound so strange when first enunciated that even the person who first suggests the idea immediately begins to doubt its validity. Therefore everyone who embarks on a brainstorming session is instructed from the very beginning that no idea, suggestion or initial thought, no matter how bizarre, strange or outlandish it appears, can be dismissed. Everything must be recorded and given due consideration:

> Brainstorming is a popular method of encouraging creative thinking. Its main advantage is deferred judgement, by which all ideas, even unusual and impractical ones, are encouraged without criticism or evaluation. Ideas are recorded as fast as they can be suggested; then they are evaluated for usefulness at a later time. The purpose of deferred judgement is to encourage people to propose bold, unique ideas without worrying about what others think about them; this approach typically produces more ideas than the conventional approach of thinking and judging concurrently. Brainstorming can last from ten minutes to one hour and require no preparation other than a general knowledge of the subject. Other advantages of brainstorming are enthusiasm, broader participation, greater risk ori-

entation, building on ideas exchanged and the feeling that
the final product is a team solution.[7]

Although the ability to run brainstorming sessions is usually assumed to require no special training they can very easily go off the
rails and people who have some experience of moderating discussions will be more likely to achieve better results. The main advantage of the technique is its ability to create a strong sense of
teamwork among members of a group. Many companies use it as a
means of encouraging more participation among executives at different levels in the organisation and a better *esprit de corps*.

However, in spite of the near-universal use of the technique it is
not without its critics. A number of studies have shown that different people thinking on their own are likely to come up with more
ideas than when they think together as a group. There are several
reasons for this. Unless the group is well practised in thinking together it is unlikely that they will be able to operate at the same
pace or that their personalities will allow them to interact in an
equal fashion. Three specific problems have been identified. The
first is the obvious one of everyone not pulling their weight: social
loafing. It is all too easy to hide in the group throwing in the odd
comment to make it less obvious. A number of studies have shown
that some people in brainstorming groups will always expect others to do the bulk of the work and this explains why the aggregate
of individuals' outputs will often be much greater than the collective output of a group.

A second problem is the fear of failure or not wanting to appear a fool in front of colleagues: evaluation apprehension. This
problem is accentuated by the common practice of having individuals at very different levels of seniority involved in brainstorming groups. In these circumstances, the junior members will react
very differently to their superiors. Some will use the opportunity

---

[7] Furnham, A., "The Brainstorming Myth", *Business Strategy Review*, Vol. 11, No. 4, 2000.

to advance their careers, others will be too nervous to fulfil their potential. Neither behaviour is conducive to the essential purpose of brainstorming.

The third problem arises because the nature of the process means that only one person at a time can speak, so other members are prevented from airing their views as they occur to them: production blocking. The waiting time can dilute their suggestions and this can lead to a decline in effort.

Regardless of any possible disadvantages brainstorming has such obvious advantages that it is likely to be the main method of insight generation for the foreseeable future and if the potential problems are kept in mind they can be minimised.

Scenario Planning

Scenario planning has a long history as man has always been fascinated with what the future holds in store; but its modern manifestation probably dates from the beginning of the last century when the possibilities of scientific discovery seemed not only endless but full of exciting and liberating possibilities. H.G. Wells could therefore be considered the father of modern scenario planning. The first formal working-out of fully fledged scenarios was the study of what the year 2000 would look like in the 1960s by Herman Kahn at the Hudson Institute in New York. The fact that less than a quarter of Kahn's predictions turned out to be true didn't inhibit people's interest in the subject.

Businessmen have always tried to envisage the future but formal scenario planning only became a recognised business tool in the 1970s when a strategic planning team at Shell were working on alternative possibilities for the future of the company and devised a range of possible future scenarios including one where the Arab oil suppliers deliberately restricted production resulting in huge price increases. When that actually happened in the aftermath of the Yom Kippur War in 1973, Shell were in the best position to respond because they had already considered what options they would be faced with through their scenario planning exercises.

Shell are still committed to scenario planning and every three years they build a set of global scenarios "to explore the overarching challenges arising from changes in the business environment that need to be faced by its businesses — these scenarios provide a useful context for testing our strategies and plans and help us to anticipate significant changes in the world around us".[8]

Peter Schwartz, who has written a number of books on the subject, defines scenario planning as:

> A tool for ordering one's perceptions about alternative future environments in which one's decisions might be played out. Alternatively a set of organised ways for us to dream effectively about our own future.[9]

It has also been described as a "sophisticated technique for stimulating a firm's management to identify creative ideas for development and implementation".[10]

Although scenario planning emerged from the recognition that a need to anticipate the future was an essential component of business planning it can be used to produce new insights for brand planning because of the nature of the process. Scenario planning in the geopolitical sense involves trying to anticipate what might happen if certain political, technological, or economic events were to arise. From a brand planning perspective we start with the conclusion (e.g. we manage to double our share of the market); we then work backwards to envisage what events would have to take place for this outcome to happen. The resulting analysis can provide very useful insights about what we could introduce into our brand plans to secure the desired outcome. A number of writers on this subject

---

[8] People & Connections: Global Scenarios to 2020, "Shell International 2002", www.shell.com.

[9] Schwartz, P., *The Art of the Long View*, Doubleday Currency, 1991.

[10] Majoro, S., *The Creative Gap*, Longman, 1998.

make the point that it is not the accuracy of the scenario that is important, it is the opportunity to open up the brand planning process to new perspectives and possibilities that would not have been considered in the normal course of events.

When using this technique for the purpose of generating better brand insights, it is probably more accurate to refer to it as scenario writing. We are writing essays about desirable futures rather than trying to predict possible futures. If, for example, we were working with the Irish "brand" in the tourism market and our target group was continental Europeans, we might envisage a world in 2010 where tourist numbers from these markets had doubled compared to the numbers for 2005. We would then have to envisage how this outcome might come about — what events would have to happen for numbers to double; what initiatives would have to be introduced for this to happen. By stretching our imaginations in this way we are forced into coming up with insights which could help to achieve the outcome:

> Scenarios, by definition, challenge the mind-set of managers by developing plausible alternatives. They take decision-makers into new substantive terrain: they require them to be willing to suspend their beliefs, assumptions, and preconceptions; they compel them to grapple with questions that were not raised or were briefly considered and quickly shunted aside — they explicitly challenge conventional wisdom, historic ways of thinking and operating, and long-held assumptions about important issues.[11]

Problem Solving Models

These models are usually associated with multinational companies who manage a range of fast-moving consumer goods brands around the world. Most of these companies have long experience and teams of experts in their head offices who have the time and

---

[11] Fahey, L. and Randall, R. (Eds.), *Learning from the Future*, Wiley 1998.

resources to codify experience from around the world into best practice manuals. Many of them have attempted to produce blueprints for brand planning and although they are not specifically insight-generating methods in the way that brainstorming is, they can be considered under this heading on the grounds that the more imaginatively a situation is defined, the more likely we are to generate creative insights that will lead to growth.

The most famous of all the multinational models is Unilever's. It originated in the 1960s under the title *Unilever Plan for Great Advertising*, but was known fondly by generations of marketing and advertising managers by its acronym UPGA. The objective of these models is to force brand managers to define the marketing background more rigorously, thus enabling a more single-minded communications direction to emerge. The following are the main areas covered in models of this type:

- **Market background:** Describe where the brand is currently positioned in the market in relation to the main competitive brands.

- **Functional benefits:** Main physical benefits or attributes of the brand in relation to the main competitive brands.

- **Emotional benefits:** Main emotional benefits or attributes of the brand compared to the main competitive brands.

- **Personality:** A summary of the overall personality of the brand which will combine functional and emotional attributes.

- **Essence:** The core proposition at the heart of the brand.

- **Insight:** An aspect of the brand — functional or emotional — which can be leveraged against a requirement of the target market.

The theory behind these models is that if we have analysed the market and our brand's current competitive position in relation to competitive brands in enough detail and with enough sensitivity we should be equipped to come up with an insight which could transform the brand's future. The resulting positioning must be both distinctive (distinguishing the brand from its competitors) and desirable (representing an attractive offer to the target group). In order to arrive at a suitable insight and brand proposition we may need to use some of the other insight generating methods described in this chapter but often the very act of filling out the model will be sufficient to generate the necessary ideas. For example, if we were working on a brand image for Ireland in the tourist market an obvious target market would be middle-class, middle-aged holiday makers in the main continental European markets, France, Germany, Italy and the Benelux countries. We could then define the main elements of a model as follows:

- **Market background:** The target market only have a hazy idea of Ireland, it does not automatically come into their initial repertoire of destinations.

- **Functional benefits:** Spectacular, rugged, unspoilt scenery, friendly engaging people, strong sense of history and vibrant culture.

- **Emotional benefits:** Transcendental refreshment — a spiritual experience for stressed out European sophisticates.

- **Personality**: Warm, friendly, easy to engage with.

Detailed consideration of that analysis might lead to the following insight: "Unlike holidays in other destinations I will be able to engage more directly with people and events in Ireland." This in turn could lead to a brand essence as follows: "In Ireland you will be a participant rather than a spectator."

Although most multinational companies have developed their own models, a number of expert commentators have produced their own and one of the most widely used is that developed by Wendy Gordon commonly referred to as the Brand Essence Model.[12]

Figure 3: Brand Essence Model

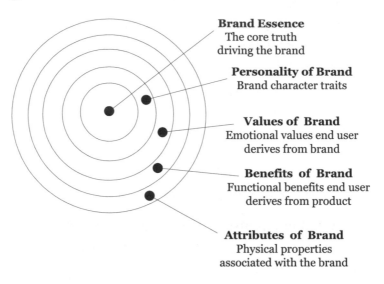

Brand Essence
The core truth
driving the brand

Personality of Brand
Brand character traits

Values of Brand
Emotional values end user
derives from brand

Benefits of Brand
Functional benefits end user
derives from product

Attributes of Brand
Physical properties
associated with the brand

A slightly more academic model which is also widely quoted and used is Jean Noel Kapferer's "Prism Model"[13] (see Figure 4).

Figure 4: Prism Model

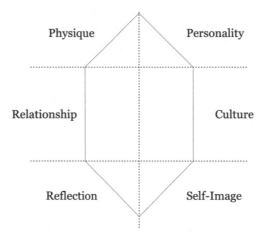

Physique · Personality

Relationship · Culture

Reflection · Self-Image

---

[12] Gordon, W., *Good Thinking*, Admap Publications, 1999.

[13] Kapferer, J-N., *Strategic Brand Management*, Kogan Page, 1992.

For example, if we applied this model to Apple, a very distinctive and well-managed brand, "physique" would represent innovative design, "personality" would be youthful and dynamic, "culture" would be creative, "relationship" would be the willingness to do things differently, "reflection" represents how the brand reflects the customer's image so in the case of Apple it would be self-confident and in control and "self-image" would be an inward sense of being at the leading edge of one's profession.

The advantage of Kapferer's model is that it gives more weight than most models to the consumer's relationship with the brand and in particular to how the consumer might use the brand in the construction of their own self-image. In this way it forces us to dig deeper into every aspect of the brand and there is no doubt that the richer the material we have to work with the more likely we are to generate better insights and propositions.

On the basis that the more detailed the analysis the greater chance we have of better insights one of the most useful models is the "Fishbone Diagram".[14] This is not strictly speaking a model like those that have already been described but it is an extremely useful method of presenting an analysis of a market and because it was not specifically designed as a branding tool it encourages us to think about the wider issues in the market. It was developed by Professor Kaoru Ishikawa of the University of Tokyo and is so called because in order to complete the exercise you work with a diagram that resembles the bones of a fish. It is also known as the cause-and-effect diagram and its purpose is to assist in categorising the many potential causes of problems in an orderly way to identify the root causes and hopefully lead on to proposed solutions. The technique can lead to a more thorough exploration of the issues behind a problem which should lead to more robust solutions. To construct a fishbone, start with a statement of the problem and write this down in the "fish head". For example, if we

---

14 Majero, S. Ibid.

revert to the Irish tourism market example we could express the problem as follows: "Why are there not more Continental European tourists in Ireland?" The next step is to draw a line across the page from the head and attach several lines, or "bones", coming out vertically from the main line. These branches represent different categories of problems with further sub categories being written below the main problem. We might end up with a "fishbone" looking like this:

Figure 5: Fishbone Diagram (1)

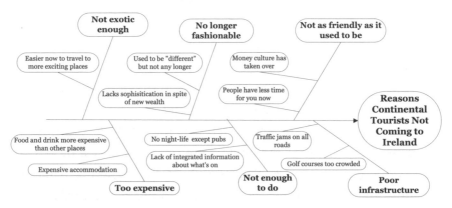

This "Fishbone Diagram" is based on judgement, anecdotal evidence and hearsay. Access to the detailed research that is usually available in the tourist industry would result in a much richer diagram which in turn would lead to better insights to improve the position.

The following example, again drawn up from judgement rather than access to detailed market research demonstrates how the technique could be used to produce a comprehensive plan for a brand of jam or marmalade:

Figure 6: Fishbone Diagram (2)

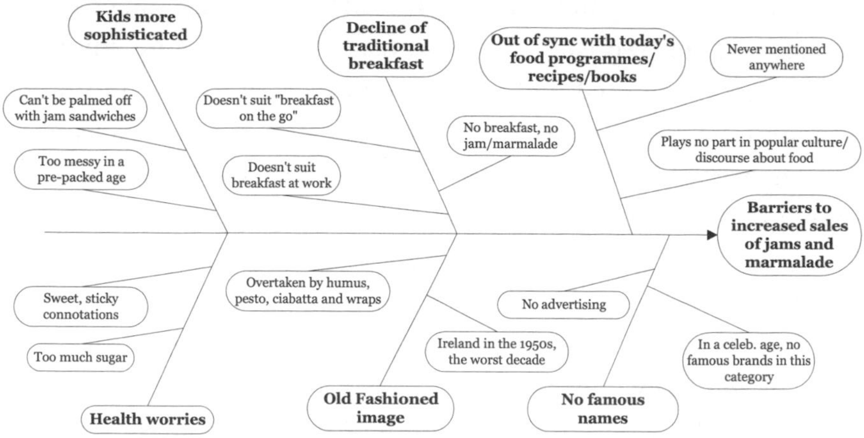

Kids more sophisticated

Decline of traditional breakfast

Out of sync with today's food programmes/recipes/books

Never mentioned anywhere

Can't be palmed off with jam sandwiches

Doesn't suit "breakfast on the go"

No breakfast, no jam/marmalade

Plays no part in popular culture/discourse about food

Too messy in a pre-packed age

Doesn't suit breakfast at work

Barriers to increased sales of jams and marmalade

Sweet, sticky connotations

Overtaken by humus, pesto, ciabatta and wraps

No advertising

Too much sugar

Ireland in the 1950s, the worst decade

In a celeb. age, no famous brands in this category

Health worries

Old Fashioned image

No famous names

New Improved Market Research

If brainstorming is the most widely used method of generating insights internally, market research is the most widely used external method. Market research originated in the period between the First and Second World Wars and was initially preoccupied in persuading business that a relatively small sample of the population could accurately reflect the views of the total population. The breakthrough came in 1936 in the US when the popular magazine, *The Literary Digest*, invited readers to fill out a postal ballot for the forthcoming presidential election. The offer attracted a huge response of almost two and a half million people and the result predicted a George Landon victory for the Republicans. Meanwhile in Washington George Gallup was conducting a statistically based poll of a few thousand people across the country. His result predicted a Roosevelt victory for the Democrats. Although very few US businessmen were impressed with the actual outcome of the election they were very impressed with the accuracy of the Gallup Poll and soon market research became an accepted feature of most businesses, especially consumer goods businesses.

Initially most companies used the new market research industry to measure their markets, their brand shares and the different segments of their consumers. But once the basic data on any market has been collected and arrangements made to update the information on a regular basis, the next question businesses want to have answered is "Why?" Why is our market share the size it is? Why don't more people buy our brand? Quantitative market research was, and still is, used to answer these questions but in the late 1950s a new branch of market research, known as motivational research, began to appear, promising more revealing answers to some of the "why" questions. The early motivational researchers were a racy lot with intriguing middle-European sounding names and a reputation for slightly sensationalist findings, often with sexual overtones. The classic finding that became a popular talking point in the 1950s was that coupes represented mistresses while sedans represented wives. The risqué overtones attaching to motivational research inhibited its growth but the 1960s witnessed the birth of what we now know as qualitative research.

Originally qualitative research involved talking to people in groups of eight or ten, known as group discussions, or sometimes talking to individuals, referred to as depth interviews. Interviewers — usually people with clinical psychology training — led the groups and asked respondents about their lives, the brands they bought, the reasons why and their attitudes to and relationship with all the main brands in the market under review. The discussion leader would have a predetermined list of question areas to be covered but respondents were allowed to talk freely among themselves as long as they didn't stray too far from the subject area. It was accepted that the more animated people became when talking among themselves without too much overt prompting from the discussion leader the better chance there was of uncovering some new insight into a market. However, during the 1960s and 1970s the main objective was to cover all the areas in the predetermined check list. This phase of qualitative research has been described as the "Discursive Paradigm" stage; here research is seen essentially as an in-formation-gathering exercise which requires the collation of that information and its presentation more or less in a reportage for-mat. Underlying this paradigm is the assumption that people are conscious of the purchasing decisions they take and the reasons for these decisions. This was followed by a new "Creative Paradigm" where it is assumed that people's behaviour and attitudes are not always consciously known by respondents and have to be "uncov-ered" using indirect questioning techniques that operate in a non-rational and often non-verbal way. A further development, the "Analytic Paradigm" was based on the premise that it was impossi-ble to understand consumer attitudes and behaviour without a thorough understanding of, "the cultural web of meaning and be-haviour which we call consumer culture".[15] In order to better un-derstand these "ways of meaning" the disciplines of ethnography and semiotics began to attract the attention of marketing commu-nication strategists in the 1990s.

Ethnography comes from the Greek word "ethnos" meaning a people, a race or a cultural group and when *ethno-* as a prefix is combined with *-graphy* to form the term *ethnography* the word refers to a sub-discipline of anthropology meaning a scientific study of a people or a group of people with the objective of de-scribing aspects of their culture and behaviour. Much of the growth of interest in this area coincided with the increasing use of that annoying business mantra, "getting closer to the customer". Instead of observing consumers in group discussions and depth interviews it was now deemed necessary to observe them in their natural habitat. This has led to an increase in market research projects involving "accompanied journeys". This could mean going along with housewives to the supermarket, observing their behav-iour and asking questions where necessary. The technique re-

---

[15] Chandeler, J. and Owen, M., "Genesis to Revelations: The Evolution of Qualita-tive Research", Market Research Society Conference (UK), 1989.

quires considerable skill on the part of the researcher to be able to ascertain when a piece of behaviour is important and could lead to a new insight into the market or about the brand under review. Sometimes whole teams of researchers will descend into areas of interest (e.g. pubs and off-licences) in an area where a particular brand is being consumed at a rate which is either significantly above or below the national average.

The growth of this technique has been facilitated by the increasing familiarity of the public with the aims, objectives and methods of market research and marketing as a whole. In Ireland today most people under the age of 40 are well versed in all of these areas as a result of the rudiments of the subject being explained in the educational system and the number of references to the subject in popular culture. Over the years market researchers have become much less reticent about sharing the underlying objectives of their research with respondents. Now that the "secret" is out in the open there is no such need. Respondents are now often recruited as willing collaborators in the search for insights.

A good example of the new ethnographically influenced turn in market research is described in a case history[16] on how Baileys Irish Cream carried out an extended study among groups of respondents who were recruited on the basis that they seemed to be able to make more insightful observations than the average respondent. The project was carried out in the early 1990s and at the time the brand had an ambitious growth strategy which relied on giving "more people more reasons to drink Baileys more often". The research team adopted an interesting approach which involved recruiting what they refer to as "rolling groups" which meant recruiting group discussion respondents in the normal way, but inviting the most "interesting" respondents back for more discussions over an extended period. A significant amount of time,

---

[16] White, T. and O'Doherty, M., "Active Listening to Consumers", ESOMAR Annual Conference Papers, 1996.

and money, was invested in the respondents. The research was carried out in a number of overseas markets but the respondents were invited as part of an initiation process on a two-day visit to Dublin for a series of briefings in the production plant and the marketing department and were even brought out to one of the farms that supply milk for the brand. A combination of mood boards, word sort cards, scatter cards, tonality tapes and video clips were used in subsequent discussions. Between groups, respondents were kept busy and involved with a series of exercises that were recorded in diaries. These exercises included writing down ten or more ways in which Baileys is different from other alcoholic drinks, introduce a friend who had never drunk Baileys before to try it and record their reactions, pick out any advertisements you see that Baileys would fit into for whatever reason. The results were used to formulate a new positioning for the brand but the whole exercise was also used to provide material for PR campaigns and to begin the process of building a substantial worldwide database.

Semiotics also derives from a Greek word, *semeion,* which means "sign", and semiotics has been referred to as the science of signs. Because any market research investigation and indeed any attempt in a wider sense to gain fresh insights into brands must take into account what's going on in the society surrounding a market we will inevitably have to have the best possible understanding of the culture in which the brand exists. And that's where semiotics comes in:

> The shape of a culture, or total way of life of a community was in fact determined by or at any rate clearly structured in the same way as that culture's language — we see and hear and otherwise experience very largely as we do be-

cause the language habits of our community predispose certain choices of interpretation.[17]

Semiotics accepts that consumers are products of whatever culture they inhabit and that they are conditioned not only by the language but by the music, the sports, the history and the popular culture of the community. Therefore we need to study that culture in order fully to understand people's relationships with the brands that are also part of community. Semiotics starts with the culture, not the consumer:

> Instead of interrogating respondents, semiotic analysis begins by directly interrogating the culture itself — it proposes that we are all creatures of our cultures and we perceive the world, draw up our value systems, and make our group meanings in accordance with the perceptions, values and meanings of the particular culture we belong to.[18]

By carrying out semiotic analysis on a particular market we should be in a position to understand the brand relationships in that market much better and the findings may result in better insights. One of the reasons why it does this and one of the main advantages of adding a semiotic dimension to our studies of a market is because it enables us to understand the wider concerns of the market and therefore keeps us up-to-date with new trends and issues that may be about to emerge.

Planning Consultancies

Ever since innovation and creativity started to loom larger and larger on the executive radar there have been an endless procession of consultants eager to guide tired and weary business people

---

[17] Alexander, M., "Codes and Contexts: Practical Semiotics for the Qualitative Research", Market Research Society Conference (UK) 2000

[18] Lawes, R., "Demystifying Semiotics: Some Key Questions Answered", *International Journal of Market Research*, Volume 44, No 3, 2002.

through the treacherous white water of "thinking outside the box". One of the best known is Dr Edward de Bono, who coined the phrase "lateral thinking" and is one of the most famous exponents of the belief that everyone can be creative, as long as they use the right techniques. Lateral thinking seeks solutions to difficult business problems by using unorthodox methods and de Bono has devised a systematic process that will achieve these objectives.

But there are also a number of planning consultancies specialising in branding and marketing communications that offer a service designed to help businesses to generate insights that will transform the fortunes of their brands. Many of them are thinly based, trading on one successful case history, poorly resourced and lacking in wider professional expertise.

There are a number who are worth considering and the following brief account of two of them will hopefully give a flavour of what they can contribute. The first example is a UK-based consultant, Adam Morgan, an ex-agency planner who wrote the well regarded book *Eating the Big Fish*.[19] Writing a bestselling business book has become an established starting point for launching a consultancy career but Morgan's book contained enough original material to justify this. His starting point was that established brand leaders could be successfully thrown off their pedestals by agile, innovative and opportunistic "challenger" brands. The book consists of an extended series of exercises designed to generate insights which could give your brand a competitive advantage. It doesn't really matter whether the brand in question is a brand "challenger" or a brand leader; the exercises apply equally to both. It could be argued that all these exercises amount to are games to play in brainstorming sessions but that would be to underestimate their imaginative nature and the capacity of different ways of looking at problems to unlock fresh thoughts about brands. All of the

---

[19] Morgan, A., *Eating the Big Fish*, Wiley, 1999.

exercises are given distinctive names, most of them referring to the well-known people who inspired them; for example:

- "Waitt": Inspired by Ted Waitt of Gateway who initially could not afford to advertise. In order to attract attention and differentiate his computers, he used a unique design based on a faux cowhide black-and-white motif for the boxes the computers were sold in. Taking this initiative as a starting point, this exercise involves coming up with new, innovative and inexpensive ways to publicise a brand.

- "Schultz": Howard Schultz of Starbucks turned waiting in line for a cup of coffee into a moment of education and sophistication in what would otherwise be a boring and irritating experience. This exercise involves trying to think of ways of turning a part of our brand experience the consumer likes least into an advantage. This could be a useful exercise for financial services brands.

- "Schrager": Ian Schrager founded a number of hotels in New York and transformed the conventions of hotel design. This exercise involves imagining someone coming in from outside the brand's normal frame of reference and trying to envisage what they would change, e.g. if Michael O'Leary were to enter the financial services market, what changes would he make and are there any lessons that we could apply to our brand now?

Morgan's book presents a comprehensive strategy for smaller brands taking on brand leaders but the essence of his theory is the series of highly imaginative exercises, some of which are outlined above.

The second example of the new wave of planning consultancies is Red Spider. It should already be apparent to any observant reader that a prerequisite of a planning consultant is the ability to come up with a constant stream of cute little titles. Red Spider do have a range of planning techniques with cute little names but at

the heart of their offering is the belief that if you continually inter-
rogate a brand it will eventually yield up a secret nugget that will
constitute a new insight. They start with the conventional planning cycle and a belief that all good answers begin with good questions. The objective therefore is to ask as many different questions
as possible so that we begin to view the brand in a different light.
One of their more innovative planning tools is called "planets and
moons".[20] This is based on the now widely accepted principle that
because it is so difficult to achieve a genuine product or service
difference among any of the brands that dominate all developed
markets, in the future the only way for people to differentiate for
the purpose of making a purchasing decision will be on the basis
of the belief systems or values of the different brands. It is basically a method of teasing out the values of the different brands in a
market. It involves a group exercise of writing down on the ubiquitous Post-It notes every possible description that could be applied
to the brand while sticking each one to a large board or a wall.
These are the "moons". Then carefully examine them all and group
them into like-minded clusters. The final step is to come up with
an overall title for the clusters which are the "planets". These are
useful techniques for gaining a better understanding of the real
nature of a brand and on the basis that the more detail we have
about what this is the more likely we are to produce better insights
to move the brand forward. But the real core of the Red Spider offering is a series of over one hundred questions designed to inter-
rogate the brand from every possible angle. We can never know in
advance which question will provide the critical insight but the
more we ask the greater our chances.

---

[20] www.redspider.co.uk.

PART TWO: REGULAR STIMULANTS FOR INSIGHT GENERATION

The following section describes sources of data and methods of working and observation which work like health supplements — when taken regularly they leave you in better shape to focus with more insight on day-to-day problems.

Futurology and Forecasting Institutes

Forecasting has always attracted its share of cranks and chancers and it is no wonder it often has a bad name. Peter Drucker's comment that the only reason the word "guru" ever came into vogue was because sub-editors couldn't spell "charlatan" strikes a chord here. In order to deflect attention from the inevitable scepticism that attaches to the genre most forecasters, or futurists as they are now called, preface their remarks with a little gentle self-deprecation: "The herd instinct among forecasters make sheep look like independent thinkers"; or "Forecasting is the art of saying what will happen and then explaining why it didn't".

However, the insatiable business demand for insights into the future has spawned a plethora of institutes, consultancies and gurus all over the world. Although it would be stretching the imagination to ascribe a degree of academic rigour to any of them, some are more reputable than others and can often provide useful general directions which can in turn kick-start ideas for our own brands and markets. Would-be purveyors of what lies ahead have been a feature of all societies down the ages but the brand insight specialists are obviously of more recent vintage.

The publication of Alvin Toffler's *Future Shock* in 1973 signalled the start of the modern preoccupation with the future from a business perspective. The main point of this six-million-copy bestseller was that we were entering a period of history when change would become endemic and successful businesses would be the ones who were best able to anticipate and respond to these changes. This is now a commonplace observation but Toffler was the first to popularise the notion and he fully justifies *Time* magazine's depiction of him as having "set the standard by which all subsequent would-be futurists have been measured". A follow-up book *The Third Wave*,[21] published in 1980, made some remarkably accurate predictions, including the fragmentation of the media and the rise of the prosumer — major preoccupations of all businesses today. Toffler effectively created a new discipline around the study of change and its impact on business and culture, a discipline now referred to as futurism.

One of Toffler's most notable successors was John Naisbitt whose 1982 publication, *Megatrends*[22] became one of the most popular business books at the time. Naisbitt put forward the idea of ten "megatrends" that would transform our lives in the immediate future. They were all broad societal trends that the astute brand manager could apply to their own markets to gain a competitive advantage either through new product innovation or by using the forecasted trends to make more relevant marketing communication messages. Some of Naisbitt's forecasts proved to be very accurate: the move from hierarchies to networking, from national economies to a world economy and from an industrial society to the information age.

More recently a futurist who attracted the attention of the marketing communications business was the suitably self-branded Faith Popcorn whose trend forecasts in the *Popcorn Report*[23] created a high level of interest and whose talent for nomenclature ensured that some of her forecasts were not confined to the business world. Her main predictions were that consumers would become more vocal and belligerent ("the vigilante consumer"); that they

[21] Toffler, A., *The Third Wave*, William Collins, 1980.

[22] Naisbett, J., *Megatrends: Ten New Directions Transforming our Lives*, Warner Books 1982.

[23] Popcorn, F., *The Popcorn Report*, Doubleday, 1991.

would start to assume multiple roles to cope with time pressure ("99 lives"); and that they would seek to shield themselves from the harsh unpredictable realities of the outside world by retreating into safe cosy environments ("cocooning"). These were useful insights into consumer society in the 1990s and her depiction of the "vigilante consumer" anticipated the Naomi Klein "No Logo" phenomenon by a decade.

For every one of these futurist publications, there were hundreds that made little impact. However, one which failed to attract the attention of the marketing communications business probably offers the most interesting analysis of the future shape of society and in particular deals with some of the issues that may lie just below the surface of current consumer behaviour. Michael Mazarr's *Global Trends: 2005*[24] was published in 1999 and is a wide-ranging survey of social, technological and political changes in the world today. Mazarr is an American professor of national security studies whose main beat is geopolitical studies, so he operates at some distance from the less ethereal world of brand management and marketing communications but his book offers some of the most profound insights into societal trends. The book describes nine themes that the author believes will be important for the immediate future:

- **Paradox:** The paradoxical and contradictory nature of the future; for example, the inevitability of expanded individualism and the likelihood of a desire for a greater sense of community.

- **Blurring of Boundaries:** The knowledge era is an interdisciplinary time.

- **Networks, Systems and Holistic Thinking:** Networks are the hard-wiring of an age that will be increasingly interrelated.

---

[24] Mazarr, M., *Global Trends: 2005*, Macmillan, 1999.

- **Process not Product:** Constantly improving rather than "being", this trend also suggests the growing importance of the "experience" which will be familiar to everyone in the world of marketing communications.

- **The S-Curve:** The necessity to be continually aware that successful products and services are always on the point of becoming obsolete as the pace of change quickens.

- **Values and Responsibility:** New value systems will be required to replace the old ones.

- **Perception Increasingly Equals Reality:** This has obvious implications for brand management.

- **Change is Costly:** Eras of major social change are disruptive and often exact an enormous social toll as many people are unable to keep up with the changes.

- **Increasing Empowerment:** In spite of the problems there will be more opportunities for most people.

Mazarr never mentions the word "brand" but his analysis should be carefully considered by all brand managers as a guide to future behaviour:

> Individual empowerment results partly from growing self-awareness among knowledge-era people. This era as we have seen is a time of diversity and individualism, a time of alienated yet empowered individuals, and a time of unprecedented information about the human condition. It therefore follows that it should be a time of intense self-awareness which can take the form of either destructive selfishness or constructive self-reflection. In its negative manifestations, self-awareness leads to self-absorption: the obsession with health and beauty; concern for one's narrow interests; an unwillingness to sacrifice for the good of soci-

ety; consumerism. Yet the same urge to self-reflection can carry immense positive value as well.[25]

Mazarr is also interesting on the importance of storytelling, the need for successful businesses to have credible and entertaining stories about themselves and the likely demands on businesses, and brands, to adopt the highest ethical standards.

As well as individual writers and commentators there are also institutes and specialist businesses devoted to the strange art of predicting the future. Two of the most respected are the London-based Future Foundation and the Copenhagen Institute for Future Studies.

The Future Foundation is a group of general consultants and re-searchers who aim to "understand what's going on in the world, to provide order within the complexity, to present a clear sense of un-derstanding and direction, to develop clear visions from the mael-strom of trends that swirl and interact to provide a seemingly constantly changing operating landscape". They organise confer-ences, publish a newsletter, work on commissions from individual businesses and sometimes organise groups of businesses with common problems to undertake research into how these problems could be overcome in the future. An interesting example of the lat-ter is a current project to put together a consortium of companies to carry out research into what they refer to as the "Assault on Pleas-ure" — the trend towards the restriction and increasing regulation of individual indulgences that has become a feature of so many markets today. They claim to have already done some work on the subject and have come up with insights which would be of interest to businesses in areas like food and drink, hospitality and enter-tainment, and media and communications. Recent reports include *Insomniac Britain*, which deals with the growth of the twenty-four-hour society, *The Digital Divide* and *The Future of Breakfast*. Some

---

[25] Ibid.

of their reports are available free of charge and a recent survey of attitudes towards the acceptance of counselling and psychotherapy provides extremely interesting insights into an area that is having a major influence on a wide range of consumer markets.[26]

The Copenhagen Institute provides a similar service but seems to rely less on market research and more on the original thinking and intuitions of their consultants. They also issue regular news-letters, organise seminars and conferences and publish books. One of the best known, *The Dream Society*[27] by Rolf Jensen, deals with the prediction that we have left the information age and are enter-ing a new age which he refers to as the Dream Society. In this soci-ety, storytelling will assume much greater importance and successful brands will have to have very clear and unambiguous storylines. More recently, the Copenhagen Institute has been pub-licising the view that as Western societies become wealthier and an increasing proportion of the workforce become knowledge workers more people will want to express their own creativity. They also argue that technology will play an important role in aid-ing this transformation, either through the internet, which facili-tates publication in a way that was never possible for the majority of mankind, and through advances in digital cameras, which en-able individual film-making. They have recently published a new book, *Creative Man*, which describes these ideas in more detail.

These are some of the main futurists but there are many more, most of them chancing their arm but some contributing random thoughts on the future, which just might spark off a fresh insight about a brand. Richard Neville, once an "enfant terrible" in 1960s' London is now back in his native Australia operating as a success-ful entrepreneurial futurist. Neville has recently focused on the issue of vanishing boundaries, for example between childhood and adulthood; left-wing and right-wing; east and west; mind and

---

[26] "The Age of Therapy", Future Foundation Project, London 2004.

[27] Jenson, R., *The Dream Society*, MaGraw Hill 1999.

body; mass market and customisation; men and women; science and art; and so on.[28]

A relatively new entrant into the insight stakes is a new type of consultant known as a "coolhunter". This exotic species came to prominence in the 1990s when a number of markets driven by fashion trends, from trainers to alcoholic drinks, began to notice that instead of trickling down, many fashion trends were trickling up. When acknowledged style leaders are setting the pace, businesses are able to keep up but when the pace and direction of change is being dictated from the street then businesses need help. This is where the "coolhunter" came to the rescue, offering to penetrate the mysteries of the underground and decipher them to the less hip types who inhabit the boardroom.

The term is reputed to have made its first appearance in the *New Yorker*,[29] as good a place as any to make your debut, on St Patrick's Day 1997 and the writer was none other than Malcolm Gladwell who went on to higher things a few years later with his world-wide best-seller *The Tipping Point*.[30] The original article mentioned that "coolhunting is not about the articulation of a coherent philosophy of cool — it's just a collection of spontaneous observations and predictions that differ from one moment to the next and from one encounter to the next". As well as searching for the streets, bars, and other spaces where street cred is likely to be at its height, a coolhunter must have an instinctive grasp of what works and what doesn't.

The heroine of the ultra-cool William Gibson's latest novel[31] is a coolhunter who is described as "a very specialised piece of human litmus paper". Coolhunters could be used to provide insights in some markets where fashion is a critical factor in purchasing

---

[28] Neville, R., *Footprints of the Future*, Richmond Ventura Pty., Sydney, 2002.

[29] Gladwell, M., "Annals of Style: The Coolhunter", New Yorker, 17 March 1997.

[30] Gladwell, M., *The Tipping Point*, Little Brown and Company, 2000.

[31] Gibson, W., *Pattern Recognition*, Berkley Publishing Group, 2004.

decisions but there is always the danger that the exercise could defeat the object of the exercise: "The first rule of cool is that you have to be one to know one, the second rule is that cool cannot be manufactured only observed and the third rule is that it cannot be accurately observed at all because the act of discovering cool causes cool to take flight."[32] So now you know!

Feng Shui

This may seem an odd inclusion into a typology of methods of achieving better insights but it constantly surfaces in the literature on the subject. Feng Shui is based on the Oriental belief that our environment has a significant effect on our internal energies. Its origins date back over 4,000 years to China and the concept of energy, which the Chinese call *qi*, the breath of life, the force that informs all our existence. The objective of Feng Shui is to align us with the flow of *qi* and in particular to remove any obstacles to the generation of new ideas and insights. In ancient China no buildings were constructed without first consulting a Feng Shui expert and a number of modern businesses are now applying the same principles as management consultants increasingly refer to a new creative age in business. One of the best-known examples of this trend is Microsoft, whose headquarters are known as The Campus. In this connection it is interesting to note that a number of advertising commentators have predicted that the advertising agencies of the future will resemble university common rooms and will be staffed by experts in different disciplines who will divide their time between consulting on client problems, carrying out research and studying.

Proponents of Feng Shui tend to concentrate on two physical components of the insight generation process. The first point they make is that the physical surroundings in which idea generation

---

[32] Ibid.

takes place have to be carefully considered as the normal business office and meeting rooms do not constitute a sufficiently creative environment. Insight generation is a collaborative process and most office meeting rooms are designed for presentation, not collaboration. Idea generation rooms would be much less formal; they would have more space and would not be dominated by a single big table. All the wall space would be capable of being written on; there would be areas where people could congregate in smaller groups; and the place would be littered with Post-it notes and marker pens. Tea, coffee, water and sticky buns would be in constant supply.

The second preoccupation of the proponents of Feng Shui is the elimination of barriers to thinking, which usually involves decisions about light, noise, temperature and interior design. Removing distractions to creative thinking is very much a part of Feng Shui but another common theme in this area is the need to create positive stimuli to better creative thinking. Two regular suggestions that crop up under this heading are the desirability of reading a different newspaper or magazine on a regular basis and the benefits of going to work by a different route or using a different mode of transport. Some of the regularly published suggestions are decidedly flaky — spend Friday afternoons playing in a steel band or with a fortune teller, or "build a tree house"! — but the underlying theoretical assumptions are the same; the greatest barrier to more creative thinking is one's imprisonment in the habits of the past. Anything that breaks up long-established ways of thinking and seeing helps to prepare the ground for new thinking and new seeing.

Case Histories

Case histories can be an important source of new insights. Their relative neglect by the marketing communications industry is indicative of the incestuous nature of the business with its suspicion of professionalism and historical provincialism. If we contrast our business with the legal profession we see that we both have a problem with predicting the outcome of our professional advice and recommendations. Lawyers and solicitors offer advice but they cannot always be certain of the outcome in a court case. We are rarely able to predict the outcome of our recommendations, whether we are talking about a particular brand strategy or a marketing communications campaign. But lawyers and solicitors can drastically reduce the odds by reference to precedent; the detailed case histories of what happened in similar circumstances provide a reassuring professional bank of knowledge with which to soothe client uncertainties. Until recently we had no equivalent resource although most people in the business could quote a few well-known successes and failures. Now that situation has been transformed with the regular publication of marketing communication case studies about what happened to brands as a result of different communication strategies and campaigns.

Although individual case studies have been around for a long time, often publicised by the agency that was responsible for them as a publicity campaign for its own business, the first really ambitious attempt to institute a formal arrangement for the regular publication of case histories was in London where the Institute of Practitioners of Advertising introduced the Advertising Effectiveness Awards in 1980. The awards have been published every second year since then so there are now thirteen volumes of detailed case studies and the IPA website contains the results of almost 1,000 cases covering almost every product and service market. Although the primary purpose of the awards is to demonstrate the effectiveness of advertising, most of the papers in describing the background to the successful campaigns demonstrate the insight-generating process that led to the final creative solution.

The success of the IPA initiative prompted other national advertising bodies to do the same and now there are a wide range of similar publications available from around the world. The following are some examples with the dates they began publication:

- AFA — Advertising Federation of Australia, 1990

- Cassies — Canadian Advertising Success Story, 1993

- Effies — New York Advertising & Marketing Association, 2000

- APG (UK) — Advertising Planning Group, 1993

- IAPI (Dublin) — Advertising Effectiveness Awards, 1996.

All of these case histories represent an invaluable repository of insights into how brands around the world have been managed and developed. They should be the first port of call for anyone confronted with a brand management issue and in future people working in brand management and marketing communications will not be able to call themselves professional without a good working knowledge of the classic cases from these publications.

She's an Artist, She Don't Look Back

Businesses, market researchers, futurists, consultants and cool-hunters are not the only ones trying to understand what's going on in our society. Artists are also preoccupied with this quest:

> Like every true prophet the artist is the unwitting mouth-piece of the psychic secrets of his time and is often as unconscious as a sleepwalker.[33]

Jung was writing here about Joyce but the same is true of present-day artists and keeping a close watch on what contemporary artists are up to can be a powerful source of ideas and insights. In a hundred years' time, when historians are grappling with early twenty-first-century Ireland they will draw on the novels, poems, paintings, music, films and sculpture of today for inspiration. All of these texts are readily available to us now and they remain an

---

[33] Jung, C., "*Ulysses*: A Monologue", *The Collected Works*, Vol. 15, Bollingin, New York, 1966.

underused resource. Current examples include the poetry of Derek Mahon and the paintings of Martin Gale. Mahon has been casting a cold eye on Irish society for some time now and his recent poetry can be read as a sustained critique of some of the values that accompany the new individualism in Irish society:

> For now, whatever our ancestral dream
> we give ourselves over to a vast corporate scheme
> where our true wit is devalued once again
> our solitude remembered by the rain.[34]

The foreword to a recent major Martin Gale retrospective stated that his work "echoes an unease about identity and place that is a fundamental determinant of contemporary Irish life".[35] A close watch on the themes and preoccupations of Irish artists can often illuminate a brand management or marketing communications problem. Artists are particularly acute observers of the "cultural contradictions" in society which can be used to advantage by brands. This subject is explained in detail in Chapter 14.

Insight Generation: The Critical Importance of Domain Skills

Although it is now fashionable to assume that we are all inherently creative and that with a little help from a few workshop exercises we can all emerge with transformational insights that will enhance the performance of our businesses, there is always the nagging suspicion that life isn't that simple. The good news is that people can be taught to be more creative, that the exercises outlined above will stimulate fresh thinking and occasionally lead to insights which when properly applied could transform the fortunes of a brand. The bad news is that spending a day in a comfortable country house hotel all dressed up in casual gear with your col-

---

[34] Mahon, D., *Collected Poems*, Gallery Press, 2001.

[35] Royal Hibernian Academy, Dublin, Martin Gale, 2004.

leagues, facilitated by a "rappateur" equipped with the latest creative exercises does not always guarantee insights that will change the world. That doesn't mean they are a waste of time. They may not solve many problems but they do open up many possibilities and they can work wonders for *esprit de corps*.

A more fruitful approach is one that inevitably involves harder, less glamorous work. There is a surprising level of agreement that people who know most about their subject are the ones who are more likely to come up with the most useful insights. Dr Teresa Amabile, a psychologist at Brandeis University who specialises in the study of creativity, believes there are three basic ingredients to creativity.[36] The first and most important is a basic mastery of the field, in the case of brand management the market under review. The second is the creative thinking skills that are outlined here and the third is intrinsic motivation, the determination or passion to succeed. As insight generation has become an indispensable part of the branding and marketing communications business, exercises for creative thinking have been the focus of much attention and the word "passion" has been flung around with great abandon but the all-important mastery of the field is rarely mentioned. This a pity because no matter how passionate you are or how many creative exercises you have in your armoury, if you don't know what you're talking about your "insights" are not going to add up to very much. Mastery of the field has been referred to as "domain skills", which means knowing as much as there is to know about the topic under review. So, if we are reviewing the beer market we should ideally be fully conversant with the brand we are dealing with, its history, ups and downs, the history of the other brands in the market, what has worked and not worked in the past, and because the product itself is a critical factor we also need to know something about the ingredients and the brewing process.

---

[36] Goleman, D., Kaufman, P., Ray, M., *The Creative Spirit*, Plume 1993.

The main argument in favour of domain skills goes to the heart of the nature of creativity, which usually involves making connections between ideas or concepts that already exist but where no one had previously made a connection, which goes back to Koestler's idea of "cabbages and kings":

> Discovery often means simply the uncovering of something which has always been there but was hidden from the eye by the blinkers of habit. The creative act is not an act of creation in the sense of the Old Testament; it does not create something out of nothing; it uncovers, it selects, reshuffles, combines, synthesises, always existing facts.[37]

A recent paper on the subject argues that the world of science is also a rich source of new thinking and quotes a variety of thinkers from Newton to Wittgenstein in support of this view:

> Insight is the thread that connects fields, forms and patterns; we gain new insights by new arrangement, not by new data — this is it seems to me a lesson that has not been sufficiently absorbed into the marketing (and research) bloodstream: it is not just about quantity, not even thoroughness, but a question of seeing things differently.[38]

Therefore the more domain skills we have, the more we are masters of our subjects, the more new arrangements we are likely to make. The exercises outlined above in Part One should contribute to solving specific brand management problems. The exercises outlined in Part Two should facilitate continuous insight generation. But none of them are likely to amount to much without the necessary domain skills.

The greatest barrier to an ability to generate insights is the "eureka" fallacy or what has been referred to as the "bed, bath or bus" syndrome; the impression that great ideas occur to us at ran-

---

[37] Koestler, A., Ibid.

[38] Tasgal, A., "Insightment: Where art meets Science", *Admap*, Dec 2004.

dom and out of nowhere. They don't; they come about as a result of a deep immersion in the subject under review, whether it is physics in the case of Einstein, whose fascination began at the age of five when his father bought him a small magnetic compass when he was ill, or some consumer market in the case of a brand manager or marketing communications manager.

7

Two Hardy Annuals: Brand Extension and Brand Valuation

Whenever the subject of branding is discussed in business circles, it is not long before two hardy annuals make an appearance. The first is "brand extension": *across how many product markets can my brand stretch?* (this question is sometimes expressed as *how elastic is my brand?*); and the second is "brand valuation": *how much is my brand worth?*

As one would expect with a subject as chameleon-like as branding, definitive answers are out of the question but an impressive amount of theoretical work has been carried out in both areas, backed up with a range of case histories. We still cannot provide definitive answers but we can offer practical guidelines.

Brand Extension

Before branding was accorded the status it enjoys today businesses were much less systematic in their approach to brand management. The most famous example of successful companies making the same products while pursuing diametrically opposed strategies is in the confectionary market. Cadbury's use their name and design style across a range of different products. However, although Mars and Nestlé use their company name for some products, they also employ a variety of different brand names. For example, Mars features on the eponymous bars but not on Twix, Snickers or M&M's. Rowntree have an impressive portfolio of strong individual brands

— Kit Kat, Polo, After Eight — but since the Nestlé takeover the corporate name is starting to appear on these individual products.

Brand Extension: Potential and Pitfalls

It would be difficult to think of any company in possession of even the most reticent brand that hasn't made some move to extend that brand in the last few decades. The almost universal acceptance of the revenue-generating power of brands, and the realisation that they represent the most valuable assets most businesses have, combined with the increasing cost and risks of launching new brands, have forced managements into trying to squeeze the last ounce of revenue from their existing brands. It has been estimated that 95 per cent of all the 16,000 new product launches in the US every year are now brand extensions of some kind.[1] Most companies have examined the possibility of extending their brands into new sub-sectors of the markets in which they operate but some brands have managed the difficult task of operating in a number of very different markets — Virgin and Bic being two examples.

The primary reason for brand extension is fairly obvious: because launching new brands is both expensive and risky, if you can give a new brand the equivalent of a silver spoon from birth in the form of an established name, it would seem a logical thing to do. But there is also another potential benefit: if the new brand represents a sub-sector of an established market it will invariably be a more fashionable and innovative sector and the new brand will then be in a position to transfer favourable attributes back onto the parent brand. Thus a brand extension can refresh the existing brand as well as improving the cost effectiveness of marketing communication resources.

If the potential for brand extension is therefore obvious, the pitfalls are slightly less so but they exist nevertheless. The biggest

---

[1] Dacin, P., Blair, E., Gelb, B. and Oakenfull, G. "Measuring Brand Meaning", *Journal of Advertising Research*, Volume 40, No 5, September/October 2000.

problem is the possibility of failure, which could in turn weaken the parent brand so that the whole process leaves the business in a worse situation than before. There is also the possibility of diluting the personality of the parent brand, leaving people confused about what it stands for. A brand extension gives to and takes from the parent brand.

Many attempts have been made to examine the very different strategies businesses use to manage their existing brand portfolios and the following put forward by Laforet and Saunders[2] is probably the most comprehensive:

Corporate Brand Names	Kellogg's and Heinz are two obvious examples. Cadbury's is also a good example, because unlike their main rivals in the confectionery market they rely almost exclusively on their corporate brand name.
House Brand Names	Sometimes companies who would probably prefer to adopt a single corporate brand name are forced by market circumstances to introduce more appropriate names for different product or market sectors. Toyota's use of the Lexus to cater for the upper end of the car market is a good example.
Family Brand Names	Family brands within a particular market sometimes adopt the family name in addition to another brand name covering a particular market sector. Dulux Weathershield is a good example: the corporate name is used in combination with a range of paints covering a very specific sector of the paint market.
Mono Brand Names	The main strategy used by many manufacturers, especially in the fast-moving consumer goods sector. Two of the major global FMCG businesses, Procter & Gamble and Unilever, employ this strategy. Both own a wide range of brands covering many different market sectors but most consumers would be unaware of who the ultimate business owner is.

---

[2] Laforet, S. and Saunders, J. "Managing Brand Portfolios: How the Leaders Do It", *Journal of Advertising Research*, September/October 1994.

The following is a summary of the possible spectrum of the effects of brand extension from the most successful to the most disastrous:[3]

- **Enrichment:** Both the core brand and the extension benefit from the association with each other.

- **Extension:** The extension benefits from being associated with the original core brand and grows more quickly than it would on its own.

- **Neutral:** The extension gains nothing from the association with the core brand; this is rare as an extension always draws some attention to its parentage and some reaction is almost inevitable.

- **Conflict:** The extension is at odds with the position or values of the core brand and it fails because consumers are confused.

- **Damage:** The extension not only fails but damages the position of the core brand; because it is at odds with the core brand it changes the consumer perception of the worth or values of the parent brand.

Examples and Case Histories

Millward Brown recently carried out a study of brand elasticity of forty global brands in eight countries. The main conclusions were as follows:[4]

1. Consumers put limits on where a brand can go; they can clearly see what is and what isn't a sensible place that a brand can stretch to. Appropriateness is very dependent on which sector is being considered; 92 per cent of consumers felt that

---

[3] Arnold, D., *The Handbook of Brand Management,* Century Business in Association with The Economist Books, 1992.

[4] Page, G. and Farr, A., "Do You Have an Elastic Brand?", Advertising Research Foundation Workshop, October 2000.

Motorola could stretch to telecommunications equipment but only 4 per cent believed they would be credible in skin care.

2. Some brands are more elastic than others. Virgin is at the top of this league with Coca Cola at the bottom. Brands like Coke, which are so dominant in their own field, tend not to be given permission to stretch.

3. Brand strength in an existing realm of expertise does not drive brand elasticity.

4. "Far in" is easier to work than "far out". A brand extension with a close relationship to the existing market sector will usually work better than a brand extension in a completely new sector.

The two brands usually put forward as being the most adaptable are Virgin and Bic. Both operate across widely diverse markets but they are not completely elastic. Bic Perfume did not work and Virgin Cola and Virgin Vodka have not been very successful. An interesting example of an unusual brand extension is Caterpillar's move from heavy building equipment into work boots. Yamaha's range, which stretches from motorcycles to pianos, would suggest that the brand has great elasticity but the general consensus in this particular instance is that the brand effect is neutral.

All the available evidence suggests that it is the nature of what the parent brand stands for that determines the degree of brand extension success. If we could imagine a continuum stretching from product expertise in a narrowly defined area at one end (e.g. Guinness and stout) and a clearly defined overall philosophy at the other (e.g. Virgin and the idea of "the little no-nonsense guy against the big bureaucrats") on the other, then the more a brand can be positioned at the latter end of the continuum, the more elastic it will be. For example, it is unlikely that a Guinness brand of wine would be successful, but a Virgin range of sensibly priced no-nonsense wine, devoid of the palaver of the dominant French mystique, could work. (The only problem now is that in the last decade the Australians have adopted this position.) However, no "philosophy" can be stretched *ad infinitum*.

In short, brands which represent a "philosophy" — for example, Virgin taking on the big bureaucratic behemoths ostensibly on behalf of "the punter" — can in theory extend into any market, but there are always limitations. It could be argued that the established airlines and banks that Virgin started to compete against fell into the above category but that their less successful entries into the cola and vodka markets failed because, although both brand leaders in these categories, Coca Cola and Smirnoff, were "big", neither was bureaucratic. Similarly, Bic's move into perfume didn't work because their core philosophy — a functional, value-for-money, honest-to-goodness alternative — was alien to the generic requirements of the perfume market.

It is obvious therefore that the key to any proposed brand extension is to define what the parent brand stands for; for example:

- Coca-Cola: based primarily on know how; limited scope

- Virgin and Bic: based on a philosophy; not universal

- Marlboro: some scope for an overall positioning of "rugged individualism" but strong tobacco associations do not help

- Caterpillar: a surprising degree of scope in any product category requiring a "hard wearing" or "tough" image

- Mitsubishi: no real benefit other than country of origin; but for electrical products, the Japanese provenance is so strong that some European businesses have created "made-up" Japanese-sounding brand names.

The key to any proposed brand extension is a thorough understanding of what the parent brand stands for:

- How well does it perform its *function*; how much "know-how" is it perceived to have?

- What degree of warmth does it evoke; how strong are its *emotional values*?

- What ideas, impressions, associations first come to mind among the target group when the name is mentioned; that is, what is its *philosophy*?

The answers to these three questions will determine the likely success of any brand extension.

Guinness Light: A Cautionary Tale

The most famous brand extension in Ireland was undoubtedly Guinness Light. It was launched in 1981 with the slogan, "They said it couldn't be done", and to this day people who admit to working in advertising will be assailed at dinner parties and other social events by crashing bores who, under the influence of drink, imagine themselves to be witty sophisticates, completing the slogan with the words, "and they were right".

The reasoning behind this particular brand extension was sound enough. The parent brand always had difficulty recruiting younger drinkers. Guinness has a more challenging taste than other beers and young people in their late teens found the transition from carbonated soft drinks to stout a little hard to handle. By the early 1980s the Irish market was well supplied with lagers, ales and cider so there was no shortage of alternatives. However, marketing executives, like Jesuits, operate on the assumption that if you fail to catch them young you may fail to catch them at all so proposals were prepared for a variation of the master brand that would be easier to drink. There were also precedents for "light" variations of long-established brands and there had been a number of successful launches of "lite" American beers. Guinness was also assumed to be more fattening than other beers and it was hoped that more women drinkers would be attracted to a "lighter" taste.

The planning of the launch was meticulous and market research results were fully supportive of the project. The launch itself was marred by an ominous lapse by the chief executive of the company who admitted that he didn't really like the taste of the product himself. It is not uncommon for chief executives of companies to be dubious about some of the products that are launched in their name, but this particular comment was overheard by the press, which effectively meant that the new brand was born with a wooden spoon. It duly failed to make much of an impact, with the exception of continually negative media coverage, and was withdrawn shortly afterwards.

If you wanted to engage in some speculative post-rationalisation, an activity not exactly unknown among the marketing fraternity, it could be argued that the launch of Guinness Light did no harm to the master brand, and in fact it may have benefited it by reminding people just how good and unique a brand it was. Something very similar happened years later in the US with the launch of a new Coca Cola which was also withdrawn in a blaze of publicity and re-affirmed people's commitment to the original product. There are, however, much less risky and less expensive strategies for coping with problem brands.

It was widely accepted after the Guinness Light debacle that the product did not deliver enough satisfaction for the drinker and to that extent the chief executive was right. The main lesson from the experience is to exercise extreme caution when interpreting market research results prior to new product launches. Contrary to popular opinion, the public, once memorably described as a collection of people with scant regard for the problems of running an advertising agency, will always bend over backwards to give favourable responses to potential new products. They sense the enthusiasm of the executives in charge of the project and it is that enthusiasm that is largely responsible for the very high level of new product failures.

It should also be borne in mind that successful brands are invariably the result of someone's commitment to, and conviction about, a product or service as opposed to emanating from a market research report looking for gaps in the market.

BRAND VALUATION: OPENING A PANDORA'S BOX

Once the concept of the brand moved out of the marketing department and into the boardroom as a result of the corporate takeover frenzy during the mid- to late 1980s, the issue of brand valuation began to make its presence felt. The corporate raiders and asset strippers of that time had spotted that companies with strong brands were undervalued by financial orthodoxy and prudent accountancy practice. The result was that brands were not represented at their true value in the balance sheets of the companies that owned them. Conventional accounting practice valued assets at their historical cost rather than at their current value, and many intangible assets were never capitalised and included in the balance sheet. This was regarded as prudent financial practice in spite of the fact that common sense would suggest otherwise.

1988: The Year of the Brand

Two hotly contested takeovers in 1988 brought the issue of brand valuation to a head. One was perhaps the most dramatic example of the growing realisation of the financial power of brands — the Nestlé takeover of Rowntree-Mackintosh whose brands included such household names as Rolo, Kit-Kat, After Eight and many more. Two Swiss-based companies, Nestlé and Suchard, wanted to get their hands on these brands and Nestlé emerged victorious but only after paying £2.5 billion for a company with a net asset value of £300 million. Rowntree's market capitalisation was around £1 billion at the time of the takeover, which meant that the stock market significantly undervalued the worth of the company's brands.

The second takeover was for RHM, another company with a plethora of household brands such as Hovis and Sharwoods, which was the subject of a hostile bid from Goodman Fielder Wattie, an Australian baking group. This time RHM made a virtue of their brands in their defence document:

> RHM owns a number of strong brands, many of which are market leaders, which are valuable in their own right, but which the stock market tends consistently to undervalue. These valuable assets are not included in the balance sheet, but they have helped RHM build profits in the past and provide a sound basis for future growth.[5]

The issue was now well and truly out in the open and methods of brand valuation began to be discussed. Having successfully rebuffed the takeover attempt, RHM went on to have their brands valued and included in their balance sheet. This resulted in an increas in their net assets from £265 million to £979 million and they were then able to leverage their newly expanded asset base to make their own acquisitions. But soon after, they were successfully taken over for a smaller sum than the original Australian offer. To some extent this seemed to justify the accountancy profession's scepticism of brand valuation as it showed that values can be volatile and critically can mean very different amounts to different companies. The *Financial Times* summed up the dilemma at the end of a dramatic year:

> Valuing "intangible" items such as brands is set to become an uncontrollable craze in the coming months — many more examples of this accounting fashion are set to appear and they will push the boundaries of companies' accounts and readers' credibility far further than at present. The accountants believe companies may choose what intangible assets they value and how they do it but they should at least be aware that they may be opening a Pandora's Box in the process.[6]

---

[5] Haigh, D., *Brand Valuation: A Review of Current Practice*, IPA, London, 1996.
[6] Arnold, D., Ibid.

Methods of Brand Valuation

In spite of the scepticism, there was considerable interest in the subject following 1988, and in 1992 Arthur Andersen produced a report which argued in favour of valuing intangible assets and that there were acknowledged methods of doing so. The three main accountancy approaches to asset valuation are cost-based, market-based and income-based. A cost-based approach to brand valuation would attempt to put a value on what it would actually cost to re-create the brand from scratch. Although this approach may have some relevance for a new brand it seems a little unrealistic to apply it to established brands as it would be next to impossible to make the necessary calculations.

Market-based valuations depend on there being existing valuations of comparable brands. This works in many markets; for example, in the housing market, if a house in an estate is sold for a certain sum it is reasonable to assume that a similar house will sell for a similar amount. Unfortunately, the market for brands is not as simple and this approach is unlikely to be of much practical benefit.

Income-based approaches come in different forms, mainly based on calculating a "royalty" value or calculating "discounted cash flows". A "royalty"-based approach is sometimes used not so much to provide a total estimate of the value of a brand as to calculate how much a brand name would add to the value of an existing asset. This is used to calculate the value of a franchise — how much would the addition of the "O'Brien's" name add to the value of a sandwich outlet or how much would the "Bewley's" name add to the value of a hotel? The "discounted cash flow" approach attempts to put a value on the future revenue that would accrue to a product or service because of its brand name as opposed to its functional or physical properties.

The fundamental nature of brands, and in particular the fact that they exist as bundles of impressions, opinions and associations in people's heads, means that there are problems of measuring their value using the traditional accountancy-based methods for assessing the value of assets.

The company that became most closely associated with new methods of valuing brands was Interbrand, a London-based consultancy that had carried out the initial valuation of the RHM brands. They favoured the "economic use" method which calculates the brand's net contribution to the current owner:

> It is based on a thorough financial and marketing evaluation of the brand, including the background and characteristics of the brand together with a financial analysis including sensitivity analysis of the key assumptions.[7]

The main advantage of this method is that it tries to come to terms with the complexity of the subject and seeks to combine hard factual information with the more subjective judgements which are an inevitable element in any assessment of brands.

The Interbrand method is based on:

> A brand's current level of profitability expressed as a weighted average of earnings over recent years — an earnings multiplier based on the brand strength assessment is applied to a brand's profitability in order to determine the brand's value — the stronger the brand the greater the multiplier with the maximum being twenty as twenty years is considered to be a reasonable time horizon.[8]

The critical issue here is the brand strength assessment and this is where expertise and judgement come in. Interbrand has devised a method based on a composite score from seven weighted factors. The following are brief descriptions of the factors with their weightings in brackets:

---

[7] Haigh, D. Ibid.

[8] Arnold, D. Ibid.

- Leadership (25): The position of a brand within its market; brand leaders or brands which are close to brand leadership have a disproportionate advantage in most markets.

- Geographic spread (25): Brands which operate in more than one market also have advantages disproportionate to their size.

- Brand stability (15): Long-established brands are more valuable than recently launched brands.

- Market stability (10): Some markets are more stable than others.

- Trend (10): Some brands in the same markets can represent the future direction of the market better than others.

- Support (10): Brands that have received consistent marketing communications support over the years are stronger than others.

- Protection (5): A registered trade mark is an added source of strength.

It should be obvious from this description that the Interbrand methodology is heavily reliant on judgement; the weightings are arbitrary and most of the measures rely on opinions rather than facts, but it makes sense and is therefore more likely to be accepted than any alternative.

The Confused Usage of "Brand Equity"

Like many of the terms used in conjunction with brands, "equity" is thrown around with abandon and it is not always clear exactly what type of "equity" is being referenced. Paul Feldwick has performed a valuable service in distinguishing between three distinct types of meaning.[9]

---

[9] Feldwick, P., *What Is Brand Equity Anyway?* WARC Publication, 2002.

The first is where brand equity is taken to mean brand value, the price that might be expected to be paid if the brand was sold or if the company who owned the brand wanted to include it as an intangible asset on their balance sheet.

The second is where equity is used as a substitute for other words like "strength" or "power", as in the degree of attachment that people have for the brand. In this sense the degree of equity is measured by some form of consumer rating scales in consumer surveys as opposed to a financial valuation.

The third meaning is where equity is simply a description that consumers ascribe to the brand.

In the same paper Feldwick cast some doubt on the usefulness of brand valuation by making the point that they are not particularly helpful in determining the long-term health of a brand because there are too many arbitrary assumptions involved. A glance at the proposed Interbrand methodology will confirm this observation. Most of the measures can only be assigned numerical values on the basis of subjective judgement. Attempting to impose an objective monetary value on brands through calculations of discounted cash flows involves forecasting and "to forecast you have to make all kinds of assumptions about the future, many of which will, in the event, turn out to be wrong".

But the most fundamental problem in attempting to arrive at an objective measure of the value of a brand is the question of ownership. Brands can have very different values to different people or different businesses. One of the reasons why Nestlé were prepared to pay so much for Rowntree Mackintosh is because they could envisage synergies between the two businesses that were not present for any of the other bidders. A more recent example was the takeover by Rupert Murdoch of the internet-based MySpace brand in the US, which was fuelled by his conversion to the new medium after considerable initial scepticism. The price paid was regarded as extremely high by financial opinion in America but Murdoch needed credible internet brands in a hurry.

A final problem is concerned with "separability" — how the brand can be separated from the rest of the business. Feldwich makes the point that many brands if separated from the support systems they enjoy under one management team, and in particular the culture of that team, may perform very differently in a different environment. One of the best examples of the ownership issue in practice was in the takeover of the iconic American soft drinks brand "Snapple" by Quaker Foods. The latter company was a long-established, traditional and professional business that naturally tried to impose their streamlined way of working on their new acquisition. However, a large part of the appeal of the brand for its consumers was the laid-back casual approach by the previous management. So when Quaker started to apply more professional standards, consumers were dismayed, sales declined and the brand was eventually sold on to new owners at a huge loss. The lesson from this little case history is that many brands are inseparable from their managements, a lesson that many successful corporate raiders have learned to their cost.

Other Applications of Brand Valuations

Providing a measure for balance sheets is not the only reason for attempting brand valuations. Most businesses are now attuned to the need to communicate to a much wider range of audiences than in the past. These include investors and financial opinion leaders, the media and above all the staff. It can be beneficial to alert all of these groups to the value of the business's brands. The more the brands are worth the more each of these audiences will admire the business and this can only be to its benefit.

There are also more specific uses of brand valuations; for example:

- *Licensing and franchising*: Some companies may wish to license their brands and therefore some form of value will be required. An example of this application in the Irish market is where Bewley's have licensed their brand to property developers for hotels. Both parties will need some form of valuation of the Bewley's brand before they can come to an amicable arrangement.

- *Litigation support*: As society becomes more litigious we are likely to see more legal cases which require a brand valuation before they can be resolved.

- *Internal marketing management*: Where companies have more than one brand, some form of valuation of the brands can facilitate brand management and allocation of resources.

Conclusion

The fact that there is no such thing as an objective valuation of a brand doesn't mean that people are not going to continue trying to value brands. Whether these valuations are included on balance sheets or not is a matter for accountants and regulatory authorities, not brand managers, but regardless of whether they do or not there are other practical benefits of carrying out the exercise.

There are valid objections to brand valuation but it is evident that they are not going to prevent more such exercises in the future. It has been argued that property values, which routinely appear on company balance sheets, are also subject to fairly subjective calculation and certainly price guidelines in the Dublin property market bear little relation to their subsequent sale price. Brand valuations are not the only financial calculation that involve informed estimation:

> To admit that the process requires informed estimation is sometimes taken as an admission of defeat. However it is clear that in all financial accounting matters, from activity based costing to asset valuations, and provisions in published financial accounts, experienced estimation is widely

used and widely accepted. In fact it is the only way of producing the figures.[10]

The key words in that quote are "experienced estimation". Because brand valuation is a relatively new concept, no one has built up a large body of experience in the area, but a start has been made and we can expect more and better brand valuations in the future.

---

[10] Haigh, D. Ibid

PART THREE

BRANDING IN IRELAND: FOUR CRITICAL ISSUES

"At the heart of every great brand — whether it is a chocolate box for its customers, a bank for its customers, pop stars for their fans or a company to its employees — is a compelling story built around an emotional character or personality."

— Scott Bradbury, *Admap*, October 2003

"Soon branding was being applied not only to products but to the companies that supplied them too, then it became apparent that the same concept could be applied to just about anything that competes for attention such as political parties, football clubs, charities, museums and universities. Eventually people started to think of themselves and each other as brands."

— Richard Tomkins, *Financial Times*, 8 September 2003

"A great brand is one you want to live your life by, one you trust and hang on to while everything around you is changing, one that articulates the type of person you are or want to be, one that enables you to do what you couldn't otherwise achieve."

— Peter Fisk, *Marketing Genius*, 2006

Chivers began manufacturing in Henrietta Place, Dublin in 1932. A new plant was built in Beech Hill, Clonskeagh, County Dublin in 1953.

8

CONSUMER GOODS BRANDING: IS THERE A FUTURE?

U ntil very recently the answer to this question would have been irrelevant because the question would have been unthinkable. Now that the question is being raised regularly we will have to consider the possible answers a little more carefully.

For most of the time that people have been conscious of brands they have automatically associated them with the range of products that could be bought in what used to be called grocery stores and are now called supermarkets. Packaged detergents probably represent the quintessential brand from the now almost forgotten Rinso to the still ever popular Persil. These brands are part of our cultural landscape with their generations of intrusive and often irritating TV advertising featuring smarmy celebrities and minor soap opera characters. In fact, the term "soap opera" originates from the early detergent manufacturers in the US who were the first sponsors of extended drama serials on radio in the 1930s.

Brands, and grocery brands in particular, only really started to emerge at the turn of the last century. Prior to that people bought their groceries from their local grocery store and placed their trust in the store owner who was of course known to them. Most of the goods they bought had no brand names; they were purchased loose and packed by the store owner. Findlaters, the Dublin retailer founded in 1823, which until the 1960s had shops in the city, was a good example of the early grocery stores although they were best known for their wines and spirits. This advertisement from 100 years ago shows their range of oatmeals sold at different prices depending on the type but with no brand name other than that of the retailer. (It is also interesting to note how much more self-confident copy writers were in 1905).

ALEX. FINDLATER & CO. LTD., DUBLIN.

IRISH OATMEAL

is far superior in every way to that made in America, the home-grown oat being larger, better developed, and more succulent and nourishing than the dried-up American grain.

FINDLATER'S

IRISH

OATMEAL.

Findlater's Finest Quality Pinhead,
per 5 lb. linen bag, 1/-

„ Finest Flake, per stone, 2/4

„ „ Pinhead, „ 2/4

ALEX. FINDLATER & CO., Ltd.

The growth of mass manufacturing at the beginning of the last century changed all that and saw the rise of powerful manufacturing giants like Unilever and Procter & Gamble, selling their branded name detergents supported by consistent and frequent advertising. By mid-century almost all the items sold in the average grocery store were manufacturer brands. There were some exceptions, especially in the "nation of shopkeepers" next door. As Napoleon had correctly observed, Britain had a powerful retail tradition and a number of the most famous like Marks & Spencer and Sainsbury's have always been known for their own label brands.

The study of brands and branding from an academic perspective was slow to begin and it could be argued that it only started when the first signs of a threat to the dominance of manufacturer brands, from the growing power of retailer brands, began to emerge in the late 1960s. It could also be argued that it was the advertising agencies rather than academia that were first to perceive the implications of this development.

The First Crisis of Branding — 1978

In 1978 J. Walter Thompson, in London, published a pamphlet entitled "The Crisis in Branding".[1] JWT resided in baronial splendour in Berkeley Square in the heart of London's West End and during the 1960s and 1970s the agency was a powerhouse of intellectual thinking about branding from senior executives, including John Treasure, Tom Corlett, Timothy Joyce and above all Stephen King. King's book *Developing New Brands*, which was first published in 1973, was one of the most important contributions to brand thinking.[2] In this book King made the remarkable assertion for the time that "branding is the central task of the manufacturer – his raison d'etre". The main point in the "Crisis in Branding" paper was that because of the importance of brands to any business, problems in this area could be regarded as a "crisis". The problem alluded to was a decline in advertising support for brands during the 1970s because of the very high inflation caused by the Arab oil embargos as a result of the wars in the Middle East. The share of total advertising for food and other household brands fell from 30 per cent to 22 per cent between 1970 and 1977, and the main reason for this decline was the erosion of above the line support because of pressure from retailers to make all kinds of payments and discounts in order to ensure shelf space. The large retailers were beginning to flex their now considerable muscles in a process that has remained a feature of the trade ever since. Manufacturers were thus faced with a "vicious spiral": the more they had to contribute to the retailer the less there was available for marketing communications support, thus leaving their brands in an even weaker position to withstand retailer demands in the next negotiation cycle (see Figure 7). The paper concluded:

---

[1] "The Crisis In Branding", 1978, J. Walter Thompson Publication, London.

[2] King, S., *Developing New Brands*, The Garden City Press, London, 1973.

Can the manufacturer brand survive? The fact is that there will always be economies of scale in distribution for own labels, and with considerable spare capacity in industry quite often lower production costs too. Unless the manufacturer devotes proper resources to adding other values to his brands, it's hard to see why people should continue to pay a premium price for them.

The main recommendation was that all brand owners should regularly carry out a health check of their brands to ensure that everything was being done to maintain their position and to act as an early warning for possible threats that might lie ahead.

Figure 7: The Vicious Spiral

It is interesting to note that the health check included areas like R&D, product and process improvement, as well as areas such as advertising and other forms of marketing communications. It also includes comprehensive comparative data on the brand and its competitors in addition to profitability breakdowns for the brand starting with net sales and splitting expenditure by "brand building" and other costs. It could be argued that very few of today's brand managers are in control of all of these aspects of their brand's performance.

It could also be argued that if every manufacturer had devoted proper resources to "adding other values to his brands", the growth of retailer brands would not have been as strong following the first crises of branding. The importance of branding did come to be appreciated by senior management, but retailers also grew in power and approximately fifteen years later there was a second crisis of branding, this time on a global scale.

The Second Crisis of Branding — 1993

If the first "crisis" was debated and discussed only within the confines of the marketing and in particular the marketing communications business, the second was a more elaborate affair which engaged the attention of all levels of business, was widely commented on in the media and for a brief fifteen minutes of fame even made the front pages under the sub-editors sobriquet "Marlboro Friday".

The exact date is the only one that makes a regular entry into brand history, 2 April 1993. On that day Philip Morris, the world's biggest producer of consumer products, reduced the price of one of its best known brands, in fact one of the best known brands in the world, by 20 per cent. By the early 1990s business news stories were beginning to migrate to the front pages of newspapers with the inevitable consequence that the fevered mind of the modern sub-editor was let loose: "brands on the run", "can the big brands survive", "the death of brands" and "brands — who needs them?" were some of the less lurid headlines that accompanied the story. The fact of the matter was that Marlboro was beginning to lose market share to discount cigarette brands but the brand had been taking annual price increases well ahead of inflation and by 1993 it was selling at \$2.00 a pack compared with discount brands at \$0.69 a pack.

If there was one obvious conclusion from the second crisis of branding it was that the public tolerance for continuous price increases and for too big a price difference between manufacturer brands and retailer brands was limited. Ultimately, they will shout "stop" and on Marlboro Friday they did, with a vengeance. Marlboro's parent company, Philip Morris, suffered a massive $14 billion fall in its share value and the shock waves from the event wiped $50 billion off the value of the top twenty five consumer packaged goods companies.[3] But media and academic reaction to the event, especially the plethora of "death of brands" articles, was way off the mark. Marlboro Friday wasn't a reaction against brands; it was a reaction to continuous price increases from one manufacturer, who mistakenly imagined it was immune to the normal behaviour in any market because of the addicted loyalty of smokers.

The events of March 1993 didn't result in the death of brands, in fact during the remainder of that decade the issue of brands and branding became even more prominent in the business press, but in the grocery sector retailer brands continued to increase their share of many markets.

The Third Crisis of Branding — 2004

A new wave of apprehension about the future of manufacturer brands started to develop during 2004. It was not as dramatic as the first two crises, and it was difficult to pinpoint a single cause, but it created the same sense of concern among the owners and managers of manufacturer brands. It would be wrong to attempt to locate this crisis on a single date but on 21 September there were simultaneous profit warnings from two of the most powerful owners of manufacturer brands, Unilever and Colgate, leading to speculation that consumer goods companies were under renewed pressure from retailers. The *Financial Times* reported that this event was being compared to Marlboro Friday, but then back-

---

[3] *Harvard Business Review*, Jan-Feb, 1996.

tracked a little by agreeing that there was no comparison and went on to accept the fact that the fears expressed about the future of brands in 1993 had proved to be unfounded. However, their commentator, Adam Jones, did make the point that "consumer goods multinationals are still under intense pressure to prove to price conscious consumers that their brands are worth that bit extra".[4]

There were two other disturbing straws in the wind in 2004. First, a number of respected commentators in journals as diverse as the *Financial Times* and *Admap* began writing articles with opening sentences along the lines of "I used to be a brand only buyer but . . .". The general theme of these articles was not about price but was largely concerned with the growing quality and sophistication of retailer brands: "no one now thinks it cheap should a guest arrive at a dinner party clutching a box of Tesco Finest Belgium chocolates".[5] Meanwhile in Ireland manufacturer brands faced renewed pressure on margins from the two leading multiples, Tesco and Dunnes, because they in turn were beginning to feel the heat from the growing market share of the two German hard discounters Lidl and Aldi, whose combined brand share in the Irish grocery market had crept over 5% per cent. The outcome of this little affray harked back to the first crisis of branding because manufacturer brands were squeezed so hard in 2004 that they were forced to cut back on above the line marketing communications thus weakening their brands still further. The vicious circle was back.

So where do grocery manufacturer brands stand now after all these travails and traumas?

---

[4] Jones, A., "Unilever Colgate Profit Warnings", *Financial Times*, 21 September 2004.

[5] Tomkins, R., "The Brand Is Dead, Long Live The Brand", *Financial Times*, 21 September 2004.

Manufacturer Brands versus Retailer Brands: Market Share Trends

It is always difficult to obtain accurate comparison figures because different research companies and consultancies tend to operate with different definitions but the figures below give a good indication of the current situation.

Figure 8 below shows the very different market shares for retailer brands across the world. The results show that Switzerland, UK and Germany are the three countries with the highest retailer brand shares. Asian countries tend to be at the bottom end of the scale and it is tempting to conclude that there is a positive correlation between economic prosperity and high retailer brand penetration. However, Japan, with only 4 per cent retailer brand share, belies this and the most powerful economy in the world, the US, is only half way up the table with a share of 19 per cent. Ireland occupies a mid-table position with a share of 26 per cent.

Figure 8: Country by Country Variation in Retail Brand Penetration[6]

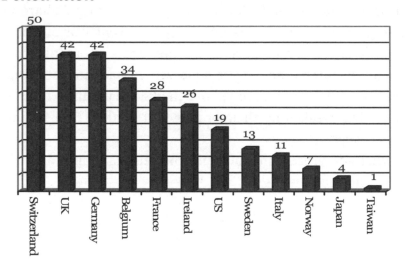

---

[6] Passingham-Hughes, H., "Will Private Label Drive Out Manufacture Brands", *Admap* October 2004.

Figure 9 shows the long-term retailer brand trends in the UK over a 24-year-period, from 1980 to 2003. The results show a steady rise in retailer brands through the 1980s and early 1990s but there hasn't been much progress over the last decade and the results suggest that the retailer brand revolution may have peaked.

Figure 10 shows the most recent trends in the Irish market where the retailer share has been rising steadily and represents a quarter of total sales.

Figure 9: Long-term Retailer Brand Trends, UK[7]

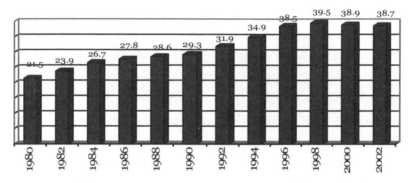

Figure 10: Branded vs Private Label Trends, Republic of Ireland[8]

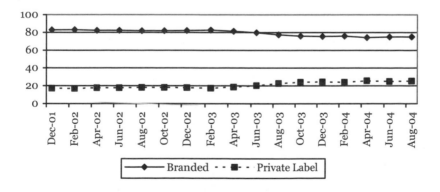

---

[7] TSN Worldpanel, Ireland, 2003-04.

[8] Ibid.

The reasons for the comparatively low share of retailer brands in Ireland has often been attributed to innate cultural differences, the inference being that the Irish psyche is fundamentally against the notion of retailer brands. Some proponents of this dubious line of reasoning argue that Irish consumers are more comfortable with the quality assurance attached to manufacturer brands and would prefer not to be associated with the traditionally more down-market retailer brands. The real explanation probably stems from the way that the retail trade developed in this country and in particular the retailer brand strategies employed by the main players. In fact, the main explanations for the variation in the penetration of retailer brands across the world are the different structures of retailer concentration in different markets and the different own-label strategies adopted by the leading retailers.

There have been significant differences in the own-label strategies of the major retailers in Ireland. The market is dominated by three main businesses — Dunnes, Tesco and SuperValu — on a national level and one major regional brand, Superquinn, which operates mainly in the greater Dublin area. Dunnes, a legend among Irish shoppers, is the longest-established of the multiples. It was launched in 1944 and quickly established itself as the leading low-cost grocery chain in the country with its long-running slogan "Dunnes Stores Better Value Beats Them All".

Dunnes was an early convert to retailer brands and launched the St Bernard own-label range in the 1960s. Although there was an obvious echo of Marks & Spencer's St Michael range in the UK, the Dunne's initiative was modelled on the conventional retailer brand thinking of the time. This involved product quality specifications which were reasonably close to, but never ahead of, the manufacturer brands and pack designs, which went as close to the brand leader's as the law would allow. Quinnsworth (now Tesco) pursued a similar strategy, as did a number of the symbol groups but none of them took the high ground and there was no equivalent retailer brand strategies of Sainsbury's and Marks & Spencer. Superquinn was the obvious candidate for a more up-market range of retailer brands but they did not really enter the fray, although they did launch a generic range of very basic products in the 1970s. It was only after Tesco's takeover of Quinnsworth in the early 1990s, and their subsequent launch of the "Tesco Finest" range, that Irish consumers were exposed to premium quality retailer brands.

In spite of these developments it is still possible to argue that the retailer brand phenomenon is exaggerated. For a start, many of the products that are now being classified as "retailer brands", like fruit and vegetables, were never manufacturer brands to begin with. Traditionally they were sold loose as commodity products but now many have been re-classified as retailer brands. This category was always weakly branded because the goods that made up this market were supplied by a myriad of small suppliers. It is, however, a growth market which raises the possibility that one of the reasons manufacturer brands have been in decline is not due to any inherent weaknesses in branded goods, but because the market categories in which they compete now account for a declining share of total grocery purchases.

There is also the fact that the recent rise of a few percentage points in the retailer brand share in Ireland may have more to do with the rise in share of the two hard discounters, Lidl and Aldi, than any consumer-led move to retailer brands. The less well-known continental brands stocked in these outlets are all classified by the market research organisation who measure this market as retailer brands.

Between 2004 and 2005 the number of Lidl and Aldi stores increased from 69 to 94 but their combined brand share remained at around 5.5 per cent. There is some indication that although the hard discounters have attracted a significant proportion of Irish grocery shoppers, many of their customers are topping up on a specific range of goods rather than using them for their main weekly shopping.

The Future of Manufacturer Brands

Anyone reading the literature of branding over the last two decades would be forgiven for thinking that by now retailer brands would be averaging more than eighty per cent of the grocery market and that manufacturer brands would be on their last legs. Faced with the accumulated weight of learned papers, books, consultants' reports of all kinds and business journalist speculations, one would be forced to conclude that the game was up. So why isn't it? Why are most of the brand leaders from the 1970s still the brand leaders today? Why, in spite of some increases in retailer brand share, has there been so little real change? Could it be that manufacturer brands are more resilient than the critics assumed? In which case, the real question should be: why in spite of the evidence to the contrary is the demise of branding still being predicted on a regular basis?

It is hard not to come to the conclusion that many of the people who write about branding disapprove of the whole idea of brands and believe that anyone who pays a premium price for branded goods is gullible, easily led and downright stupid. There always seems to be an air of quietly suppressed glee when pontificating about the "death of the brand", an unspoken feeling that they deserved what was coming:

> There seems to be gloating pleasure that advertisers and brand owners are under attack almost as if they deserve a thrashing because of the excesses they enjoyed during the ostentatious 1980s.[9]

At an evening meeting of the Marketing Society in 1999 a paper presented by the Amarach consultancy stated with the *chutzpah* that characterises consultants' predictions that "most brands will not survive in the new millennium".[10] As usual no evidence was

---

[9] Gordon, W., "Meeting the Challenge of Retailer Brands", *Admap,* March 1994.

[10] Amarach Report, "Why Brands Have No Future in the New Millennium", Marketing Society, 1999.

given for this dramatic pronouncement, which has so far proved to be completely unfounded. The presentation went on to state that retailer brands at the time accounted for twenty per cent of all grocery sales in the US and would ultimately account for 100 per cent. Again, no evidence was given for this remarkable prediction and the only real reason given was a vague theory that brands had acted as nannies for all those silly twentieth-century women; but the women of the new millennium would not be so easily fooled. Nevertheless, it is clear that retailer brands have increased market share in recent years.

Why Are Retailers Gaining the Upper Hand?

The three main reasons that are usually advanced for the increasing market share of retailer brands are better consumer information, better access to consumers and better marketing strategies.

Better Information

Traditionally manufacturers had much better information about the buying public because of their investment in market research. The introduction of "loyalty cards" in the early 1990s changed all that and tipped the balance of information power firmly into the hands of the retailers. In the UK, Tesco boss Sir Ian McLaurin famously remarked a few months after the introduction of the Tesco Clubcard that they had found out more about their customers in the last few months than they had in the previous fifty years.

In Ireland it has been estimated that in 2002 Dunnes had over 900,000 store card members, Tesco had around 850,000 and Superquinn had 300,000 members. This means that all these retailers must have amassed a vast amount of information about their customers, but it also means that there must be a reasonable degree of over-lapping ownership of so-called "loyalty" cards.

Retailers were now within striking distance of marketing nirvana, the ability to conduct real one-to-one communication with their customers armed with detailed knowledge of their purchasing behaviour. They had vastly more information than manufacturers could ever dream of or be in a position to pay for. The use of military analogies in marketing literature can be tedious but it may be worth pointing out that military commanders who possess the most accurate and up-to-date information tend to end up victorious and, as the twentieth century came to a close, the leading retailers were in no doubt that they had won.

Better Access

Like so many of the battles in the war between manufacturers and retailers, the latter's strengths were achieved partly as a result of the former's weaknesses. The fragmentation of mass media audiences coincided, but had nothing to do with, increasing traffic or footfall within the leading grocery outlets. Traditionally manufacturers had used the mass media to bypass the retailer and speak to them directly; now it was claimed the retailer was in a position to reverse the process. Mass audiences were becoming harder to build up and were more likely to be found in the new temples of worship, the shopping centres. Tesco, always the innovator, took this development to its logical conclusion by opportunistically launching its own TV station within some of its UK stores, thus enabling them to beam messages directly to consumers as they shopped. But of course retailers also had more indirect ways of communicating with customers by controlling shelf facings, special displays and in-store messages of all kinds. Retailers which offer online shopping facilities have even more ways of directing messages to their customers.

Better Retailer Brand Strategies

With better customer information and better media access all that was required for retailers to complete their victory was better products. Accurate quantitative data and perceptive qualitative insights have always been at the heart of the best manufacturer brand strategies. In the past, retailers underinvested in this area and tended to regard it with a certain amount of suspicion — a little too airy-fairy for the macho hard-man world of retailing where real men bought in bulk and women did the shopping. But armed with the data explosion, created by loyalty cards and information technology, retailers began to develop more sophisticated own-label strategies.

When retailers first dipped their toes into own-label products in the 1960s and 1970s they were content with slightly below-par offerings in terms of quality. They would also brief design agencies to come up with a pack design which was as near to that of the brand leader as was legally possible. Sometimes over-enthusiastic designers went too far and there were a number of high-profile "copycat" court cases in the early days of own-label brands. Retailers initially approached the leading manufacturers requesting them to make their own-label products for them; most manufacturers refused but even then a number succumbed. Soon, however, independent manufacturing plants emerged with the specific purpose of servicing the retailers' requirements. As the retailers began to embrace the world of marketing strategy they started to think more in terms of what their customers would prefer as opposed to what they could supply. In some cases they completely ignored what manufacturers were up to and created entirely new product lines based on the changing requirements of their customers. In general, retailers were quicker off the mark than the traditional manufacturing giants in spotting the time-pressure phenomenon which was creating an intolerable burden for a younger generation of consumers, particularly working women. In response they created a whole range of ready-to-eat meals. Although a number of manufacturers had tried their hand in this area — Unilever's Vesta range in the 1960s comes to mind — the modern retailers' offerings were much more sophisticated.

But it wasn't just new product categories. For the first time in the 1990s retailers began to segment their own-label strategies.

Again Tesco were to the fore. They began to divide their own-label brands into different categories beginning with Tesco own-label, a standard retailer brand with product quality very close to the main manufacturer products and selling at a slight discount and with a pack design fairly close to the brand leader. But they also introduced Tesco Value, very low-priced products with packaging designed to convey this message. This range has some similarities to the "generic" retailer brand concept that enjoyed a brief vogue in the 1970s. Two additional products complete the Tesco offering: Tesco Finest, an upmarket range of products with a level of quality that sometimes surpasses the main manufacturer brands and with with sophisticated contemporary pack designs; and Tesco Healthy Living, which is aimed at a small but growing segment of the population who are increasingly concerned with nutritional issues.

The following example from the sausage market illustrates the new development, by showing the prices per kilo of the different brands on display at one Tesco outlet during a week day in early January 2005.

Table 3: Sausage Prices in Tesco's, January 2005

Description	Price Per Kilo
Tesco Value	€3.64
Tesco Pork Sausages	€4.76
Oldhausen	€5.27
Dennys Gold Medal	€5.27
Kearns	€5.27
Granby	€5.64
Galtee Sizzlers	€5.95
Boyers	€5.95
Clonakilty	€6.08
Shaws	€6.18
Tesco Finest	€6.35
Tesco Healthy Living	€6.39

The main point to note about this table is that Tesco now operate a segmented retailer brand strategy, and more significantly are positioned both above and below the manufacturer brands in price. The Tesco value range, sold at a significant discount to all other brands, has a uniform design which exemplifies its low price position. The packaging for the traditional own brand, "Tesco Pork Sausages", conforms to traditional retailer brand strategy imitating the design formats of the brand leaders. The design of the "Tesco Finest" range bears no relationship to any of the manufacturer brands and is deliberately positioned at the very top of the market.

How Manufacturers Contributed to the Rise in Retailer Power

With some notable exceptions, Kellogg's being a classic example, manufacturers contributed to the rise in retailer power by ignoring many of the principles that had created their own success at the very time when retailers were beginning to exert their dominance.

Andrew Seth, who had been in charge of Lever Brothers marketing in the UK during the 1980s, has argued that manufacturers effectively allowed retailers to increase their share of the market by elevating short-term profitability at the expense of long-term survival:

> Marketing turned from a strategic business leading job to one where operational effectiveness was the hallmark of success —brand managers no longer championed the big issues of innovation and how to create consumer demand; instead they co-ordinated a range of tactical administrative and largely internal functions —brand owners have ceded research and development, innovation and integrated consumer inspired marketing to their trade customers. They (marketing departments) appear out of place in the more demanding business environment of the 90s. Marketing departments are essentially a spending function. Caught in a period of cost savings and reductions they have few roles

that are uniquely their own or decisions which fall directly within their remit.[11]

This is a damning indictment from an experienced professional but he was not alone; the weaknesses of marketing departments have been commented on regularly for some time.

A widely quoted report from Coopers & Lybrand following Marlboro Friday concluded:

> Marketing as a discipline is more vital than ever – marketing as a department is increasingly failing to match up to expectations.[12]

How Manufacturers Can Regain the Initiative

Almost without exception everyone who has commented on the rise of retailer brands and the decline of manufacturer brands has come to the same conclusion about what manufacturers must do to halt the decline: continuous product innovation. Improved product quality is the only guaranteed way to keep ahead of the all-powerful retailers and there is a widespread perception that manufacturers have begun to slow down in this area, and in some market segments have even allowed retailers to take the product development initiative. The fact that there has been a steady stream of new product initiatives from relatively small companies – for example the emergence of the Innocent brand in the UK and the success of a number of small Irish food companies, such as Clonakilty, with the encouragement of Bord Bia – shows that this is not an impossible task. Imagination, insight and courage are more important than physical and monetary resources.

It is also true that the two main weapons employed by manufacturers in the past to maintain their advantage are just as relevant today: consumer understanding and marketing communica-

---

[11] Seth, A., "Creative Review", *Financial Times,* 7 December 2004.
[12] "Marketing at the Crossroads", Coopers & Lybrand, 1994.

tions. Manufacturers cannot cede this ground to the retailer. In spite of some retailer successes, for example ready-to-eat meals, manufacturers should have much greater expertise in their own product area and they must continue to be committed to new product development. One of the world's leading manufacturer-branded businesses appears to be heeding this message. P&G have recently been reported as "rediscovering their creative heart" and the recent introduction of a number of new cleaning products in the US (Autodry and Magic Eraser) are reported to have "helped keep the supermarket private label at bay".[13]

The second area where manufacturers need to regain the initiative is in consumer understanding. Throughout the twentieth century manufacturer brand owners have been aided by the vast array of consumer research techniques to gain a better understanding of the needs, aspirations and desires of consumers. But it is now being claimed that loyalty card data, which is only available to retailers, has effectively trumped this advantage by giving them infinitely superior information.

Although the introduction of loyalty cards was claimed to give the retail trade dominance in the area of consumer understanding, not everyone agreed that this has been the case:

> It seems increasingly evident that loyalty programmes are a waste of a company's time, effort and money and that over time such investment would be better spent on making sure that a business gets all the basics right such as product, service, value for money, convenience and availability.[14]

No amount of loyalty card data can ever compete with the accumulated consumer understanding of the manufacturers. Retailers are unlikely to have the detailed consumer understanding of indi-

---

[13] Buckley, N., "The Power of Original Thinking", *Financial Times*, 14 May 2004.
[14] Mazur, L., "Loyalty Cards are a Waste of Company's Time, Effort & Money" *Market Leader*, Issue 4, 1999.

vidual markets that can only come from active listening to consumers and acute observation of their behaviour.

The third area where manufacturers can still maintain their traditional advantage is in marketing communications. Most great brands, from the world-famous names that originated in the late nineteenth century to the newly established twenty-first-century brands, are built up through marketing communications, mainly advertising. The long-established brands have a rich and formidable advertising history and it may not be a coincidence that at the very time that manufacturers of fast-moving consumer brands are facing a crisis of confidence the advertising business is also facing its own dark night of the soul. Fragmenting media audiences, cynical ad-literate consumers and increasing costs are all being put forward as evidence that advertising isn't working as well as it used to.

But no matter how much image advertising retailers engage in, the majority of their marketing communication budgets will be devoted to price-related ads. The big multiple retailers can never allow a competitor to upstage them in this area. In the Irish market Superquinn has traditionally been regarded as providing a better service and a more sophisticated range of goods than its rivals. Independent shopping basket surveys showed that they were a little more expensive than their competitors, but enough people were still prepared to pay the price for the superior service and shopping experience. Superquinn could never allow the perception of a price gap to become too wide so they had to devote most of their advertising budget over the years to showing selected goods at special promotional price offers. Shoppers need the reassurance that they are not paying too much above the odds and that they are capable managers of the household budget. The promise of low prices is a generic attribute of the grocery market which must always be communicated to shoppers, but the constant re-iteration of prices weakens the impact of retailer advertising.

Another inhibiting factor for retailer advertising is the need to play safe because they must appeal to a wider target group than the vast majority of manufacturers. It would be difficult to envisage a major retailer engaging in the sort of sexually explicit advertising, which worked so well for Häagen Dazs, for their own-label ice cream.

But advertising is not the only form of marketing communications, and in all the different forms of communication manufacturers are much more likely to extend the bounds of creativity in an attempt to engage with consumers. Hovis's dramatic new packaging in the UK bread market is a good example. It led to a huge increase in sales[15] and also prompted the following comment in a book on the UK grocery sector, which is one of the first to suggest that the rise of own brands may have reached a peak:

> Supermarket customer opinion has now swung back in favour of branded products; shoppers are willing to pay a little more for the assured quality of a well-known brand in preference to a cheaper own label product that is possibly inferior. For example in 1996 own label bread accounted for 50% of supermarket bread sales – by 2004 that was down to a mere 30% after bakers such as the family-run Warburtons and RHM, which makes Hovis, actively pushed their brands and customers responded.[16]

Professor Douglas Holt's theory of cultural branding[17] could also offer manufacturer brands an opportunity to devise marketing communication strategies which are likely to be effective with the public and are unlikely to be matched by retailer brands. Holt's thesis argues for marketing communications which take a positive stance on cultural contradictions within a society at any given point, which is likely to create greater resonance with the public and have a better chance of standing out from the clutter of mass communications. An interesting example of this approach is currently being

---

[15] IPA, Vol 12 & WARC, 2003.

[16] Bevan, J., *Trolley Wars*, Profile Books, 2005.

[17] Holt, D., *How Brands Become Icons*, Harvard Business School Press, 2003.

adopted by one of the best-managed brands in the world, Persil. Persil have always been associated with a caring, sharing, emotionally based brand image, but their latest "Dirt is Good" campaign celebrates creativity in childhood with the inevitable messy consequences — and Persil is there to clean up the mess. The concept is referred to internally in Unilever as "Modern Parenting". This is a topic of much greater interest to the target market than incremental improvements in detergents. It is also a topic which is likely to create a much greater degree of loyalty to the brand and one that retailers would find it very difficult to match.

A Tale of Two Markets

The following table shows the contrasting fortunes of manufacturer brands in two Irish markets:

Table 4: Contrasting Brand Fortunes

	Incidence of New Product Development	Ad Spend 2001-2004 as a % of Market Value	% Retailer Brand Share (Value)
Ready-to-Eat Cereal	Continuous	20%	12%
Natural Block Cheddar	Sporadic	7%	48%

Source: McConnells estimates

Although there may be special factors which have influenced the retailer brand share of each market, this table would suggest that in a market where the manufacturer brands are continuously introducing new products, carrying out regular market research and have a deep understanding and embedded knowledge of the attitudes and behaviour of consumers, retailer brands will struggle to gain market share, regardless of how big they are or how much loyalty card data they have. The fact that the ready-to-eat cereal market is dominated by three multinational companies, and the cheddar cheese market is dominated by three Irish dairy businesses who were preoccupied by takeovers, rationalisations and internal re-organisations during the last five years, may help to explain why the cheddar cheese market was not as well looked after as the ready-to-eat cereal market, but it does not negate the central thrust of the argument.

Conclusion

Superior consumer understanding and more creative marketing communications are two powerful weapons in the brand manufacturer's armoury but in future they will not be sufficient to guarantee success against the onslaught of retailer brands. Ultimately, the continuing success of manufacturer brands will depend on product innovation. Ever since 1837 when two immigrants, Irishman James Gamble and Englishman William Procter, swept up the scraps from the slaughterhouses of Cincinnati and rendered the fat to make soaps and candles, thus founding P&G, the people responsible for the development of the first manufacturer brands were characterised by an obsessive concern for product improvement and product quality. They were messianic in their belief that their creations could improve the lot of ordinary people. Dr John Harvey Kellogg and his brother William pioneered the breakfast cereal as a means of preventing digestion problems. William Colgate introduced the first collapsible toothpaste tube, which made cleaning teeth easier and more hygienic. Henry Ford dreamed of building a "motor car for the multitudes". A pharmacist from Georgia invented a secret recipe for a cola-based drink which eventually became Coca Cola and was originally launched as a brain tonic. And in the early twentieth century Isaac Carasso launched Danone yoghurt because he noticed children in Barcelona suffering from intestinal disorders. Not all of the brand pioneers were driven by altruistic motives but they were all driven by an obsession with product quality.

Nowadays most of the great brands are effectively owned by financial institutions on behalf of shareholders and are therefore driven by the need to maximise shareholder value. It may be that a return to an obsession with product quality would be the best defence against the erosion of margins and market share by the retail trade, and would be the best guarantee of shareholder value in the long run.

9

SERVICE BRANDS:
IS THERE ANY DIFFERENCE?

The theory of branding was mainly constructed from the experience of fast-moving consumer goods brands. Even today, when the term is applied indiscriminately to everything and anything by the general public and the mass media, there is still an underlying assumption that brands are mainly things that you buy in the shops. The main evolution that has occurred is that where the term was previously associated with goods purchased in supermarkets only, it is now applied to all retail outlets.

Academic analysis of branding has long assumed that service businesses can be regarded as brands. It is now over forty years since Professor Ted Levitt famously included accountancy and cold rolled steel as well as hot cross buns within the branding remit.[1]

The Problems of "Tangibility" and "Homogeneity"

In theory the principles of branding should apply in exactly the same way to services as to manufactured goods. Where there are a number of competitive offerings in a market the people who comprise the universe for that market will have some kind of image of the companies supplying the services and it is therefore in the interests of each supplier to manage that image as best they can. In practice two critical differences between product and service

---

[1] Levitt T., *The Marketing Mode*, The Free Press, 1969.

were identified in the earliest writing on the subject. The first was the difficulty in service branding of coping with an "intangible" service compared to a "tangible" product. It was argued that it was easier to brand a product that could be attractively packaged than an "intangible" service where the main focus was less clearly identifiable. However, this was at a time when the whole subject of branding was still heavily concentrated on functional benefits and the logo and pack were seen as two of the most critical areas for differentiation.

A second difference between product and service brands that was also widely commented on from the beginning was the "homogeneity" issue. A key element in branding had always been consistency, an implied guarantee that the product would not only look the same no matter where it was purchased but would perform its function in exactly the same way. A bar of confectionery or a pack of detergent could deliver on this promise but a service could not because a service was ultimately delivered by people who by definition were not homogeneous. The essence of the brand service experience lay in hundreds, thousands or in some cases millions of "moments of truth" — usually contacts between the service, in the form of a staff member, and the consumer.

Because of these differences it has always been assumed that it was much more difficult to brand a service than a product. Early examples of service branding made valiant attempts to overcome the difficulties by ruthlessly eliminating as many differences as possible to create a uniform standard of service. McDonalds is probably the best-known example and the famous "Hamburger University" was designed to produce a service experience that came as close to "homogeneity" as was humanly possible.

The Growing Prominence of Services Branding

A number of developments in the 1980s simultaneously focused more attention on the branding of service businesses and served to narrow the gap between product and service brands. These developments are outlined below.

In Search of Excellence

The publication of *In Search of Excellence*, the first management blockbuster, in 1982, written by two McKinsey consultants, Tom Peters and Robert Waterman, was a publishing phenomenon, selling over two million copies worldwide and spawning almost as many copycat volumes. The basic theme of the book was that excellent companies were characterised by extraordinary levels of commitment by staff at all levels and that the only way this could be achieved was to allow them much more freedom to operate than the traditional "command and control" style of management used to tolerate. Ironically, in many service organisations these staff were often the least well-paid and regarded. Although the book wasn't about branding *per se*, by focusing on the culture of business organisations it was dealing with what brand commentators were beginning to conclude was the critical issue in service branding:

> Without exception the dominance and coherence of culture proved to be an essential quality of the excellent companies — moreover the stronger the culture and the more it was directed towards the marketplace the less need there was for policy manuals, organisation charts or detailed procedures and rules — in these companies people way down the line know what they are supposed to do in most situations because the handful of guiding values is crystal clear.[2]

Company as Brand

Around the same time in the early 1980s a number of brand commentators were coming to the conclusion that companies would have to start thinking of themselves as brands. Hitherto the main businesses associated with brands, the leading fast-moving con-

---

[2] Peters T. & Waterman R., *In Search of Excellence*, Harper & Row, 1982.

sumer goods manufacturers, had concentrated on their individual brands and apart from the City and financial opinion leaders had kept the company name well in the background. In 1985 Stephen King made the following case:

> I think there will have to be far more emphasis on company as brand — this has been obvious in retailing and services for some time since in most services the people are already more important and a greater discriminator than the "products" they offer — there is no reason why manufacturing companies should not have a clear-cut corporate personality and stand for something very specific —think of IBM, ICI, Sony, Kellogg's.[3]

Once manufacturing companies started to consider themselves as brands the distinction between service and product brands began to erode.

Servitisation of Brands

A further element in this erosion was the "servitisation"[4] of all businesses. This clumsy expression refers to the growing belief that in order to survive all brands must add a service element. It's not enough for Persil to make your whites white; it must also provide a twenty-four hour helpline just in case you wonder whether it's safe to mix your coloureds with your whites. This service was provided in Ireland by Persil from around the mid-1990s. Again, the net result of this development was to further blur the distinction between product and service brands. In recent years the development of brand websites has added another service element to many product brands.

---

[3] King S., "Another Turning Point for Brands", *Admap*, October 1985.

[4] Fanning, J., "Tell Me a Story", *Irish Marketing Review*, Vol. 12, No. 2, 1999.

Relationship Marketing

The growing interest in relationship marketing in the 1980s was another factor which brought product and service brands closer together. Relationship marketing was a direct descendant of direct mail, which had always suffered from the reputation of an uninvited guest. Developments in information technology revolutionised this branch of marketing communications and some of the more aggressive proselytisers of relationship marketing regularly propounded the view that one-to-one communication was the only way to go. Needless to say, this did not come to pass but some of the underlying principles of this form of communication were adopted by the marketing community and because relationship marketing adds an additional service to a product offering there was a further erosion of the distinction between the two.

For all of the reasons outlined above, the special position of service brands has almost disappeared and there are now some doubts as to whether any real distinction between product and service brands exists:

> Thus the services marketing literature re-evaluates and questions the dichotomy between products and services — it indicates that a continuum is more appropriate than a dichotomy, that offerings may be more appropriate than services versus products and that because consumers act as co-producers of value there is a need to ensure consistency between all aspects of the consumer's experience.[5]

To that extent there is an element of "we're all service brands now" and it depends on the degree to which front-line staff play a role in determining the final brand image of the business. This could range from almost no part at all for a confectionery bar to the total brand

---

[5] de Chernatony, L., Khan, S. and Segal-Horn, S., "Characteristics of Successful Service Brands", Market Research Society (UK) Conference Papers, 2000.

image for a hairdresser or a firm of accountants. Retailers would fall somewhere in between because although the staff play a role in determining the brand image of the retailer it is the range of goods and the prices offered which probably play the dominant role.

Four Examples of Service Branding

To explore further the nature of service branding, and to show how the problems of brand management could be tackled in this area, it may be useful to examine four very different case studies.

Bus Éireann

Bus Éireann is one of the three constituent companies within the CIÉ Group. It is a state-owned business which operates inter-city long-distance bus services in Ireland. It also operates other services including the city bus services for Cork, Limerick, Galway and Waterford, and provincial school bus services. Since its inception as a separate company in 1987 Bus Éireann has faced competition for one of these services — long-distance inter-city — and this competition has intensified over the years. Research carried out in 1987 and 1989 showed serious image weaknesses for the Bus Éireann inter-city service compared to the private operators.[6]

Table 5: Image of Bus Éireann vs Private Operators

	1987		1989	
Attributes Rating	**BE %**	**PO %**	**BE %**	**PO %**
Value for Money	34	43	27	41
Friendly Service	44	38	32	31
Modern Coaches	60	44	52	32
Services a wide range of towns	65	38	56	26
Is very punctual	49	29	42	24

---

[6] Bus Éireann Marketing Department.

Given the company's healthy lead on most attributes, these results could be regarded as encouraging, but the widening gap on the critical "value for money" issue suggested otherwise. Bus travel has always been regarded as the cheapest form of transport; therefore price is a critical factor in dictating choice. Bus Éireann was slightly more expensive than the private operators because of higher overheads and they would always be perceived to be more expensive because they were a large state-owned operation. The following communications strategy was adopted:

> Promote the company name strongly, build the Bus Éireann brand, create a brand symbol to convey emotional warmth and devise an advertising strategy to convey the impression of a modern efficient professional business-driven organisation.

The red setter logo was designed to project the values of reliability, speed, friendliness and Irishness and to create a warm persona for the company. A series of TV commercials have been made since the late 1980s designed to fulfil these objectives, with the red setter playing a central role and American road music deliberately chosen to create a more contemporary image for the brand. Internal training programmes were also carried out with front-line staff, designed to impress upon them the urgency of the competitive situation and the need for enhanced customer service. The fleet was upgraded to provide a more comfortable passenger experience.

The results have been impressive: passenger numbers have grown from just over two million in 1987 to over eight million in 2004 while revenue has increased from just over €900,000 in 1987 to €5.3 million in the same period.[7]

---

[7] Ibid.

Table 6: Number of Passengers

	Intercity (Expressway) 000's	Rural (Bus Service) 000's	Four Cities (Cork, Limerick, Galway, Waterford)
1987	2,040	12,340	18,876
1993	4,852	12,984	20,510
1998	5,472	12,672	18,900
2001	7,108	16,154	20,051
2004	8,549	17,762	21,070

Attribute ratings improved significantly and by the turn of the century Bus Éireann was rated better than the private operators on value for money.[8]

Table 7: Changing Perceptions of "Value for Money"[8]

	1998		1999		2000		2001	
	BE %	PO %	BE %	PO %	BE %	PO %	BE %	PO %
Best Value for Money	27	27	26	27	25	25	28	24

- **Lessons from the Bus Éireann case study**: Public service businesses that adhere to the principles and best practice of branding — careful choice of brand symbols, music and marketing communications, consistency over the long term and a focus on consumer requirements rather than operational issues — can transform the image of the business over time.

Behaviour & Attitudes

Behaviour & Attitudes is a medium-sized market research company which offers a comprehensive range of market research services. The company was established in 1985 and has created a strong

---

[8] Ibid.

brand image among its target market of research buyers in the Irish marketing community. The image they have created is the much-sought-after position for any business-to-business service company: the brand that brings more insight to bear in its field of operations.

Traditional market research firms presented the data they had collected as objectively as possible, answered any technical questions about the fieldwork and the statistical significance of the data but were reluctant to be drawn into discussions about the implications of the results in terms of future action. That traditional attitude was changing at precisely the time B&A was established and the company successfully caught the new wave from the beginning. In addition to genuinely offering a more interpretive service, the company used marketing communications to build the desired brand image of a service provider willing and able to act as a strategic adviser based on their research findings. B&A's target market is very small, perhaps not more than 5,000 people in the wider marketing communications community and less than a few hundred core buyers of market research. Advertising would be a possibility but although it is now possible to target increasingly narrow specialist audiences, they chose a combination of sponsorship and relationship marketing.

The traditional form of relationship marketing for small service organisations is the annual party, usually at Christmas but sometimes organised around sporting events like football matches, race meetings or golf outings, but although they are much appreciated by the attendees there is little opportunity to create any distinctive brand message or build a brand image because so many businesses are engaged in the same exercises. B&A chose a different route: they commissioned an original print from a well-known artist and sent them to their core target group at Christmas. Apart from their visual attraction and the prospect of capital appreciation, the real benefit of this enterprise is that the underlying message, or sub-text if you prefer, is in tune with the image the company wants to project for itself. B&A not only collect data from the Irish public, they interpret Irish society for the benefit of their clients, and that is also what Irish artists do, albeit for very different reasons. The company's marketing communications is perfectly in tune with what it wants to stand for and how it wants to be positioned.

- *Lessons from the Behaviour & Attitudes case study*: everything a business does, even the choice of a Christmas gift, forms part of the image of that business. It follows therefore that even seemingly innocuous decisions can pay handsome brand image dividends if they are carefully considered in the light of what stance or positioning the business wishes to adopt.

KPMG

Like the previous example, this company operates in the business-to-business market but they are a substantial firm employing over 1,000 professional advisors and their marketing communications are the norm for the main accountancy firms. Like the other "Big Four" in the Irish market, KPMG operate a combination of relationship marketing programmes — very important clients are invited to very exclusive entertainment at a variety of mainly sporting but some cultural events, with less important clients invited to less exclusive events. This is balanced by regular publications and briefings directly related to the professional expertise of the firm.

This is a common pattern in the major business-to-business sectors. Until recently very few of them would have considered themselves from a brand perspective but the relentless focus on the power of brands in the business press, academia and from management consultants has forced service businesses to pay more attention to the image they reflect. The net result is that all the major accountancy firms now have well-designed uniform suites of corporate literature and structured relationship marketing programmes. To some extent all of this branding activity tends to cancel itself out, but everyone has to keep pace to stay in the race. Because of the uniform nature of the service the big firms provide it is difficult to create a distinctive identity.

Surveys among leading Irish business people up to a few years ago would have produced some image differences among the leading accountancy firms with one having a more defined and distinctive image than the rest. That firm was Arthur Andersen, the US-based multinational accountancy giant which sensationally collapsed almost overnight in 2002 following its involvement in the Enron scandal. Prior to that, Andersen's had managed to achieve what some brand commentators thought was impossible: a brand image which enabled it to stand out very clearly from all of its competitors who offered exactly the same services and were staffed by people with exactly the same qualifications. As a result they managed to achieve what strong brands do in any market: a premium price. Andersen's were regarded as more professional, more hard-working, more thorough and more expensive than their competitors.

The way they achieved this competitive advantage has implications, both good and bad, for all service companies. It was not because of any functional advantage; service companies rarely achieve this because technical expertise is too easily replicated. It was essentially due to a unique company culture backed up by a genuine commitment to internal training. For certain types of service brands internal training can provide a critical advantage and it also creates a very strong internal culture. The Andersen culture was legendary — competitors, and even some of their clients, regarded them with a combination of awe, fear and disdain. Not for nothing was the word "Android" used in connection with them. To some extent, and with the grateful benefit of hindsight, the seeds of their downfall may have been buried in their awesome company culture, with Enron an accident waiting to happen. A strong corporate culture can be the most powerful branding device for a service firm, but if it is so all-pervasive that it shields the firm, not just from the reality of commercial life but from the grubby reality of everyday living, it can be counter-productive.

With Andersen's now out of the picture, image differences between the "Big Four" are very difficult to detect, but using more projective market research techniques KPMG emerges as having a slightly more innovative, progressive image. The explanation, common to many service firms, lies in the history of the company and in particular the aggressive hard-driving reputation that Stokes Kennedy Crowley achieved in the 1960s and 1970s when the first shoots of native economic growth emerged. SKC eventually joined the global revolution under the KPMG banner but parentage casts a long shadow.

- ***Lessons from the KPMG case study:*** In spite of the fact that many successful consumer brands base their positioning on aspects of their history, often in highly idealised form, service brands are curiously reluctant to follow suit. But this approach could provide KPMG with a more distinctive image and arguably accounts for a critical element in their current image.

Ballynahinch Castle

Ballynahinch Castle has a long and romantic history, and is situated in a spectacular 450-acre setting in Connemara, facing the Twelve Bens mountain range, and surrounded by what used to be the most famous salmon-filled river in Ireland. Now that the salmon have virtually disappeared, the castle is a commercial hotel which must compete with a number of other premium-priced hotels in the immediate vicinity and, like them against the competing attractions in other parts of the country and beyond.

The hotel is open all year round with the exception of a short break in February and enjoys an occupancy rate of over 80 per cent. It has managed to attract an extremely loyal customer base and the manager Patrick O'Flaherty has a very clear idea of what the Ballynahinch brand stands for: Intimacy, Professionalism, Unpretentiousness. This is both a succinct and comprehensive brand proposition and shows the benefit of having such a clearly held view of what the brand stands for; in fact, it is not unknown for companies to pay six-figure sums for this type of analysis. A well-defined brand strategy guides the manager in making all other marketing and marketing communication decisions. The Ballynahinch strategy is obviously primarily dependent on the staff; only they can deliver on the three elements of the brand platform, and considerable skill, tact charm and confidence are required in balancing all three — especially "professionalism" with "unpretentiousness". This is why much of O'Flaherty's time is taken up with staff issues: training, listening, guiding and above all selecting.

Another key element of the Ballynahinch "experience" is the decision to welcome local people into the bar of the hotel, as the manager illustrates: "A few weeks ago a waitress went into the bar to take a dinner order from three guests — a high court judge, a prominent Dublin businessman and a European commissioner — but they were engaged in an animated conversation with three locals — a gillie, a fisherman and a small farmer. The waitress quietly withdrew and the kitchen was told to wait a little and although the meal was delayed the three visitors had a special experience, a unique insight into a way of life that has a particular resonance with the Irish psyche."

Consciousness of the brand stance also guides the main marketing communication strategy of the hotel: relationship marketing. A database of customers is very carefully maintained but there are no mass mailings; that would not be in keeping with the spirit of the brand proposition. An example of how the data is used would be in planning for the year ahead. If, for example, in January advance bookings for March or April are below target, a careful trawl through the bookings for that time in previous years will be made and if there are some on the list who haven't booked this time round and who haven't booked at an alternative time they will be sent a personalised postcard signed by key members of the staff, enquiring how they got on over the festive season, commenting on the wonderful early spring weather in Connemara and offering them a special package of an upgraded room, depending on availability, and a bottle of wine, if they are interested in a holiday break in March or April.

In addition to the relationship marketing programme, a limited advertising campaign is carried out using the "Special Notices" page in *The Irish Times*; and more recently a PR company has been appointed, mainly to ensure that the hotel is featured regularly in the trade press, where coverage has an important influence on potential staff.

Lessons from the Ballynahinch Castle case study: In some service industry sectors "personality" is more important than "knowledge" in creating a distinctive and desirable brand image. But it could be argued that creating this kind of culture is the most difficult task of all. Ballynahinch has managed to achieve this objective because the brand values have been so clearly defined and articulated.

The Critical Role of Staff in Service Branding

The biggest problem facing the service brand manager is the need to align all staff with the values of the organisation. This has been known for some time and numerous internal programmes have been designed to achieve this objective but there are still very few real success stories. The problem is that living the brand requires more than a few internal training courses and away-days. It often requires a complete change in culture, especially from the top, and this is where the problem lies: living the brand is impossible without a level of democracy that not all companies are prepared to tolerate. The essence of a successful business culture is not so much knowing what the brand values of the organisation are but a feeling of being trusted to implement these values on your own terms. It has been pointed out that a surprising number of businesses that have succeeded in this area are located in either "socially democratic Scandinavia or counter-culture West Coast America".[9]

Southwest Airlines is cited in numerous books and academic papers as a classic case of superior customer service. Having fun is often a key characteristic of successful service brands and humour appears to be a core attribute of the airline, to the extent that people are hired partly because of their sense of humour and pilots and flight attendants are encouraged to make their announcements in a creative and witty manner. Flight attendants are known to pop out of the overhead bins to organise "biggest hole in the sock" competitions and to sing "Happy Birthday" to anyone on board who is celebrating a birthday. A classic Southwest story involved a particularly rough and bumpy landing, at the end of which the flight attendant announced "when Captain Kangaroo finally manages to bring the plane to a halt you may unfasten your seatbelts". This must have been very reassuring to anyone travelling — you don't make announcements like that unless there is absolutely no danger and it shows a refreshing degree of self-confidence, camaraderie and style among the staff. It was also a brilliant branding exercise. It exemplified the core values of the airline and the story was bound to be repeated by all passengers, thus creating an invaluable level of word-of-mouth communication favourable to the airline.

The strength of the Southwest brand and the fact that the case history has been written about so often has acted as a spur to other companies to follow a similar route, and there were many attempts to do so in the 1990s. Very few succeeded because although on the surface it may appear easy to follow it is very difficult for established companies to change the deeply ingrained habits of a lifetime and be prepared to empower their staff to the same extent. In most of the failed experiments too many senior managers expected the staff to change without being prepared to change themselves.

---

9 Ind, N., "Inside Out", article on www.nicholasind.com.

It has also been pointed out that a disproportionate number of successful service business case histories involve either start-up companies or companies involved in what would be considered to be exciting business areas. It is obviously easier to generate a sense of enthusiasm, commitment and excitement among a small group of people who are starting a business than in a long-established business where there will inevitably be a much wider range of age and interest groups, problems of unrealised ambitions and an element of inertia. Any programme designed to enable people to "live the brand" must take these obstacles into account.

The issue of the nature of the business should not present the same problems. It is true that many of the most successful case studies are from the travel or entertainment businesses, but there are an equal number from more mundane occupations. One of the best books on the subject, O'Reilly and Pfeffer's *Hidden Value: How Great Companies Achieve Extraordinary Results with Ordinary People*,[10] includes Southwest as a case history but there are also some examples from very traditional businesses.

Figure 11, which is adapted from the book, shows the difference between looking at a business from a conventional strategic viewpoint and from the perspective of making the staff the critical drivers of brand strategy.

One widely quoted example included in *Hidden Value* but also written about elsewhere[11] is Men's Warehouse, a leading discount retailer for men's clothing in the US. The company has an enviable ability to turn normally reluctant male shoppers into loyal customers. The secret, as for many successful service companies, is in staff selection: "We don't look for people with specific levels of education and experience, we have one criterion for hiring, optimism, we look for passion, excitement, and energy. We want peo-

---

[10] O'Reilly, C.A. and Pfeffer, J., *Hidden Value*, Harvard Business School Press, 2000.

[11] Ransdell, E., "The Sell Suits with Soul", *Fast Company*, Issue 18, October 1998.

ple who enjoy life." The company looks for people with a high level of emotional intelligence and is fanatical about regular training. All prospective employees must attend a "Suits University".

Figure 11: Conventional View of Strategy vs a Values-Based View of Strategy

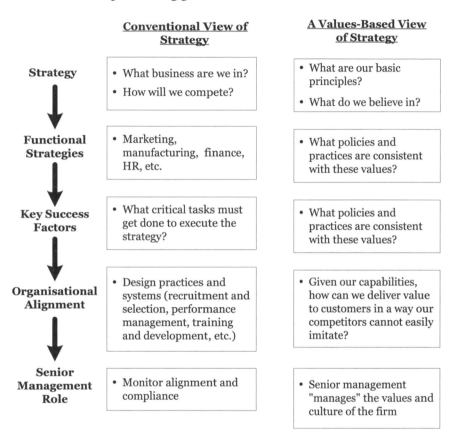

	Conventional View of Strategy	**A Values-Based View of Strategy**
Strategy	• What business are we in? • How will we compete?	• What are our basic principles? • What do we believe in?
Functional Strategies	• Marketing, manufacturing, finance, HR, etc.	• What policies and practices are consistent with these values?
Key Success Factors	• What critical tasks must get done to execute the strategy?	• What policies and practices are consistent with these values?
Organisational Alignment	• Design practices and systems (recruitment and selection, performance management, training and development, etc.)	• Given our capabilities, how can we deliver value to customers in a way our competitors cannot easily imitate?
Senior Management Role	• Monitor alignment and compliance	• Senior management "manages" the values and culture of the firm

Difficulties with Distinctive Differences

Another big problem with service branding is the fact that there is often less scope for differentiating positioning strategies than for product brands. In the detergent market the two leading brands, Persil and Ariel, have completely different core propositions. Persil stands for caring, sharing parenting values whereas Ariel stands for scientific efficiency. Both positionings are successful but service brands have a tendency to cluster around the same type of positioning. Respondents in market research surveys often have difficulty in articulating differentiating factors amongst service brands, compared to purchasers of detergents who have no such difficulties. Meanwhile all of the professional services firms selling to a business audience are tripping over themselves trying to convince their customers and potential customers not just of their professional competence but of their ability to make a real strategic impact due to their commitment to "fully understand your business".

Even the sedate world of the law is beginning to throw a few shapes at brand positioning. The following are the brand positioning statements of the "Big Five" Irish law firms taken from their websites:

- **McCann's**: "We are always looking for a result that will best deliver your particular business objectives; we must therefore first understand your business circumstances and the issues that are of real concern to you."

- **William Fry**: "One of the key factors in the service provided by the firm is the depth of experience and the level of expertise it can bring to bear for the benefit of clients."

- **Goodbody's:** "We understand the dynamics and requirements of the business environment. We use our skills and experience to judge the balance between legal and commercial risk. The result is an effective solution-focused approach that helps our clients grow their businesses."

- **Cox's:** "We identify ourselves with our client requirements and work with our clients to help them achieve their goals. In operating a policy of direct partner involvement in client matters and a system of regular reviews we ensure that all clients are provided with a top-class service and all matters are handled in an efficient and cost-effective manner."

- **Matheson Ormsby Prentice (MOP's):** "We consider quality of advice to be of paramount importance."

Although there are some variations — McCann's and Cox's major
on "understanding your business", Goodbody's on understanding
business in general, Fry's on experience in general and MOP's on
quality — a prospective client who had never heard of any of them
before would be hard-pressed to make a decision based on a pref-
erence for a brand positioning. So if one of the "Big Five" wanted
to make a more serious attempt to create a more distinctive brand
positioning, how would they go about it?

The first step, as always, is to consult the consumer, the people
in whose minds you want the image to exist. A survey should be
carried out among a representative sample of the target audience —
for example, a sample of senior business executives in Ireland — to
check out awareness of and attitudes towards the major law firms.
Let's assume that we have carried out this research and the results
show very little variation in attitudes towards the five firms, and
that any variation that does exist is based on the degree of familiarity respondents have with the firms themselves and is not due to
any brand image differences. So how do we go about building a distinctive image? The following are three possible routes:

1. **Brand Vault**: This is an exercise taken from Adam Morgan's
   book about insight generation, *Eating the Big Fish*.[12] It refers
   to the fact that in most long-established companies there are
   stories — some true, some apocryphal — buried in a meta-
   phorical vault which are capable of acting as a source of inspiration to staff and a point of differentiation for the firm. Most
   successful service companies were started by larger-than-life
   personalities whose vision and passion, often bordering on obsession, were responsible for the business becoming estab-

---

[12] Morgan, A., *Eating the Big Fish*, Wiley, 1999.

lished in the first place. Emerson's line that "every institution is the lengthened shadow of a single man; his character determines the character of the organisation" may not be as accurate a guide as it was in the nineteenth century but it still has a surprising degree of validity, especially for professional service businesses. Bringing these personalities and stories out into the open establishes a point of difference in a way that the tired clichés of contemporary management-speak characterised by the website excerpts quoted above could never do.

2. **Intellectual Leadership**: This was discussed under the "Third Age of Branding" and it is a well-established strategy in service businesses. It involves attempting to become the firm that is continually defining the future direction of the sector through publications, lectures and other material. Adopting this strategy means that senior executives must be prepared to play an active role in the third-level educational institutions that feed into the sector, and must specialise in aspects of the business so that when issues connected with the sector arise in the media their staff are most likely to be called upon to comment. This is a demanding stance to adopt but it can usually be guaranteed to establish a distinctive identity.

3. **More Distinctive Marketing Communications**: This would not be very difficult for any of the "Big Five" law firms who all spend a reasonable sum of money on identical company announcement-type advertising which does nothing to distinguish them from each other. It wouldn't tax any creative brains to come up with something more distinctive and even the choice of a different medium should achieve a result. A Dublin accountancy firm, Horwath Bastow Charleton, made a big impact recently with a simple radio campaign, partly because they were the only accountancy firm engaged in this type of advertising. A London firm of solicitors, Olswang, have made a big impact in the UK market and their website is worth

a visit if only to see how well-crafted copy combined with tasteful design can create a distinctive and positive image.

The Rise of the Prosumer

Another difference between product and service branding which has received some attention is the concept of the "prosumer". It is assumed that the consumer plays a more active role in the production of a service than a product. A product is produced in a factory or plant of some kind and then purchased in a retail outlet with the consumer playing little or no part in the production process. In contrast, the consumer often plays an active role in the "production" of a service. Hairdressers provide a service but the customer usually specifies what type of haircut they require. Restaurants provide a service but the consumer usually specifies how they want their meat cooked, except of course if they are in McDonalds. The idea of the prosumer has been around for a long time. In 1980 Alvin Toffler predicted a blurring of the distinction between the producer and the consumer and he went on to discuss the likely rise in the incidence of "prosuming". He was preoccupied with the complete break that had occurred between the producer and the consumer as a result of the Industrial Revolution, which he believed had damaged the "underlying unity of society — creating a way of life filled with economic tension, social conflict and psychological stress".[13]

He believed that "The Third Wave" would represent a partial return to the pre-industrial first wave where people produced goods for their own consumption or became more involved in the production process. More recent comment on the prosumer from C.K. Prahalad[14] regards it less as a move towards a more balanced way of life and more as a way to customise the goods and services that we buy. Information technology has aided the process and

---

[13] Toffler, A., *The Third Wave*, William Collins, 1980.

[14] Prahalad, C.K. and Ramaswamy, V., *The Future of Competition: Co-Creating Value with Consumers*, Harvard Business School Press, 2004.

_nies like Dell, a manufacturer, and Amazon, a service com-
_ have been to the forefront of this development. The recent
successful, though small-scale, launch of BMW's Mini Cooper in
the US is a good example of this trend where customised models
were available via the company's website, accounting for 86 per
cent of buyers. A huge variety of factory-fitted items, such as different body styles and colours, and dealer-fitted accessories, like
alternative lighting, audio systems and wheels, meant that few
models sold were exactly the same.[15]

To some extent therefore all businesses should think of how
they can make their customers more involved in the production of
goods and delivery of services. It is a business issue, not a branding issue, although businesses which take an early lead in this area
can build a greater capacity for customised products and services
as an integral part of their brand positioning.

The Future of Service Branding

As the distinction between products and services begins to blur,
more businesses will have to consider the special aspects of service
branding. As we have seen, the theory and much of the practice
remain the same but in service branding there is a special emphasis on the culture of the business and how closely staff, especially
front-line staff, are aligned to the overall values of the business.

The key to successful service brands is well summarised by the
following quote:

> Successful services brands thrive when managers develop
> both internal systems to design consistent value delivery
> processes and a culture that educates staff about their brand
> values and supports staff in enacting those brand values.[16]

---

[15] "Crowned at Last: A Survey of Consumer Power", *Economist* supplement, 2
April 2005.

[16] de Chernatony, L., Ibid.

This places a huge onus on the staff that have to "perform" their role to perfection in the creation of the brand; "the interaction between service staff and customers in people processing services in particular is comparable or analogous to a theatrical performance."[17] As service becomes a source of competitive advantage, more demands will be made of the staff and a recent book from Cranfield contains a neat summary of the new skills that will be required:[18]

- Imagination — making our work memorable
- Irreverence — challenging the status quo
- Improvement — a little better every time
- Initiative — making the first move.

Any service business that embraces all of these principles should be able to create a more powerful brand but no amount of theatrical excellence will be allowed to compensate for sloppy delivery. Information technology will play an increasing role in the future delivery of services and the concept of the "fusion brand" has been put forward as a potentially important development. Fusion branding will be discussed in more detail in Chapter 13.

Service brands need to define what they stand for more carefully, they need to heighten the service "experience" wherever possible but they must never lose sight of the critical importance of logistics and excellent delivery systems.

---

[17] Daly, A., *Marketing Institute Quarterly,* Issue 1, 2004.
[18] Baker, S., *New Consumer Marketing*, Wiley, 2003.

10

LOCAL BRANDS: IS THERE ANY HOPE?

If fast-moving consumer goods brands face a threat from the growing concentration of retailer power, local or indigenous brands are faced with the same threat from the retailers and an even more daunting challenge from global brands. To understand this threat we need to examine the whole issue of globalisation (one of those words that have been described as "fat", i.e. a word that raises emotions and can have widely different meanings for different people). We then need to consider the nature of local brands and how they are performing in the market, especially when in competition with global brands.

This chapter concludes with a discussion of the importance of local brands and whether it matters if they are successful or not.

Globalisation — An Overview

The issue of globalisation has been the subject of intense debate in the recent past, a debate that has generated more heat than light. Even the word "globalisation" itself has many different meanings for different people in different contexts and is too often used indiscriminately. It is usually considered to be a business and economic phenomenon, a development of global and financial markets, the growth of the transnational companies and the resulting decline in power and influence of national economies. From this perspective, globalisation is seen as a relatively recent phenomenon — a development that differentiates the present day from 50 or even 25 years ago. In this context globalisation is usually attributed to two key developments: the collapse of the socialist-run economies of Eastern Europe around the late 1980s; and the advances in information technology during the same period. Both paved the way for the dominance of free-market economics and the growth of global companies selling global brands.

The main proponents of this view of globalisation argue that it is not only good for the individual; it is economically the only way forward:

> It is important to understand why economic integration is a force for good and why globalisation, far from being the greatest cause of poverty, is the only feasible cure.[1]

However, alternative definitions of globalisation suggest that it may be a more complex phenomenon than it would appear on the economic surface:

> The intensification of worldwide social relations which link distant localities in such a way that local happenings are shaped by events occurring many miles away and vice versa.[2]

This definition is interesting for a number of reasons. It doesn't specifically mention business or economics, thereby suggesting that globalisation may have much wider, particularly cultural, implications. Even more significant however, it suggests that the process is not all one-way traffic, in that the opening up of small local communities might mean that they too could have an influence on the wider world.

Another useful insight is the repudiation of the assumption that globalisation is a recent phenomenon. In fact the exact opposite would appear to be case — the world may well have been globalising

---

[1] "Globalisation and its Critics", *The Economist*, Special Edition, 29 September 2001.

[2] Giddens, A., *Runaway World: How Globalisation is Reshaping Our Lives*, Routledge, (UK), 2000.

since the beginning of time — "humans have been weaving commercial and cultural connections since before the first camel caravan ventured afield".[3] It is also true that there have always been sceptics who feared for the loss of existing order. A historian writing in the second century BC complained that "Formerly the things which happened in the world had no connection among themselves — but since then all events are united in a common bundle".[4]

Regardless of how long the process has been happening there is little doubt that it moved up a gear in the last two decades. Thomas Friedman's *The Lexus and the Olive Tree* [5] captured the mood of this period with his powerful exposition of the view that any country which is prepared to adopt liberal economic policies could expect to enjoy the fruits of economic prosperity. Unlike some of the more starry-eyed and sometimes triumphalist free-market evangelists, Friedman's liberal (in the American sense) New York background ensured an element of caution. The terms he used to summarise the process are very revealing — global capital movements are referred to as "the economic herd" and the policies recommended to countries that wish to attract global capital are referred to as "the golden straitjacket". "Herds" imply being trampled on and "straightjackets" are very restrictive, so in spite of his apparent endorsement and enthusiasm for the globalisation project Friedman is aware of possible problems. He has no doubts about the validity of the overall philosophy but is concerned about local sensitivities and the fact that there may be unfortunate side-effects: "globalisation in a very short time could wipe out the ecological and cultural diversity that took millions of years of human and biological effort to produce".[6]

---

3 Zwingle, E., *National Geographic*, August 1999, page 12.

4 Robinson, R., "Mapping the Global Condition" in *Global Culture: Nationalism, Globalisation and Modernity,* Featherstone, M. (Ed.), Sage, London, 1990.

5 Friedman, T. *The Lexus and the Olive Tree*, Harper & Collins, UK, 1999.

6 Ibid.

Another passionate advocate of globalisation is the *Financial Times* chief economics commentator Martin Wolf. His recent book, *Why Globalisation Works*,[7] offers a robust rebuttal of the critics who condemn the process as a malign force that "impoverishes the masses, destroys cultures, undermines democracies, imposes Americanisation, lays waste the welfare state, ruins the environment and enthrones greed".[8] Wolf makes a convincing case, citing Ireland as a prime beneficiary of the phenomenon and urges everyone else to follow suit. He tackles each criticism in turn and provides detailed statistical evidence to refute the critics but his refusal to countenance any negative effects ultimately serves to weaken his argument.

A number of commentators have drawn attention to the fact that the claims of historical inevitability and economic determinism which were once a feature of left-wing thinking and subject to derision from the right have now been wholeheartedly adopted by the right. To some extent a more ambitious attempt to allay the fears of the anti-globalisation camp is Tyler Cowen's sophisticated survey of globalisation's effect on world cultures. Less polemical than Wolf, he reaches some enlightening conclusions:

> The concept of cultural diversity has multiple and sometimes divergent meanings; cultural homogenisation and heterogenisation are not alternatives or substitutes; rather, they tend to come together. Cross-cultural exchange, while it will alter and disrupt each society it touches, will support innovation and creative human energies.[9]

Cowen make a persuasive case that the advantages of cosmopolitanism outweigh whatever is lost as a society becomes more open to global influences.

---

[7] Wolf, M. "Why Globalisation Works", *Yale Nota Bene* 2005.

[8] Ibid.

[9] Cowen, T., *Creative Destruction: How Globalisation is Changing the World's Cultures*, Princeton University Press, 2002.

But the most thorough examination of globalisation is probably Manuel Castell's monumental three-volume study *The Information Age*. He accepts that the process of globalisation has been around for a long time but claims it has been speeded up exponentially by the new information technology:

> A world economy, that is an economy in which capital accumulation proceeds through the world, has existed at least since the sixteenth century. A global economy is an economy with a capacity to work as a unit in real time or chosen time on a planetary scale . . . it was only in the late twentieth century that the world economy was to become truly global on the basis of the new infrastructure provided by information and communication technologies and with the decisive help of deregulation and liberalising policies by governments.[10]

One of Castell's main conclusions is that revolutions will inevitably create their own backlash and that as a result there will be an increase of interest in and enthusiasm for local identity all over the world:

> We have experienced the widespread upsurge of powerful expressions of cultural identity that challenged globalisation and cosmopolitanism on behalf of cultural singularity and people's control over their lives and environment.[11]

Partly this is a natural human reaction because as the world becomes more of a global unit people will feel disenfranchised, remote from the real centres of power and frustrated by their increasing inability to affect any decisions. In these circumstances the natural reaction is to cling to as many local comfort blankets as possible. All the evidence we have therefore suggests that the globalisation process will continue but will be met with equally determined resistance

---

[10] Castells, M., *The Information Age*, Blackwell, 1999.
[11] Ibid.

from people all over the world, but especially in smaller countries who will become more fiercely attached to their own identity and seek tangible methods of demonstrating this attitude:

> Indeed one of the results of the convergence of large institutions since the end of the cold war is that people around the world are now even more conscious of the cultural differences that separate them.[12]

Local brands are one way that people can, without too much cost or effort, proclaim their identity.

Globalisation of Markets

It is now over twenty years since Professor Ted Levitts' famous assertion that cultural differences across the world were likely to erode so fast that in no time at all global brands would dominate most consumer markets.[13] Levitt's thesis has been enthusiastically adopted by the leading multinational branded goods companies who viewed it as an ideal intellectual underpinning of their quest for world domination. To some extent this thesis has proved correct — the ubiquity of global brands has become one of the defining features of modern life.

US companies have been the most zealous proselytisers of the global brand thesis — after all, they own more of the world's leading brands than anyone else and they have greater financial resources. It's also in their character; Americans, more than most people, believe that their institutions and values (democracy, individual rights, the rule of law and prosperity based on economic freedom) represent universal aspirations that will ultimately be embraced by people all over the world. They believe that American society — and therefore American brands — appeal to people of all

---

[12] Fukuyama, F., *Trust*, Hamish Hamilton, (UK), 1995.
[13] Levitt, T., "The Globalisation of Markets", *Harvard Business Review*, May–June, 1983.

countries. Britain, with its "special relationship" with the US, tends to support this argument.

The continental Europeans who are not always prepared to follow the Anglo-American view have been spearheading the intellectual backlash against global marketing, in particular standarised marketing communications in every country. The leading proponent of cultural differences is Geert Hofstede,[14] a Dutch professor of organisational anthropology and industrial management, who believes that different countries can and often do have very different cultures and that culture is a dominant influence on consumer behaviour. Consequently instead of standarising marketing communications around the world, multinational companies should be trying to analyse the culture of different countries so that they can tailor specific marketing communication messages and maximise efficiency by taking account of cultural differences. Hoftstede designated five dimensions of national culture:

- **Power Distance**: the extent to which less powerful members of a society believe and accept that power is distributed unequally:
  o France – high level of acceptance
  o Britain and Germany – low level

- **Individualism/Collectivism**: the extent to which people believe that they should look after themselves and their immediate family over the community at large:
  o Northern Europeans more individual
  o Southern Europeans more collectivist.

- **Masculine/Feminine**: masculine societies put more emphasis on achievement and success. Feminine societies are more concerned with the quality of life:
  o US — highly masculine
  o Sweden, Norway — more feminine.

---

[14] Hofstede, G., *Culture & Organisations*, McGraw-Hill, (US), 1997.

- **Uncertainty Avoidance**: the extent to which people feel threatened by ambiguity and try to avoid these situations:
  o   Italy, France — high
  o   Britain, Holland — low.

- **Long-Term Orientation**: the extent to which society is dominated by short-term issues or whether they take in more long-term view:
  o   US — short-term
  o   China —long-term.

Hofstede analysed over fifty countries on these five dimensions and found significant differences between them. If this is the case and these differences show no signs of eroding over time it would appear to contradict Levitt's thesis. Dr Marieke de Mooij, who runs a brand consultancy in Holland, has been the most determined advocate of the existence and growing importance of cultural differences across different markets and has been the most determined opponent of standarised marketing communications. Using Hofstede's five dimensions she has studied a range of consumer markets in different European countries and has demonstrated significant differences in consumer behaviour as a result.[15] For example, the individual/collective dimension is claimed to account for the significant differences which occur in European countries in the personal stereo market — ownership is very high in Holland, an individualist society, and very low in Spain, a more collectivist society. Differences in the markets for men's clothing and home furniture can also be explained with reference to different scores on the power distance and uncertainty avoidance dimensions.

If major variations in consumer behaviour in different markets can be explained by Hofstede's five dimensions, it is obvious that this must have huge implications for the content and delivery of all

---

[15] de Mooij, M., "Mapping Cultural Values for Global Marketing and Advertising", ESOMAR, Annual Conference Papers, 1997.

forms of marketing communications. It is easy to see why communications which feature certain situations and actions could perform well in one society and be completely unsuitable for another.

Another academic brand commentator, Jean-Noel Kapferer, also European, has argued that local brands can forge deep-rooted, social and cultural bonds with local communities:

> In developing countries consumers certainly want quality but as individuals they also want to retain a sense of national pride and identity. They are not necessarily waiting for international brands like the "second coming". This little-published phenomenon is in stark contrast to the general and undisputed theory of brand globalisation.[16]

However, in spite of this evidence, it is unlikely to impress senior management in the leading multinational brand companies, most of whom are locked in unceasing wars of attrition with the increasingly powerful multiple retail trade on the one hand and the increasingly voracious demands of financial analysts and shareholders on the other. One of the key strategies they are forced to adopt is to drive all unnecessary costs out of their businesses and the last thing they want to hear is an argument for different marketing communication campaigns in different countries. Professor Levitt's thesis suits them down to the ground and it is unlikely that they would be prepared to listen to anyone else. But it does leave a window of opportunity through which local brands can compete. The central theme of this chapter is that if local brand managers can understand the real nature of the cultural drivers within their own society they will be able to create marketing communication campaigns which can withstand the superior financial resources of multinational brands.

---

[16] Kapferer, J-N., *Reinventing the Brand*, Kogan Page, 2002.

Professor Douglas Holt's theory of cultural branding[17] is also worth noting in this context. He has put forward the view that marketing communications based on deeply rooted cultural contradictions in individual societies are likely to be effective in rising above the noise and clutter of today's marketplace. Although he doesn't specifically refer to multi-national campaigns, the implication is that communications based on local cultural issues are likely to strike more of a chord than standardised global campaigns, or as Jeremy Bullmore put it more eloquently, "as the global gospellers begin to sound ever less persuasive it is the coded tribal messages we should increasingly look at with respect".[18]

It is now time to look in more detail at some of the leading indigenous Irish brands.

What is an Irish Brand?

There should be an easy answer to this question but there isn't. The increasingly complicated ownership structure of modern business makes it very difficult to assign specific locations to different brands and the problem is compounded by the fact that the very large global corporations deliberately try to make their brands "country neutral" in the belief that this makes life simpler internally and is likely to be more profitable externally. The former is probably true but the latter case is not proven. Bushmill's Whiskey is a good example of the problems of definition. It was given a legal licence in 1608, making it the world's oldest official distillery. The licence was originally given to a local landlord, Sir Thomas Phillipps. It subsequently changed ownership many times among local families until it was merged into the recently formed Irish Distillers Group in 1972. So, having been a Northern Ireland brand for over 350 years it became a Republic of Ireland brand.

---

[17] Holt, D., *How Brands Become Icons*, Harvard Business Press, 2004.
[18] Bullmore, J., "Behind the Scenes in Advertising" (Mark 111), WARC 2003.

However, a decade later, following a bitter and protracted take-over battle, Irish Distillers was taken over by the French drinks company Pernod Ricard, so in terms of ownership Bushmills became a French brand. In 2005, as part of the fall-out from the Pernod Ricard takeover of Allied Domecq, Bushmill's was off-loaded to the British-based multinational Diageo. Yet most people consider it an Irish brand — it's made only in Ireland and it refers to itself as an Irish whiskey. Therefore ownership is obviously not the critical factor in trying to answer the question, "What is an Irish brand?"

Where the product is made is another starting point but even this factual issue creates problems. Many of the world's best-known brands are now made in whatever part of the developing world is the most cost-efficient. Naomi Klein, among others, has been heavily critical of the practice of outsourcing:

> The astronomical growth in the wealth and cultural influence of multinational companies over the last fifteen years can be traced back to a single seemingly innocuous idea developed by management theorists in the mid-1980s: that successful corporations must primarily produce brands, as opposed to products.[19]

So if ownership or location doesn't determine the nationality of brands, what does? The answer to this conundrum probably lies in one of the key aspects of brand definition, one that many people have difficulty with — that because brands are collections of ideas, opinions and impressions in people's minds, it is people themselves who determine their nationality. But although it is true to say that ultimately it is the people who determine the image of a brand, including its nationality, many of the ideas, opinions and impressions are determined by the manufacturer in the first place through design, packaging, advertising and other forms of market-

---

[19] Klein, N., *No Logo*, Flamingo, 2000.

ing communications. A local brand is therefore a brand that people in the local market assume originated within that market, although it may also be exported, be owned from outside the market, and not be overtly positioned as an indigenous brand.

In most cases it is immediately obvious whether a brand is Irish or not, but there are many anomalies. Under the above definition, Lyons Tea would be considered an Irish brand, mainly on the grounds that most Irish people assume it is an Irish brand. Although it was owned by an Irish company, the name originated in Britain and is now owned by the Anglo-Dutch company Unilever and is not sold anywhere else but it has been the long-term brand leader in Ireland. However, Irish Spring, a range of toiletry brands owned by the multinational company, Colgate, and positioned on an overtly Irish platform but not sold in Ireland would not be considered an Irish brand. Some brands will remain difficult to categorise, with Goodfellas being a good example. This brand was established by an Irish entrepreneur, who later sold the company to a British holding company. It is still made in Ireland, but has always been positioned as an Italian/American pizza.

Indigenous Irish Brands: A Proposed Categorisation

In order to come to an understanding of the strengths, weaknesses, opportunities and threats facing indigenous brands I want to propose a possible classification system and then discuss the problems facing some brands that might be representative of some of the categories. The following are the proposed nine categories:

- **Iconic brands:** brands that are much loved by Irish people, that are often looked forward to by Irish people who have been abroad and are regarded as being uniquely and quintessentially Irish. Typical brands in this category are:

  o Guinness stout, Tayto crisps, Club Orange, Barry's tea, Jacob's biscuits, Galtee bacon.

There are two other iconic Irish brands, Kerrygold butter and Jameson whiskey, but because they are widely available overseas, their export success means that they are denied the wistful nostalgia that is such a central element of the Irish emigrant experience. Guinness is also widely available overseas but there is a widespread belief that it tastes different, and better, in Ireland.

- **Classic brands**: brands that have withstood the test of time and are regarded as high-quality brands but for a variety of reasons have not been accorded iconic status. Typical examples are:

  o Avonmore milk and cheese, Dairygold spread, Denny's sausages, Brennan's bread, Erin soup, Batchelors beans.

- **Celtic Tigers**: brands that are relatively recent in origin and are associated with entrepreneurial activity arising from the economic transformation of the country since the early 1990s. They are characterised by overtly "Irish" names. Typical brands in this category are:

  o Ballygowan spring water, Donegal Catch fish, Boru vodka, Fiacla toothpaste.

- **Aspiring brands**: new, mainly speciality brands, which occupy niche positions but which could have considerable long-term potential. Typical brands in this category are:

  o Clonakilty black pudding, Bunalun organic foods, Dubliner cheese, Cully & Sully ready-to-eat meals.

- **Low Voltage brands**: brands with a familiar long-established name, trusted for their reliability and dependability but without any developed brand personality. Typical brands in this category are:

  o Siucra sugar, Shamrock foods.

- **Relics of Old Decency brands**: once very popular quintes-sentially Irish brands, now regarded as being in decline, but whom people would not like to see disappear; brands that are past their hey-day, but not their sell-by date. Typical brands in this category are:

  o Smithwick's, Gateaux, Odlums, Ballyfree.

- **Departed brands**: dead but not entirely forgotten. Typical brands in this category are:

  o Urney's, Lemon's Pure Sweets.

- **Cuckoo brands**: Irish-owned brands which adopt the prove-nance of another country because of that country's perceived expertise in the product field. Typical brands in this category are:

  o Roma, Goodfellas, Big Al's, Cuisine de France.

- **Orphan brands:** brands considered surplus to the require-ments of multi-national companies that are sold to local entre-preneurs. Two Irish examples of such entrepreneurs are Liam O'Rourke and Michael Carey, who both operated in senior ex-ecutive positions at Unilever and Kellogg's respectively and have snapped up impressive portfolios of brands from multi-national companies. Brands in this category in the Irish mar-ket now include:

  o Chivers, Chef, Goodalls.

Indigenous Irish Brands: Progress Report

For the last six years the grocery magazine, *Checkout*, has com-piled a list of the top hundred grocery brands and a comparison of the results for 1999 and 2004 provide the following conclusions:[20]

---

[20] "The Top 100", *Checkout* magazine, Vol. 31, No. 8, Aug. 2005.

- The number of local brands in the top one hundred has remained steady at around one-third of the total;

- Nine of the top twenty brands were local in 2005;

- Of the top twenty brands with the highest advertising to sales ratios, only one was Irish.

The main conclusion therefore is that local brands are well represented in the Irish grocery market in spite of being outspent in terms of advertising support by the multinational brands.

Indigenous Irish Brands: Marketing Communications Strategies

The following are five brief case studies of Irish local brands, all faced with multinational competition, who are thriving in the market using a variety of marketing communication strategies.

Fiacla

This brand is indicative of the increase in indigenous entrepreneurial activity which took place in Ireland in the 1980s and 1990s. Fiacla was developed by Richard Brierley and launched into the fiercely competitive toothpaste market in the late 1980s. The market was dominated by three of the biggest global consumer goods companies, Unilever, Procter & Gamble and Colgate, but Fiacla achieved a 10 per cent market share in a very fragmented and competitive market. Fifteen years later it had managed to hold on to this share in spite of almost no marketing communications support except for regular pack design changes. The only distinguishing feature of the brand is the Gaelic name, the Irish word for teeth.

Research carried out for the brand in the early years showed that there is a significant minority of consumers in this market who are not particularly concerned or convinced about the type of product improvements announced regularly by the multinational toothpaste brands. They believe, and many in the dental profession would agree, that it is the brushing action of the toothbrush that counts; what toothpaste you use is of little consequence. Although the brand owner didn't set out with the intention, Fiacla has a significant share of this group, who are obviously prepared to buy Irish if all other things are equal.

- **Conclusion:** playing the Irish card is a dangerous strategy and can imply inferior quality unless accompanied by regular product and design innovations, but it can work in some markets.

Club Orange

The soft drinks market in Ireland, as in most small countries around the world was dominated by poorly resourced local manufacturers until the arrival of the big American colas in the 1950s. They were welcomed with open arms by the youth of the repressed conservative Ireland of that time, eager to embrace the heady freedom America stood for. The local brands didn't stand a chance and most of them died a quick death; but one brand with slender enough resources persevered with consistent marketing communications support and survives today with a healthy and profitable market share. Club Orange is a much-loved carbonated orange drink long associated with "orange bits" which can be tasted and are visible on the side of the glass. The brand cannot afford the type of budgets available to the bigger players — in 2004 it had a brand value to advertising spend ratio of 0.39 per cent compared to 3.57 per cent for 7UP, 2.10 per cent for Coke and a massive 8.07 per cent for Sprite[21] — but the advertising message remained consistent, concentrating on the quality message but mindful of the need for the high-level production values and style that younger target audiences demand. In fact this audience often equate product quality with marketing communications production values.

---

[21] Ibid.

- **Conclusion:** continuous emphasis on product quality is essential for most indigenous brands because there is often an assumption in smaller countries that the quality of the multinational brands is higher.

Goodalls

A long-established brand of seasonings and spices in the Irish market, the brand was owned for many years by the multinational CPC but it was sold to an Irish entrepreneur in 1999. This phenomenon appears to be on the increase as more multinational businesses follow the example of Unilever who in the late 1990s cut the number of brands in their portfolio from 1,600 to 400.

The market for seasonings and spices is not large enough in Ireland to provide the funds for continuous advertising but there is always the need to communicate regularly to the public and in particular to reassure the public that the brand is being kept up-to-date and generally being looked after. Brands, like houses, need continual refurbishment.

Goodall's solution was to achieve this objective through packaging. There are a wide range of individual seasonings and spices so a change in pack design receives a considerable amount of shelf space, thus increasing visibility among consumers. The brand owner noted a change in kitchen design around the time he was acquiring the brand from CPC so he changed the pack from cardboard to a more "steely" looking pack to fit in with the new fashion in kitchens.

- **Conclusion:** design is a neglected form of marketing communication. All packs need some form of design and good design doesn't cost much more than bad design, so it makes sense to treat design as an integrated form of marketing communication. At a time when visual literacy and aesthetic appreciation are increasing, it is surprising that more brand owners don't exploit the potential of this medium to the full.

Kerrygold

One of the few Irish food brands to have achieved success in international markets, it has long been regarded as one of the great Irish brand success stories. The brand is owned by the Irish dairy industry under the auspices of Bord Bainne and shares the Irish market with some of the individual local brands from the dairies that make up the industry. Irish brands account for most of the volume in the butter market but there has always been the threat that an overseas brand could launch an attack on the market so the industry decided to develop and maintain the Kerrygold brand in the domestic market. Regular advertising campaigns are run featuring entertaining vignettes of interaction between French and Irish characters but always making sure to communicate the fact that the brand is well known and used in France, a country with an impeccable reputation for taste and discernment in matters of food.

- **Conclusion:** export success is a guaranteed audience winner in a small country. Irish self-confidence may have improved dramatically in recent years but we still crave international recognition and success.

Ballygowan

One of the most interesting indigenous case histories because it seemed to capture the mood of a new more self-confident entrepreneurial Ireland when it was launched. At that time, the late 1980s, the market for bottled water was very small and was dominated by the French brand leader, Perrier. Local entrepreneur Geoff Read launched the brand and within two years it had become the brand leader and doubled the size of the market. Today the market has grown tenfold and Ballygowan is still the brand leader. It is a brand which has had to face up to all of the threats that any successful local brand will come up against. It was launched in a blaze of PR glory when its telegenic founder was given an extended slot on Ireland's most popular TV chat show to talk about himself and the brand. The value of the resulting publicity was incalculable, which was just as well because the advertising budget, €12,000, was very small, even in the 1980s. A major debate took place about whether or not to capitalise on the brand's Irish origins. It was decided to ignore them on the grounds that the name and the PR would deal with this, so the launch advertising was an ultra-sophisticated take of a popular restaurant review column in *The Irish Times*. At the time the market for bottled water was small and sophisticated so it was necessary to counteract any possible advantage Perrier might have in this area. The campaign won many awards including €120,000 worth of free press advertising from the National Newspapers of Ireland.

Within five years Perrier had withered away but Ballygowan's success spawned a host of imitators so that for a time it looked as if every county in Ireland had branded bottled water. In the mid 1990s the campaign strategy was changed to an overtly Irish platform emphasising the brand's original Irish roots. This helped to stem the tide of imitators but the new millennium saw the emergence of two new threats: retailer own brands began to enter the now very large and profitable market; and more ominously a new generation of consumers began to regard the brand as being more suitable to their parents' generation. It was time for another change in direction and the advertising reverted back to its roots with an ultra-sophisticated and suitably "cool" campaign based on dance and music.

- **Conclusion:** Local brands cannot rely on brand loyalty. They have to be continuously alert to sociological change in the market and respond to these changes in their marketing communications.

Do Local Brands Matter?

The answer seems obvious: the more local brands that are manufactured, the more people are employed and the more local brands that are owned by people in a community, the wealthier that community should be. But economists who study the wealth of nations on a professional level would disagree. One of the most important ideas in economics is the theory of comparative advantage. The implication of this theory for national economies is that countries should specialise in areas where they are relatively more efficient compared to other countries. The Irish economy has been one of the most successful in the world during the last decade and one of the main reasons for that success is that we have developed a "comparative advantage" at providing mainly American companies, operating in the electronics and healthcare markets, with a combination of a stable political, legal and tax environment and a well-educated, productive and committed workforce. Taking the economic argument to its logical conclusion, we should concentrate on consolidating our advantage in this area. But taking arguments to their logical conclusions is not always a good idea and there are a number of reasons for not pursuing the theory of comparative advantage to the bitter end.

Firstly, there is the need for balance. A healthy society needs to have a mix of businesses and occupations both to reduce dependence on too narrow an economic focus and to provide different outlets for the different talents of its people.

Secondly, local brands are an important, if generally neglected, asset for a tourist industry. Tourism is important in Ireland, especially in certain parts of the country, and it is a part of the tourist experience to try out the local brands.

A third reason is that indigenous brands constitute an important part of indigenous culture. Taking the theory of comparative advantage to the limit, it wouldn't really matter if everyone in Ireland drank Coke or Pepsi all the time rather than Club Orange, as long as everyone could afford the multinational colas. However, a reading of Robert Putnam's sociological bestseller, *Bowling Alone*[22]

---

[22] Putnam, R., *Bowling Alone*, Simon & Schuster, New York, 2000.

suggests an alternative view. At the core of this book is the concept of social capital. This is defined as the quantity and quality of the connections between individuals and the societies in which they live and the main premise of the book is that the more individuals come into contact with other people, through membership of clubs, societies and voluntary organisations, the more there will be an accumulation of social capital which will satisfy social needs and lead to a substantial improvement in living conditions for the whole community.

There may be an equivalent concept of consumption capital or, perhaps more accurately, indigenous consumption capital. This would be measured by the proportion of goods consumed by a society which were produced by that society. If the proportion is very low then something more than the wealth created by the number of jobs involved is lost. If a society only eats multinational food, only drinks multinational drinks, wears multinational clothes and consumes only multinational products and services then it could be argued that it is a less healthy society than one with enough self-confidence and pride in its own worth to sustain a reasonable share of what it creates itself.

Equally, the communication of local brands creates images and signs which form a part of the character of a society. Communication shapes culture because "we do not see reality as it is but as our languages are — and our languages are our media, our media are our metaphors, our metaphors create the contents of our culture".[23] Local brands and their packaging and marketing communications represent an important contribution to local culture. They are part of the sights and sounds and smells that give a place its character.

A few years ago one of our most famous brands transferred its advertising to a London agency. One of the resulting campaigns was a series of outdoor posters, some of which are reproduced here from a photograph taken at the time near Butt Bridge.

---

[23] Castells, M., *The Information Age*, Blackwell, 1996.

I'm not sure what godforsaken market these were supposed to work for but it certainly wasn't the Irish one. Contrast this with the poster below for another well-known drink brand occupying a site in the same area.

This is stylish, witty, makes you think and smile and is based on a sound understanding of the idiosyncrasies of Dublin life.

The best advertising is not only "creative" — in whatever way we choose to define that sometimes elusive concept — but is advertising which could only have been created for and work within the society in which it originates.

This does not mean that only local produce should be consumed; people will always want the best from all over the world. The concept of "needs : states" may help to explain the rationale for local brands. This was introduced by Wendy Gordon[24] to demonstrate how it is perfectly consistent for the same person to purchase different brands in the same product category on a regular basis. She argued that each person is made up of very different personas which require different brand solutions on different occasions. People choose different brands when they want to be seen as "sophisticated me", "practical me", "family me", so it is reasonable to assume that they will also at certain times want to demonstrate "*dinnseanachas* me" — when they want to proclaim that although familiar and at ease with the world, they are also proud of their local roots.

The most successful local brands of all are those that are successful in export markets. Apart from the revenue that accrues to the nation, there are two very important benefits of local brands which prove successful in overseas markets:

- Good for national morale and pride. People of all countries, but particularly those from smaller countries, take particular pride when local brands are successful overseas. The most poignant example of this phenomenon came from a report in the Jamaican newspaper, *The Daily Gleaner*, in 1962 when that country gained independence from Britain and suggested that the real date of independence was in 1928 when Red Stripe Beer was first imported into the UK and "we established our self-respect and self-confidence through the production of a beer far beyond the capacity of mere colonial dependants".[25] In much the same way, even the most world-weary Irish sophisticate experiences a pleasurable frisson when they spy a

---

[24] Gordon, W., "The Challenge of Retailer Brands", *Admap*, March 1994.
[25] Anholt, S., *Brand New Justice*, Butterworth-Heinemann, 2003.

bottle of Jameson in some unlikely watering hole in a far-distant land.

- Successful brands can increase awareness of a country as a whole and help develop its image overseas. The image of Germany is to some extent defined by the engineering and technological excellence of its automotive brands, BMW, Mercedes, Volkswagen and Audi.

11

BRANDING IRELAND:
IS THERE ANY POINT?

The very idea of discussing the nation state in the context of branding is relatively new but has already evoked some controversy, "the concept of the nation as a brand seems to evoke visceral animosity in some people; it is not the concept they detest so much as the word brand, which for some people is seen to have trifling and superficial implications unworthy of the nation state".[1] The poor image of marketing and advertising among the chattering classes doesn't help: "marketing however is seen by many as a dirty and unprincipled business dealing with surface and illusion, vanity and deception: lies in short".[2] Given the widespread distrust of marketing in general it is easy to see why applying the same principles to nation states should be a cause for concern. But if we could disregard the terminology, which after all is only terminology, the fact remains that countries have always had brand images and have even been engaged from time to time in re-branding exercises.

Wally Olins, the UK design expert, recently quoted[3] a French academic, Michel Girard, as saying that a country carries a specific dignity, unlike a marketed product, and the idea of France engaging

---

[1] Olins W., "Branding the Nation — The Historical Context", *Brand Management*, Vol. 9, Number 4–5, April 2002.

[2] Anholt S., "Branding Places and Nations", chapter in *Brands and Branding,* The Economist, London, 2003.

[3] Olins W., ibid.

in any such exercise was completely unacceptable. Olins then went on to demonstrate how France had consistently and consciously re-branded itself on a number of occasions, from the deliberate changes introduced after the revolution in 1789 when the tricolour replaced the fleur-de-lys and the *Marseillaise* became the new national anthem, to the later re-packaging by Bonaparte and, in more recent times, in Vichy France when the brand slogan, *Liberté, Egalité, Fraternité* was replaced by *Travail, Famille, Patrie*.

The realisation that when countries were engaged in exercises like this they were acting as brand managers was slow to emerge but in the last few years as the whole issue of branding has come out of the marketing closet as an increasing number of countries, including the world's most powerful, the US, have begun to debate the issue seriously.

It has been pointed out[4] that the brand image of a country can affect its economic performance in three ways:

- Its ability to attract foreign direct investment, which is increasingly central to all country's economic growth, especially smaller countries.

- Its ability to attract tourists, now the biggest industry in the world.

- Its ability to export; the words "made in _____" can exert a powerful influence on the public's perception of that country's goods and services.

There are also some intangible benefits which accrue to countries with distinctive and desirable images, from being more attractive to talented migrant workers to a general sense of enhanced morale among the population at large.

---

[4] Fanning, J., "Countries as Brands: Can the Image be Managed and Measured?", ESOMAR Annual Conference, Monte Carlo, 1990.

Ireland can claim to have been one of the first countries to consciously manage its brand image. State involvement in branding the country as a tourist destination dates back over 50 years and the IDA began advertising the country as a location for overseas investment in the late 1960s. The IDA's successful "Young Europeans" campaign in the 1970s and 1980s was the first attempt to consciously brand the country and this was followed in the 1990s by Bord Fáilte's "Brand Ireland" campaign which created a more unified tourist image across all destinations. This campaign was based on the trinitarian approach that seems to dominate so much of marketing communications thinking: *people* (warm and friendly), *place* (beautiful scenery), and *pace* (unhurried and leisurely). Ireland's success in effectively re-inventing itself from an economic basket case to an economic showcase in a few decades did not go unnoticed and during the 1990s countries all over the world began to dip their toe in the branding pool amid a growing realisation that economic prosperity was becoming increasingly dependant on a country's brand image.

The Increasing Importance of Country Brand Image

Managing a country's brand image is becoming a more important priority for two main reasons.

Globalisation

Although smaller countries and regions are likely to become more vociferous in their claims to difference, globalisation and the integration of the world's economies are likely to continue apace, facilitated by the information technology revolution. There is no contradiction between asserting one's claims to difference and at the same time competing as strongly as possible for a share in the global economy. The process of asserting one's claims to difference has much in common with managing a brand image in the commercial world.

Competition

We have seen how managing a country's brand image is being taken more seriously, and the more this trend continues, the greater the imperative for all smaller countries to take a more active and professional approach to brand management:

> The coherence of communication is necessary because in the globalised world in which we now live every place has to compete with every other place for share of mind, share of income, share of talent, share of voice. Unless a place can come to stand for something it stands little chance of being remembered long enough to compete for any of their precious attention.[5]

More Countries Join the Brandwagon

Countries have always had brand images and countries have been advertised as tourist destinations for the last hundred years but the idea of connecting the two — of considering a country from a brand perspective — only took hold in the last two decades. In 1997, one of the first acts of the newly elected Labour government in the UK was to produce a booklet called "Branding Britain", but although there was an initial flurry of activity, with the "Cool Britannia" sobriquet featuring in the national media the project soon became a little discredited. However, the need to manage the image of Britain is still being argued:

> Most British companies are in denial that national reputation has any effect on them. Most who trade extensively overseas say they are global companies "from nowhere". This is to muddle aspiration with fact. It is true that many such firms encourage their staff to see the company as truly stateless, but all their business customers and suppliers, and very often their end customers, know full well where the

---

[5] Anholt, ibid.

company has its origins and attach their prejudices to these origins.[6]

One of the earliest appointments of the Bush administration in the US was Charlotte Beers, an ex-Madison Avenue boss, as Assistant Under-secretary in the State Department. She developed the "Shared Values Initiative" designed to improve the image of the US in predominantly Muslim countries. She described her job as handling the most elegant brand she had ever worked with and carried out research to find out what the image of America was in Muslim countries, discovering in the process that there were vast differences in their respective value systems. She then made a series of TV commercials designed to correct these imbalances by showing Muslims integrating into American culture. The experiment was not regarded as a success and Ms Beers resigned after 17 months, citing ill health.[7]

Given the basic thrust of US foreign policy in the Middle East it is hardly surprising that the campaign didn't work but the experiment should be a salutary lesson to those who believe that marketing communications can operate in isolation. However the brand image of America is still a big issue and the US business community is now becoming anxious about the possible negative effects on sales of the most overtly American brands. A group of senior businessmen have recently set up a new organisation, Business for Diplomatic Action, because they are so worried about consumers in Europe expressing their opposition to the war in Iraq by boycotting the more overtly American consumer brands.

But in spite of the failures there have been some notable successes. The Spanish have been engaged in a long-running campaign

---

6 Powell C., "Why Britain's Reputation Abroad Matters" *Market Leader*, Issue 20, Spring 2003.

7 Kendrick, A. and Fullerton, J.A., "Advertising as Public Diplomacy: Attitude Change among International Audiences", *Journal of Advertising Research*, Vol. 44, No 3, Sept. 2004.

to change their tourist brand image from one of "sea, sun, sand and sex" to a more upmarket, sophisticated and cultural image.

Japan and South Korea are two countries whose images have been transformed. In the 1950s and 1960s, Japan's image in the west was dominated by its ability to make cheap imitation goods and South Korea was hardly known. Now both countries are well-known and highly regarded for their sophisticated range of high quality consumer goods. It could be argued that this transformation had nothing to do with a conscious national re-branding operation; but the administrations in both countries were very brand conscious and were aware that this was a route to greater economic prosperity. Both governments have a long history of active involvement in industrial policy and the South Koreans have gone so far as to set up a "Brand Academy" "to train about 500 specialists every year in brand management, character design and industrial packaging".[8]

New Zealand has been involved in a number of national branding initiatives in the last ten years, most of which involved close co-operation between government and private enterprise. The most recent was an attempt to cash in on the success of the filming of *Lord of the Rings*, when the national airline painted its Boeing 747s with warlocks and advertising referred to the country as "Middle Earth". Other countries that are currently reported to be considering a more active nation-branding approach include Croatia, Finland, Estonia and Portugal.

Managing the National Brand: Problems and Pitfalls

If the brand manager of a baked bean company noticed that sales were flat and carried out market research among consumers which suggested that many of them thought that the sauce was too sour, they would have little difficulty in persuading the board and the production manager to sweeten the sauce. Within a very short time, every supermarket in the country would be re-stocked with a

---

[8] Anholt, S., *Brand New Justice*, Butterworth-Heinemann, 2003.

new improved sweetened sauce and an advertising campaign cele-brating the re-launch would be rolled out.

It doesn't work like that for national brands. The reason is that all of the countries referred to above are democracies and, in spite of fashionable management jargon about empowered workers and flat structures, businesses are essentially dictatorships. This means that managing a country's brand image faces special difficulties in three critical areas of brand management:

- Agreeing the core proposition — what the country stands for;

- Ensuring consistency of communication;

- Long-term planning.

Agreeing the Core Proposition

This can often be a contentious issue in a commercial business but when dealing with a national brand there are a number of addi-tional problems. The first is due to the potential for genuine politi-cal differences about possible alternatives positionings. The most obvious source of conflict is where a country is trying to attract more tourists and more inward investment, where the require-ments of the two target groups may be very different. But even if a country was only trying to position itself as a location for inward investment there may be difficulties agreeing on a core proposi-tion. The main requirements for businesses in this target group are likely to be: availability of skilled labour; a well-educated work-force; access to other markets; telecommunications and transport infrastructure; a benign tax regime; and a generally favourable of-ficial attitude to business. The first four requirements are unlikely to cause any problems, the latter two might, and agreeing a core proposition may need to be carefully handled.

The second problem for the "national brand manager" in trying to seek agreement on a core proposition is one of curbing the en-thusiasm of the number of interest groups who feel they have a contribution to make and who have very definite but widely different views on what the core proposition should be. It is always difficult trying to explain to people with legitimately passionate views that marketing communications works best when it is at its most single-minded:

> On more than one occasion I've been faced with the tricky task of gently explaining to a proud and patriotic minister that the world will not be enthralled with the fact that the world's first all metal suspension bridge was invented by someone whose grandfather came from this country or that over sixty different species of wild grass grew along his eastern shoreline.[9]

The third problem arises from the number of different constituencies who have a legitimate right to be part of the decision-making process and the awkward little detail that a general election could throw all plans into disarray.

Consistency of Communication

In some ways this is the most serious problem facing the "country brand manager". Economic imperatives will eventually overcome the problems of agreeing a core proposition but even in the most ruthless dictatorships the administration can never control the flow of information about a country in the same way that a business could expect to be able to do. When the IDA's "Young Europeans" campaign was at its height in the US in the 1980s, Ireland was often in the news for terrorist attacks, but there was never any question of abandoning the campaign. One of the ways in which the IDA sought to add an element of consistency was to persuade the government that any time a minister was addressing an overseas audience, on whatever subject, they should insert a paragraph about the excellence of Ireland's educational system and youthful population, the twin themes of the campaign. Hopefully this initiative added a little to the overall campaign but the fact remains that

---

[9] Anholt, S., "Nation Brands of the 21st Century", *Market Leader*, Issue No.12.

it will never be possible to achieve complete consistency of message in nation-branding communications.

Long-term Planning

The constituent parts of even the most complex products or services can usually be changed much more quickly than changes that may be required in a country's infrastructure or legislative system. The requirements of the fixed inward investment target market may require complicated and politically sensitive legislative change; the requirements from the tourism target market for an upgraded standard of cuisine will take years of training to implement and changes in the physical infrastructure, e.g. a national conference venue, take a long time to come to fruition.

Managing the National Brand: A Strategic Approach

Some of the differences between nation brands and commercial product and service brands have been outlined but the basic approach to the management of a nation brand is identical to managing any other brand. The same planning cycle, discussed in Chapter 4 — "Where are we now?"; "How did we get there?"; "Where do we want to be?"; and "How do we get there?" — that is employed in the commercial world is also the best starting point for the management of a nation brand.

Where Are We Now?

Under this heading we need to define the overseas countries, or markets, where we are going to concentrate our efforts; no country is going to try to appeal to the whole world. In the case of Ireland, America is by far and away the most important market for fixed inward investment, although other important business centres (e.g. London) also exert an influence. For the tourism market, Britain, the US and three or four continental European countries are the most important target markets, and all of these countries are important markets for Irish exports. Those responsible for marketing Ireland need to carry out surveys in all of these areas to establish: awareness levels; what people think are the main advantages of investing/visiting in Ireland; and the main disadvantages. These surveys would be carried out among those sections of the populations in each country that offer the best prospects, not among the total population. One of the main reasons for the success of the IDA over the last forty years is that they have been very careful to target emerging industry sectors and concentrate single-mindedly on them, from electronics and healthcare in the 1980s to biotechnology and life sciences in recent years. Brand managers need to know in as much detail as possible what people in the main target groups think are the chief points in their favour and against them and require the same data for their main competitors. Only when this information is available will they be able to formulate a plan for the future.

How Did We Get There?

Knowing how a brand arrived at its current situation is an invaluable but often overlooked aspect in formulating future plans. Historical market research is one of the most useful methods of finding out how we came to be where we are but in the case of nation brands there is a wealth of information to be found in media coverage of the nation in overseas media, the portrayal of that nation in literature, film and other artistic forms and any references to the history of the nation that is taught in overseas markets. The cultural output of a country has been compared to a large advertising campaign for that country.[10] It would be impossible, for instance, to understand the image of America around the world without reference to the enduring popularity of Westerns and road movies. It has been suggested that the image of Scotland owes much to the novels of Sir Walter Scott and that the image of Ireland is partly the deliberate creation of a group of writers and intellectuals of the late nineteenth century, in particular W.B. Yeats.

---

[10] Anholt, S., "Nation Brands of the 21st Century", *Market Leader*, Issue No. 12.

Where Do We Want to Be?

The critical exercise that must be undertaken by every brand manager is how to maximise the ideal match between what the product or service has to offer and what consumers want. When dealing with countries, especially Ireland, there is an immediate issue because there is often a conflict between the requirements of two key target groups: the business community who might be persuaded to invest and the general population who might be persuaded to visit. The latter group are impressed with images of a bucolic, ancient, underdeveloped past but these images can send out the wrong messages to potential investors. We will consider how this conflict can be resolved later but the first task of the nation brand manager will be to draw up an inventory of what the country has to offer and what are the ideal requirements of the target group, or groups. Before deciding on a marketing communications platform it may be necessary to examine whether some of the target group requirements which are not catered for at present could be provided. There will be some requirements that can never be achieved (e.g. constant sunshine in Ireland), but there are others that the brand manager can influence if the political authorities are in agreement. Nation brand managers in national tourism organisations usually have a development remit in addition to their overseas marketing role and Fáilte Ireland have introduced many initiatives aimed at raising standards throughout the country to meet overseas customer requirements. But the real benefit of asking "where we want to be" is to force marketing executives in development agencies and policy makers at the highest level of government to come to a clear vision of where they want the country to be "positioned" in the future, which enables them to implement the necessary measures to achieve the objective.

How Do We Get There?

Deciding on a vision of where we want to be is the most critical part of the nation brand-planning exercise. The IDA was always very clear about their vision for Ireland, about how they wanted the country to be seen by their target group. It wasn't just a vision of a location with a favourable tax regime for overseas investment; the objective was always to create a more rounded image and in particular to position Ireland as a nation with not only a high standard of education but of a people with a yearning for and love of education. As a result of this clarity of vision, they were able to brief third-level educational institutions about the qualifications that would be required from a new generation of Irish graduates.

A good example of the benefits of a clear vision to facilitate long-term planning is the transformation of the image of Spain, particularly but not exclusively, as a tourist destination over the last twenty years. When the first wave of mass tourism started in the 1960s Spain was a popular choice because of climate and low prices. Success quickly became a problem when the country developed an image dominated by "sun, sea, sand and sex". A long-term advertising campaign was introduced that was designed to communicate the wide variety of attractions the country had to offer other than those of popular cliché, and to remind people of richness of Spanish culture. It has been argued[11] that the representation of a country's culture enriches that country's image and adds an all-important element of dignity which commercial brands can do without but nation brands cannot. For example, the widespread perception of Germany as the birthplace of more of the great classical music composers than any other nation provides an extra dimension to that country's image. It could also be argued that the long-term vision of the Spanish authorities was an invaluable aid in guiding decisions about the development of the infrastructure over the last twenty years. The transformation of the North-East region by the enormous success of the Guggenheim Museum in Bilbao has been well documented, as has the transformation of Barcelona into a popular cultural centre, but the earlier decision by the authorities to secure the Thyssen-Bornemisza collection for Madrid was equally significant. In 1988

---

[11] Elwes, A., "Nations for Sale", BMP DDB Needham (London), 1994.

the Spanish government and the Thyssen-Bornemisza family reached an agreement whereby the priceless collection of 775 paintings would be on display to the public in Madrid and some years later, following the restoration of the Palacio de Villahermosa, the acquisition was made permanent. Other cities were also considered, including London, but it is arguable that the Spanish were successful because they had a clearer vision of how they wanted the brand image of their country to be developed.

Resolving the Contradiction between the Requirements of the Tourism and Investment Target Markets

This has been referred to briefly above and it is an issue that has a particular relevance to Ireland. However, it is a dilemma that has faced many countries and has been a subject of controversy long before the market for fixed inward investment was developed. One of the doyens of advertising, David Ogilvy, confronted the issue in typically robust style when advertising Britain in the US market over 30 years ago:

> When you undertake to advertise a foreign country you have to be prepared to take a lot of flak. Research told me that what American tourists wanted to see in Britain was history and tradition — so that is what I featured in the advertisements only to be slaughtered in the British press for projecting an image of a country living in the past. Why did I not project a progressive industrial society? Why did I not feature the nuclear power stations that the British had just invented? Because our research had shown that American tourists had no desire to see such things, that's why.[12]

Offending the delicate sensibilities of the popular press is one thing but creating a possible conflict between the objectives of the tourist industry and those responsible for attracting fixed inward investment is potentially a more serious issue. However, it is only likely to

---

[12] Ogilvy D., *Ogilvy on Advertising*, London, Macmillan, 1983.

cause any damage when a country is starting out to attract overseas investment. At that point a country's image is likely to be most seriously skewed towards the bucolic, at best, and the educationally backward with a poor or non-existent infrastructure, at worst. Once a country has managed to attract some inward investment it should be possible for the positionings of the tourist and industrial interests to live side-by-side. Britain is probably the best example of this accommodation; its tourism positioning still relies heavily on tradition but it has a very successful record of attracting investment.

During the 1970s Bord Fáilte had been running advertising campaigns positioning Ireland as a tourist destination for some time and the IDA were starting to promote the country as a modern location for business investment. There was a high level of dissonance between the two messages as can be seen from the following examples. The first two images below are from the 1950s and the 1970s respectively, showing how fixed the image was over that period of time.

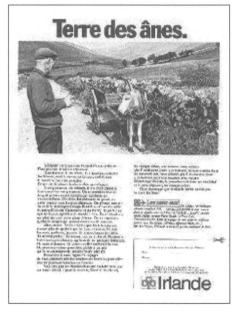

However, in the intervening thirty years there has been a notice-
able convergence between the imagery portrayed by the two promotion bodies. Surveys carried out by Bord Fáilte in the 1990s revealed that although potential tourists in the main markets wanted
to experience alternative lifestyles and culture, they also required
high standards of accommodation, entertainment and cuisine and
a generally more sophisticated experience than had been portrayed
in earlier advertisements. The latest Fáilte Ireland advertising
represents a significant shift away from the more rustic images of
the 1960s and 1970s, as can be seen from the ad below:

It has been argued that the image of many brands is still dominated by the personality of some founder figure or dominant personality from the long distant past. This is also true of countries
and in Ireland the enormous shadow of William Butler Yeats is arguably the most powerful influence on the brand image of the
country up to and including the present day.

Yeats and the Irish Brand Image

It is impossible to discuss the image of a country without becoming embroiled in the treacherous currents of nationalism and national identity. However, it is my intention to remain at the shallow end of that murky pool, albeit at the risk of treating such a vast and complex subject too lightly. It is generally agreed that "nationalism emerged and became a dominant force in the Western World in the second half of the eighteenth century",[13] but there are many scholars who argue that the origins of nationalism should be sought in much earlier times. Nevertheless, the American Declaration of Independence in 1776 and the French Revolution in 1789 are critical dates in our modern understanding of the subject. During the nineteenth century very conscious attempts were made all over the western world to define nationalism and national identity in more fixed and self-conscious ways than ever before.

The many studies which have been carried out on the subject have led to a debate between those who believe and argue that national identity is something which had created differences between people from the beginning of time and those who believe that it is a product of the modern age. The former group — the primordialists — believe that nationalism is rooted in history and determined by the physical characteristics of the homeland. The latter group — the modernists — believe that it is a condition of the modern age and is hugely influenced by the examples of the American and French revolutions. Most of the intellectual analysis of the subject supports the latter view and one of the best known, Benedict Anderson's *Imagined Communities*,[14] apart from giving the game away in the title, argues that identities are forged by human endeavour rather than by divine ordinance; that identity is artefact and not natural and therefore is a dynamic rather than a static process. Eric Hobsbawm follows the Anderson line and in a book

---

[13] Cronin, M., *Sport and Nationalism in Ireland,* Four Courts Press, 1999.

[14] Andersen, B., *Imagined Communities*, Verso: revised edition, 1991.

he co-authored called *The Invention of Tradition*,[15] a title which again gives the game away, argues that many of the so-called "traditions" which nationalists in different countries regard as being an essential part of the fabric of their society for centuries past were merely inventions of more recent times, designed by ambitious and often unscrupulous politicians to further their hold over their constituents. The contemporary Irish philosopher Richard Kearney goes even further in stating that "the idea that there exists some immutable 'essence' of national identity, timelessly preserved in a mausoleum in a sealed tradition and impervious to critical investigation, is a nonsense".[16]

It is indicative of the confusion that surrounds this whole subject that Kearney has also written, albeit in a different context, that "from the beginning the Irish mind remained free, in significant measure, of the linear, centralising logic of the Greco-Roman culture which dominated Western Europe".[17] More recent discussion of national identity shows that the debate is still far from being resolved:

> Nationalists, of course, always held that nations (in particular their own) were primal national communities that needed only to be awakened to full consciousness of their historical destiny. Social scientists, on the other hand, realised that the emergence of nationalism met a vital social need in the 19th century.[18]

It is interesting that this study goes on to argue that the "vital need" arose because of the rapid process of modernisation, industrialisation, mass communication and secularisation that was destroying traditional societies at the time, and that nationalism pro-

---

[15] Hobsbawm, E. and Ranger, T., *The Invention of Tradition*, Cambridge University Press, 1992.

[16] Kearney, R., *Irishness in a Changing Society*, Barnes & Noble, 1988.

[17] Kearney, R., *The Irish Mind*, Wolfhound Press, 1989.

[18] Townshend, C., "The God of Modernity", *Financial Times Magazine*, 12 January 2004.

vided an antidote to bring people together under a new social order. It could be argued that we are currently undergoing a new process of "modernisation" that now goes under the name of globalisation, which is currently putting traditional societies and, importantly, national identities, under the same kind of pressure.

It is not my intention here to adjudicate in this debate but it is probable that both sides have a point. The late nineteenth century was characterised by a frenzy of national identity constructions carried out by patriotic intellectuals but the material used in these constructions was often dredged from songs, stories, folklore and myth that were centuries old:

> The reputations of places have been managed and occasionally invented by those leaders who have often borrowed from others to augment their political strategy — poets, orators, philosophers, film-makers, artists and writers.[19]

Ireland in the last two decades of the nineteenth century was one of the most active "construction sites" where a remarkable generation of mainly literary people engaged in a conscious effort to create a renaissance that would underpin a revitalised national identity. The foremost of those was William Butler Yeats.

"For the world's more full of weeping than you can understand"

Ireland suffered badly during the nineteenth century. The failure of earlier and mainly half-hearted revolutions against English rule was temporarily assuaged by the success of O'Connell's campaign for Catholic Emancipation and the excitement and sense of self-confidence generated by the monster meetings for Home Rule. However, the appalling tragedy of the Famine and the unprecedented waves of emigration that followed it brought the country to its knees. To make matters worse, as Ireland grew progressively

---

[19] Anholt, S., "Brands & Branding", *The Economist*, 2003.

weaker, its colonial masters were reaching the height of their power and influence all over the world.

> Irish history strokes the sense of grievance that features so prominently in the Irish psyche, just as English history strokes the sense of superiority towards foreigners — many see the alleged Irish obsession with history as a distinctive characteristic in the Irish psyche. It invariably derives from a comparison with English normalcy. England constituted normalcy, Ireland therefore deviance. This deviance can be explained as a psychic condition.[20]

During the middle and late nineteenth century Irish failure was consistently lampooned in the English media, in particular in the influential magazine, *Punch*. The Irish were portrayed as a feckless, half-witted people incapable of organisation or development. But at the end of the century a determined and talented literary generation consciously sought, not only to reassert the dignity of the people, but to position them more favourably in relation to the British:

> This opposition, archaic, peasant but spirited Ireland versus modern, urbane and materialistic Britain, became an article of faith among the literary revivalists. The Irish countryman would never fall victim to the idolatrous materialism which afflicted the unfortunate Englishman because his race, memory, imagination, even his very landscape, was saturated with the ideas of an alternative world.[21]

Yeats, more than all of the many and varied contributors to the literary revival, was conscious of the deliberate nature of the enterprise. Roy Foster's definitive biography of the poet makes it clear that Yeats wanted Ireland to "lead the way in a war on materialism, decadence and triviality, as well as affirming her own individuality

---

[20] Lee, J., "The Irish Psyche", *The Irish Journal of Psychology*, Volume 15, Number 2 & 3, 1994.

[21] Watson, G.J., *Irish Identity and the Literary Revival*, Croom Helm, 1979.

— Ireland's spiritual idealism must be forged into a new world outlook for the dawning century."[22] The huge output of the Irish literary revival, especially the haunting lyrics of Yeats himself, forged a new consciousness of Ireland around the world. That consciousness was based on a distinctive and highly attractive positioning. Of course, Yeats, like everyone else at the time, would not have used terms like "positioning", let alone "branding", but the Foster biography makes it clear that he was a shrewd and formidable manager who was always acutely conscious of the results he wanted to achieve. Declan Kiberd, in his study of the literary output of the period, has concluded:

> That enterprise achieved nothing less than a renovation of Irish consciousness and a new understanding of politics, economics, sport, language, philosophy and culture in its widest sense. It was the grand destiny of Yeats' generation to make Ireland once again interesting to the Irish, after centuries of enforced provincialism following the collapse of the Gaelic order in 1601. No generation, before or since, lived with such conscious national intensity or left such an inspiring legacy.[23]

Following the war of independence and the subsequent civil war the newly formed Free State settled down to a more mundane existence but leading politicians picked up on the themes first enunciated and orchestrated by Yeats. The dominant political leader of the time, Eamon de Valera, in a broadcast to the nation in 1936 made the following point:

> The Irish genius has always stressed spiritual and intellectual rather than material values. It is these characteristics that fit the Irish people in a special manner for the task, now a vital one, of helping western civilisation. The great material pro-

---

[22] Foster, R., W. B., *Yeats: A Life, Part 1: The Apprentice Mage*, Oxford University Press, 1979.

[23] Kiberd, D., *Inventing Ireland*, London: Jonathan Cape, London, 1995.

gress of recent times, coming in a world where false philosophy already reigns, has distorted men's sense of proportion.[24]

It is interesting to note that in spite of our low level of economic
progress, the country's leading brand manager was in no way inhibited from setting extremely ambitious brand goals.

Progress of the Brand Vision since Yeats

Although Irish people became increasingly uncomfortable with
some of the crude manipulations of Yeats's vision of Ireland, it has
stood the test of time in establishing a distinct identity, especially
in those countries which are critical to our economic prosperity.
The main methods of measuring a country's image in other countries is through regular market research surveys. Alternatively, we
could carry out a content analysis of the way a country is portrayed
in the media and literature of other countries.

The most systematic measurement of the Irish image overseas
has been collected by Bord Fáilte (now Tourism Ireland), the organisation responsible for the attraction of tourists to Ireland.
They have carried out many *ad hoc* surveys over the years but the
most detailed studies of the Irish image were carried out in the
mid-1990s when a determined effort was made by the organisation
to mount a unified brand image campaign across all markets.

A market research report from 1995 suggested that Ireland was
seen among continental Europeans as "a saved country and culture
undisturbed by European history — a mythical island — a real and
authentic destination that could offer escapism and freedom".[25]

Research carried out in 2002 suggests that the image of Ireland
has to a remarkable extent remained true to Yeats's original vision:

---

[24] Dowling, M., "The Ireland That I Would Have: de Valera and the Creation of an
Irish National Image", *History Ireland*, Summer 1997.

[25] Bord Fáilte, Market Research Reports, 1995.

> Ireland continues to exist in the potential visitor's mind as a historic, green, scenic and cultural destination within Europe — much of the imagery is stereotypical in a classical manner but very much of the stereotyping is appealing, the place, people, pace, dimension.[26]

Although there is some evidence that Dublin is developing a slightly different image to the rest of Ireland, the country in general is seen as "untouched nature and traditions". Research carried out for Tourism Ireland in France in 2004 summarises the image of Ireland as "greenness, exciting landscapes, unique people, conviviality, open, warm, a nice place for escapism and for intense inside emotions". Research in the UK as part of the same project epitomised the image of Ireland as "regaining what has been squandered and lost in one's own country and life — a return to health — an escape to fun, a return to innocence, spiritual enrichment derived from the unspoilt places and people".[27]

Another way of looking at a country's brand image is to examine how that country is portrayed in advertising and marketing communications campaigns which use Irishness as their main point of differentiation. A recent survey[28] by Diane Negra of the most prominent US advertising campaigns that have focused on "Irishness" once again confirmed that "the pre-industrial theme park image still predominates". Negra analyses three campaigns and notes a consistency of approach in which Ireland is portrayed as "the repository of such values as simplicity and community — the category of Irishness set up as the primitive, the underdeveloped or the romantic means that to travel to Ireland is to participate in the past and to be free from rules of contemporary life".

---

[26] Ibid.

[27] Ibid.

[28] Negra, D., "Consuming Ireland: Lucky Charms Cereal, Irish Spring Soap and 1-800 Shamrock", *Cultural Studies*, 15 (1) 2001.

Yeats's vision contributed to the formation of the Irish brand in two major respects:

- *Distinctiveness*: Although there are no statistics available, there is widespread anecdotal evidence that awareness of Ireland around the world is completely disproportionate to the size of the country. In a celebrity-obsessed age, fame is an essential image attribute.

- *Desirability*: Yeats's brand vision for Ireland, although a hundred years old, still represents a powerful mental model. It suggests an alternative to the materialistic rat-race — an alternative which involves a return to a simpler lifestyle, an acceptance of the enduring need for the transcendental and acquiescence to the natural rhythms of the seasons. These ideas were fashionable among certain sections of the intelligentsia in late Victorian England as a reaction to the Industrial Revolution, but Yeats's genius was to appropriate them for an entire country. His concept was profoundly transformational and still appeals to a great number of people. "I will arise and go now, and go to Innisfree" has huge emotional and intellectual resonance all over the world and people who have never read any of the subsequent lines in the poem and who might not be even aware of the identity of the poet empathise with the ideal of simple living and escape from the hassle and stress of modern urban life.

"Romantic Ireland's Dead and Gone"

The predominant image and world-view of Ireland was formed at a time when the Irish economy was in the doldrums and when our great nemesis, the British, were at the height of their economic power. A recent study, *The Culture of Defeat*[29] found that countries or regions that have been defeated in war, or that fall under the

---

[29] Schivelbusch, W., *The Culture Of Defeat: On National Trauma, Mourning and Recovery*, Metropolitan Books, 2003.

economic and political yoke of a more powerful neighbour, often take solace in creating a romantic literary, non-materialistic image of themselves. France and the American South are two prime examples.

However, in economic terms, the late nineteenth and early twentieth century could hardly be more different than the late twentieth and early twenty-first. The last decade has witnessed a dramatic transformation of the Irish economy. After years of post-independence economic failure, characterised by the disastrous economic policies of "ourselves alone", we finally hit the jackpot in the latter part of the twentieth century to the extent that we are now an economic role model for other countries. From being one of the poorest countries in Europe, we have become one of the richest and somewhere in the late 1990s we even managed to out-strip the UK in terms of per capita GDP. The question that must now be asked is how our newfound wealth has affected our brand values. The image of a happy-go-lucky, spiritual, non-material, literary and romantic people is difficult to equate with our status as one of the most successful economies in Europe.

Something has to give and some domestic commentators are in no doubt that it has:

> From being a community-minded people living in fear of God, we have, in a short space of time, become an individu-ally minded people living in fear of negative equity.[30]

But before we get carried away by the "tabloid" tendency towards the apocalyptic we need to consider the possibility that a large part of Ireland's image was always out of line with reality. For most of the nineteenth and early twentieth century we were dealt a poor economic hand. We were denied the raw materials that economic success at the time demanded and we didn't have the political

---

[30] O'Connell, M., *Changed Utterly: Ireland and the New Irish Psyche*, The Liffey Press, 2001.

freedom to do much to counteract the situation. Inevitably, attempts were made to imply that the fault lay in the inherent characteristics of the Irish people. One of the most notable pronouncements came from an American academic, Kirby Miller, who argued that a combination of the Catholic religion, the Irish weather and the Irish language meant that we could never expect to enjoy economic success. The Catholic religion emphasised success in the afterlife as opposed to life on earth. Therefore there wasn't much point in striving for success in this life when we were guaranteed it in the next. The Irish weather was so unpredictable that planning — a prerequisite for success in any business — was well-nigh impossible and the Irish language, still present in our speech patterns if not actually spoken, laid stress on the passive rather than the active: "The semantic structure of the Irish language reflected and reinforced an Irish world view which emphasised dependence and passivity."[31] The reality, of course, has nothing to do with any of these and is more to do with our disastrous attempts to insulate ourselves economically from the rest of the world during the first three decades after Independence. These policies were made redundant by the Whitaker/Lemass initiatives of the late 1950s and early 1960s. It coincided with the time when the nature of income-generating assets was changing:

> A century ago the international division of labour was primarily based on the spatial distribution of natural resources such as the fruits of the earth and untrained or semi-trained human capital. Today the capabilities of a country to produce wealth rests increasingly on the extent to which it can create new resources or assets — such as information, technological capacity, management techniques and organisational competence.[32]

---

[31] Miller, K., *Emigrants and Exiles*, Oxford University Press, 1985.

[32] Dunning, J., "Globalisation: The Challenge For National Economy Regimes" (Geary Lecture), ESRI, Dublin: 2003.

This interpretation would fit in with the view of some commentators who have argued that we were always quite ruthless and single-minded. In an interview with *Fortune* magazine in 1999 a leading Irish cultural critic, Declan Kibard, stated:

> Far from being sentimental the Irish are one of the most ruthless, future-orientated people — jettisoning the Irish language for commercial purposes in the nineteenth century and embracing a global culture in the late twentieth century.[33]

This echoes Louis MacNeice's prophetic lines written in the late 1930s:

> Why do we like being Irish — because it gives us a hold over the sentimental English.[34]

But whether or not our image was always out of sync with reality, the fact remains that it is more seriously out of sync with the reality of the twenty-first century. Apart from the difficulty of finding any maidens, comely or otherwise, in modern Ireland, every crossroads in the country is now so heavily gridlocked that there's no longer any room for dancing. Our legendary charm and carefree attitude have been replaced by what has recently been described as a general "grumpiness" and Fáilte Ireland's exit surveys of overseas visitors suggest that this has not gone unnoticed by recent tourists. Just over a decade ago a book on Irish tourism claimed that Ireland was seen as a refuge from the tyranny of time:

> This chronocracy, the hegemony of unidirectional time in the post-renaissance west is subverted by the disguised and anachronistic disrespect for its implications in daily life in Ireland.[35]

---

[33] Kiberd, D., *Fortune*, 25 October 1999.

[34] MacNeice, L., *Collected Poems*, Faber & Faber, 1996.

[35] Cronin, M., "Fellow Travellers: Contemporary Travel Writing In Ireland", Essay in *Tourism in Ireland*, Cork University Press, 1993.

We've come a long way from this fanciful vision in today's cash-rich, time-poor society but overseas commentators continue to believe in a vision of the country that owes more to W.B. Yeats than to the reality of modern Ireland. This report appeared recently in the *Financial Times*:

> Itinerant life puts you in close touch with the legendary charm of the Irish at every turn. The chattering is infectious and addictive. Walking beside papa or riding on the platform I struck up conversations with strangers to whom once I would have given no more than a nod. The lives of old ladies gathering kindling, mothers hanging out washing, farmers on their tractors and children playing intertwined with ours. Some kept us talking for hours.[36]

These views may come as a surprise to the stressed-out, status anxiety-ridden commuters of today's Ireland but they will strike a chord with experienced brand managers in the commercial world who are continually frustrated by how difficult it is and how long it takes to change established brand images.

Conclusion

The image of Ireland created by the Literary Revival was an exaggerated idealised vision which never accurately reflected reality. However, this is true of all great brand visions. No matter how successful or talented a brand owner is, ultimately brand ownership resides in the minds of the public. The brand owner can send out all the signals they like but it is the public who create the brand. The Irish brand image has been successful partly because so many people all over the world want it to be true. In dealing with nation states there is also a tendency for people to live up to their image, to behave in the way they think is expected of them. Thus the whole proc-

---

[36] Davanport, P., "Slow Food in the Slow Lanes", *Financial Times* 28/29 August 2004.

ess becomes a self-fulfilling prophecy. But the economic transformation of the late twentieth and early twenty-first century has changed some of the attributes of the Irish brand image. The beautiful landscape has survived in parts but increasing prosperity with its attendant traffic and often ill-advised property developments has changed its character to some extent. The characteristics of the people have also changed; they're working harder and more concerned with acquisition and material goods and as a consequence have less time for social intercourse. However, the literary tradition remains a living one and has been replenished by a remarkable upsurge of talent in recent years. So if we can no longer offer the prospect of an agrarian, underdeveloped society or a landscape unaffected by the concrete, the chemicals and contrariness of modern life, we can still offer a rich cultural heritage and a vibrant literary tradition. These are attributes which have very positive associations in the three areas of economic activity influenced by a nation's brand image:

- *Fixed inward investment*: a vibrant literary tradition is compatible with an educated, innovative workforce.

- *Tourism*: cultural tourism is the fastest-growing sector of the tourist business.

- *Exports*: this can only be a positive association for our goods and services.

Ever since Yeats and his colleagues formulated an Irish brand image we have stood for something distinctive and desirable. Although this image is an important economic asset it is largely unacknowledged and unappreciated by the political, economic and civil service establishment.

This chapter has shown that the image which has been a valuable asset in the past still has the capacity to be a valuable asset in the future. But like all assets it needs to be managed and, because the brand image of a country is a relatively new idea, we may be in danger of neglecting a potentially powerful asset. The fact that a country's brand image cannot be managed in the way that businesses manage their consumer brands doesn't mean that we should allow it to be mismanaged through omission or neglect. Nor should we be deterred by the fact that the very use of marketing terminology in relation to a nation state is regarded as distasteful in many quarters.

Businesses are now being advised to identify and evaluate their non-material assets with a view to incorporating them into the overall strategic management of the firm. A firm's non-material assets include expertise and competency in dealing with non-market forces: government, media, special interest groups and, through all of them, the public. Ireland's favourable image in overseas markets constitutes a significant non-material asset which would be difficult for other countries to replicate. Take the example of St Patrick's Day, arguably the most famous national holiday in the world in terms of the number of other countries where it is celebrated. In marketing communication terms this is a unique sales promotion opportunity for the country. Therefore, instead of the usual begrudgery that accompanies government ministers flying out of Ireland to distant locations at that time, would it not be better to exploit the vast potential of this annual event to an even greater extent?

In fact there is a strong case for a more co-ordinated and active management of our brand image and there may be some merit in setting up an inter-departmental committee with responsibility for the following areas:

- Formulating proposals for developing the cultural resources of the country and disseminating Irish culture in overseas markets through performance, exhibitions, lectures, for example, the 2004 cultural expedition to China and the 1998 "L'Imaginaire Irlandaise" event in Paris. The recent establishment of Culture Ireland under the auspices of the Department of Foreign Affairs is a step in the right direction but it is too early to assess the results.

- Overall responsibility for measuring and monitoring the country's image in the main overseas markets on a continuous basis;

- Engaging the population as a whole in the process; this is an exercise that would have to be handled with caution, but nation-branding falls into the same category as service branding and it is often the people who are the primary communicators of service brand messages.

- Engaging the diaspora, who may actually welcome the opportunity to become involved.

PART FOUR

THE FUTURE OF BRANDING

"Brands will be built in the demand economy based on their ability to immediately incorporate, respond to and satisfy personalised customer requirements, much like the shopkeepers of yore."

— Nick Wreedon, *Fusion Branding*

"But what we are now faced with and have been faced with for some time is more and more customers are looking behind the brand and saying, 'I want to know who that comes from because I want to know whether the people who provide me with the brand are behaving like responsible corporate citizens'."

— Niall Fitzgerald, *Wall Street Journal*,
31 January 2002

"We trust global brands more than local brands in developing countries, but trust local brands more than global brands in developed countries."

— Henley Centre Research,
quoted in *Marketing Genius*, 2006

C&C was founded in 1852 by Dr Thomas Cantrell, apothecary and surgeon, in Belfast, and Sir Henry Cochrane, in Dublin.

12

THE MYTH OF THE MANIPULATED CONSUMER

In March of 2005 there were a number of important stories engaging the attention of news editors in Ireland. The McCartney sisters were increasing pressure on Sinn Féin and the British and Irish governments to bring the killers of their brother to justice; a pensions scandal in the Department of Health was starting to explode; and over €5 billion was wiped off the value of one of the leading shares on the Irish stock exchange — but the story that dominated all of the media at the time was the opening of a shopping centre in an unremarkable South Dublin suburb.

The majority of the coverage was favourable and exuded an air of breathless anticipation for the new centre, especially for the shops that would be opening for the first time in Ireland. But when the heavyweight columnists were called in to comment, their reaction varied from patronising condescension to outright condemnation: "Shopping malls are the cathedrals of the new religion of the necessity to buy and buy, the metaphysical nonsense that somehow you only are what you buy."[1]

---

[1] McGurk, T., "Why I never want to go into Dundrum Shopping Centre", *Sunday Business Post*, 6 March 2005.

The Long History of Intellectual Antipathy to Consumerism and Marketing Communication

To anyone working in the marketing communications business the critical comments about the new shopping centre came as no surprise. For the whole of the twentieth century the intellectual establishment had been critical of consumer goods in general and the marketing communications aimed at encouraging their purchase in particular. From the influential English critic F.R. Leavis's perfunctory dismissal of "unremitting persuasive masturbatory manipulation" to George Orwell's denunciation of advertising as "the rattling of a stick in the swill bucket of capitalism'" the world of consumer goods and marketing communications has had a bad press.

One of the founding fathers of the Irish independence movement made his position clear when he complained in his memoirs:

> My dealings with advertising agencies produced in me a distaste for the profession, if it could be dignified by that word, which has never been eradicated. I still regard it as a pernicious manifestation of the capitalist system. I believe it has been the creator of unreasonable expectations, popular discontent and unhappiness in society.[2]

However, as the *Financial Times*'s estimable Lucy Kellaway remarked:

> I bet all the people who write articles and books about what brands do to the national psyche feel that their own psyches remain in fine fettle because they are too intelligent to be manipulated. It is the less intelligent masses they fear for. This is unforgivably patronising.[3]

The most trenchant critics have tended to come from North America, which is not surprising because, in spite of being the epitome of a mass consumer society, a strong puritan streak is always bub-

---

[2] Andrews, C.S., *Man of no Property*, Lilliput Press, 2001.

[3] Kellaway, L., *Financial Times*, 16 July 2001.

bling close to the surface. From Vance Packard in the 1950s to Naomi Klein in the present day by way of countless others, including the substantial arguments of the noted economist, J.K. Galbraith, there has never been a shortage of critics of consumer society on that continent.

Packard's book *The Hidden Persuaders*[4] was a huge bestseller which preyed upon the paranoia rampant in 1950s America when McCarthyism was at its peak. The idea that advertisers were able to exert a profound influence on people using subliminal messages transmitted through advertising seems pretty daft now but there were plenty of willing believers in America at the time. Galbraith's criticism of the marketing ethos and the manipulated consumer had more substance but betrayed the economist's traditional lack of understanding of any purchasing behaviour that was not based on strictly rational grounds and a traditional left-of-centre frustration with the proles for being so easily led astray by consumer baubles. Galbraith was echoing a common view of advertising among economists at the time that marketing communications, and in particular advertising, distorted competition by creating a body of "loyal" consumers who couldn't be budged or dislodged by smaller competitors or new market entrants. We now know that the concept of the "loyal" consumer was always exaggerated and in the intervening period, for the type of markets that Galbraith was referring to, the balance of power has shifted significantly away from the manufacturers towards the retailers in spite of the so-called power of advertising. Unlike other critics, however, Galbraith writes like an angel and is prepared to concede his elitist standpoint:

> There is an instant tendency among solemn social scientists to think of any institution which features rhymed and singing commercials, intense and lachrymose voices urging highly improbable enjoyments, caricatures of the human oesophagus in normal or impaired operation and which

---

4 Packard, V., *The Hidden Persuaders*, Longmans Green (UK), 1957.

hints implausibly at opportunities for antiseptic seduction as inherently trivial.[5]

We also know now that the opposite of "rational" is not "irrational" and that emotional factors play an important role in all our decisions; but left-of-centre frustration with the purchasing behaviour of the masses remains a potent force, as we shall discuss later.

It is yet another testament to the current preoccupation with brands that the latest bestselling critic of the consumer society focuses her attention on specific brands as opposed to consumption in general. Naomi Klein's *No Logo* is partly a justifiable assault on the dubious employment conditions of the mainly third-world workers who are responsible for much of the manufacturing of consumer goods which ultimately find their way into the shopping centres of the developed world. But the second major theme running through the book is not dissimilar to the long-standing annoyance of left-wing critics with consumers who are prepared to pay over the odds for fashionable brand names that are sold on the basis of what they mean as opposed to what they do:

> The goal now is for brands to animate their marketing identities to become real world living manifestations of their myth — brands are about meaning not product attributes; brand-based companies are no longer satisfied with having a fling with their customers they want to move in together.[6]

The classic case study of how the world's most famous brand almost committed corporate suicide shows up the real flaw in Klein's argument. In 1985 Coca Cola was coming under severe pressure from its arch-rival Pepsi in the US market. Blind taste tests showed that more people preferred the taste of Pepsi to Coke, so the brand leader decided to introduce a new secret formula Coke that tasted smoother and sweeter than the original — in other words, which

---

[5] Galbraith, J.K., *The New Industrial Estate*, Hamish Hamilton, 1967.
[6] Klein, N., *No Logo*, Flamingo, 2000.

tasted closer to Pepsi. On 23 April 1985 the new formula was introduced under the name "New Coke". It was the first formula change for 99 years and the public reaction was as dramatic as it was unexpected. The people were outraged, the company were inundated with angry calls, mass demonstrations were held and societies for the preservation of the "Real Thing" were formed. Within two and a half months the company relented and the original formula was re-launched as Coca Cola Classic. In retrospect, it is extraordinary that the most successful brand in history should have made the fundamental mistake of failing to understand that brands are a combination of rational and emotional factors. By basing their decision on the rational aspect of the taste, they ignored "the fact that Coca-Cola had been an integral part of American life for more than a century — that it was part of the American identity — Coke was much more than a cola-flavoured drink; it was an American institution — a national icon".[7]

In the same way, when people buy a pair of Nike trainers they are buying much more than a running shoe made on an assembly line; the real value is in the stories and myths surrounding the brand that have been created by advertising and other forms of marketing communications. That's why wearing Nike makes you feel that you just might be able to "do it". The technical specifications of the product are important but not all-important and that is where critics of the consumer society come unstuck.

Two of the most recent critiques of consumer society come from an American social commentator, Juliet Schor, and an Australian economist, Clive Hamilton. Schor outlines her case in *The Overspent American* and makes the point that consumption is not making people any happier. The main thesis of the book is that although "competitive consumption" — the need to keep up with the Joneses — has always been a feature of American life, there

---

[7] Fog, K., Budtz, C., Yakaboylu, B., *Story Telling: Branding in Practice*, Springer (Berlin), 2005.

has recently been an "upscale emulation" because instead of comparing one's income with that of one's immediate neighbours Americans are now comparing their consumption levels with the rich and famous. The evidence for this shift in emphasis is attributed to the proliferation of media comment on the lifestyles of the rich and somewhat bizarrely to the fact that as more women enter the workforce they become more exposed to more diverse lifestyles and "become more likely to gaze upwards".[8] She states quite correctly that the 1990s saw an increase in conspicuous consumption: "trophy homes, diamonds of a carat or more, granite countertops, and sports utility vehicles are the primary consumer symbols of the late-1990s". She goes on to argue that the increased emphasis on the acquisition of consumer goods is damaging the quality of American life because the money spent on these goods could have been saved or put to better use. Schor accepts that criticising consumer culture risks being "intrusive, patronising or elitist" but ploughs on regardless, questioning how well informed consumers really are and whether each consumer's preferences are independent of other consumer's preferences. In particular, she questions the idea that the current market model is best:

> It exaggerates how rational, informed and consistent people are; it overstates their independence; it fails to address the pressures that consumerism imposes on individuals with respect to available choices and the consequences of various consumption decisions; understand these pressures and you may well arrive at very different conclusions about politics and policy.[9]

There are undoubtedly some valid points here and the fundamentalist reverence for market-based solutions to every problem did get a little out of hand during the 1990s but the underlying as-

---

[8] Schor, J., "The New Politics of Consumption" from *Do Americans Shop Too Much?*, *Boston Review*, 2000.

[9] Schor, ibid.

sumption that the real problem with so many people is that they don't really know what's good for them is as suspect as ever. People know what's good for them; it's just that what's good for them may not be all that much use to other people:

> I think that much of our current refusal to consider the liberating role of consumption is the result of who has been doing the describing. Since the 1960s the primary "readers" of the commercial "text" have been the well tended and tenured members of the academy. For any number of reasons; the most obvious being low levels of disposable income, average age and gender, and the fact that these critics are selling a competing product, high-cult (which is also created in dream values) — the academy has casually passed off as "hegemonic brainwashing" what seems to me at least a self-evident truth about human nature. We like having stuff.[10]

Clive Hamilton's critique of consumerism is more wide-ranging and is really only part of his attack on the growth imperative in today's economies. He argues that our "growth fetishism" cedes too much power to business, which in turn equates happiness with an abundance of consumer goods. He does make the valid point that the supposed plethora of choice often masks the growing homogeneity of the world in which one shopping centre looks very much like any other because all the shops are the same, selling almost identical lines of goods: "The individuality of the marketing society is an elaborate pose people adopt to cover up the fact that they have been buried in the homogenising forces of consumer culture".[11] This criticism is a throwback to the Marxist critics of the 1940s and 1950s who argued that so-called consumer choice was really a "mass deception":

---

[10] Twitchell, J., "The Stone Age", *Boston Review*, Summer 1999.

[11] Hamilton, C., *Growth Fetish,* Pluto Press, 2003.

How formalised the procedure is can be seen when the mechanically differentiated products prove to be all alike in the end — that the difference between the Chrysler range and General Motors products is basically illusory strikes every child with a keen interest in varieties — what connoisseurs discuss as good or bad points only serve to perpetuate the semblance of competition and range of choice.[12]

But the fact that all cars essentially enable people to go from A to B doesn't necessarily mean that they are all alike and the conspiracy theory arguments advanced by Adorno are no longer taken very seriously.

The main focus of Hamilton's argument is that all this choice and the abundance of consumer goods do not appear to be making us any happier. Although the sensitivity of the instruments at our disposal for measuring such an elusive concept may be suspect, there does appear to be some evidence that the more wealthy a society the greater the likelihood of an increase in the incidence of depression, stress, alienation and a pervasive feeling of discontent. Hamilton allocates most of the blame to the manipulation of consumers by an unholy conspiracy of unfettered big business, devious marketing communications agencies and governments turning a blind eye:

In the post modern world people create their own selves but they do not create them just as they please, they create them under circumstances and with materials made and transmitted by the ideology of growth fetishism and the marketing machine.[13]

But surely the real reason why people don't feel all that much happier after they have bought a load of goods in the shopping centre

---

[12] Adorno, T. and Horkheimer, M., "The Culture Industry: Enlightenment as Mass Deception", 1944 (from *Dialectic of Enlightenment*, New York: Continuum, 1993).

[13] Hamilton, Ibid.

is the nature of the human condition: the acquisition of goods leads to an intensification, rather than a reduction of wants. This has always been the case. There are two differences which may make our current predicament worse than at any time in living memory; we are wealthier and therefore can afford more goods, so the inevitable post-purchase *tristesse* is all the greater; and secondly, in a post-Christian world we have no countervailing arguments to provide us with an alternative perspective. Hamilton almost admits this himself:

> This is the pattern of restless over-consumers who deploy their wealth as a means of avoiding confrontation with the essential meaninglessness of the life that they fear may lie just below the surface.[14]

Although critics of what is usually described as the "culture of consumption" have many valuable contributions to make to debates about the future of society, their concentration on the consumer society leaves them open to ridicule from the new tough-minded market fundamentalists:

> What these academic economists have trouble with is not consumption but taste; buy a rare edition of John Milton's *Comus* for $400,000 and you won't hear a peep from the lefties over in the Econ department — but buy a videocassette of *Debbie Does Dallas* for four dollars, show it on your big screen TV in your entertainment centre with the Bose wrap-around speakers and all hell breaks loose. Although modern consumption may share a few characteristics with Victorian consumption it is not a disease to be controlled by Dr Tax and Dr Shame; it is a response to life as we are living it. When you think about consumption from this point of view you realise that it's not objects, even luxury objects, that are the problem; it is the meaning of life that has become perplexing in a world bereft of bloodlines, family

---

[14] Hamilton, ibid.

pews, social clubs and the like. Face it, you are what you consume, not what you make; you are the logo on your T-shirt, not a descendent of a Mayflower passenger.[15]

The Even Longer History of Consumption and the Role of Consumer Goods

The most coherent defence of consumption that the marketing communications business has been able to come up with is that consumer goods have been a feature of every society and was therefore present long before shopping centres, marketing or advertising ever existed. For the last thirty years the work of anthropologist Mary Douglas has been ransacked to add some intellectual ballast to this defence. Her studies of primitive societies led her to the conclusion that goods had never been seen in a purely utilitarian sense, as the critics of mass consumption would have preferred, but that they had always been used to define people's position in a particular society. She also discovered that the value of goods is not defined solely by the owner or purchaser; the evaluation of our goods by our friends, neighbours and peers is of critical importance to how we value them ourselves. Douglas's main conclusions are as valid today as they ever were:

- All consumption activity is a ritual presentation and the sharing of goods becomes classified as appropriate to particular social categories which themselves get defined and graded in the process.

- An individual's main object in consumption, after his "lower order" needs have been met, is to help to create the social universe and to find in it a credible place.

- Successful consumption requires a deployment of goods in consumption rituals that will mobilise the maximum marking services from other consumers.[16]

---

[15] Twitchell, J., "The Stone Age", *Boston Review*, Summer 1999.

The fact that these findings flew directly in the face of the main arguments of the critics of mass consumption was grist to the marketing communications businesses mill and marketing academic heavyweights like Ted Levitt lost no opportunity to ram the point home:

> Like the inhabitants of isolated African regions, where not a single whiff of advertising has ever intruded, we all encrust ourselves in rings, pendants, bracelets, neckties, clips, chains and snaps.[17]

Even T.S. Eliot's famous line about human beings not being able to bear very much reality was called in for the defence; but as often happens in debates of this type the critics ignored the arguments and went on a new offensive not so much concerned with how people used goods but how they were being cynically manipulated to purchase these goods in the first place.

The Emerging Study of the History of Consumption

Underlying all of the criticisms of consumption is a deep-rooted belief that people are being manipulated by big business, aided and abetted by the black arts of marketing communications, into passively engaging in a dumbed-down consumer culture which is continually forcing people to seek more stuff but can never make them happy. However, recent findings from the emerging study of culture and consumption tend to dispute this belief.

The history of consumption and an appreciation of its role in forming the history of the modern world is only in its infancy but it is part of a quiet revolution in historical studies. Until very recently history tended to concentrate on the great generals,

---

[16] Douglas, N., *Relative Poverty, Relative Communication: Traditions of Social Policy, Essays in Honour of Violet Butler*, Ed A.N. Halsey, Oxford, Basil Blackbird, The Blackwell, 1976.

[17] Levitt, T., "The Morality of Advertising", *Harvard Business Review*, July–August, 1970.

churchmen, politicians and all of the names, dates and battles that we learned from our school histories. Modern historians are beginning to look beyond all that to uncover what was happening at a wider societal level with a view to gaining a better understanding of what really influenced events. We are now beginning to see a "bottom-up" view of history instead of the more traditional "top-down" view. Simon Schama's *Citizens*,[18] which gave a fresh perspective on the French Revolution by looking at it through the eyes of ordinary citizens, is one of the best-known examples, and Diarmaid Ferriter's recent history of twentieth-century Ireland[19] differs from previous studies of the same period by paying much more attention to what was happening to trade unions, the women's movement, art, literature and sport.

Neither of these historians included changing patterns of consumption in their respective books but it is surely not very long before someone does. A number of studies of consumption from the sixteenth to the nineteenth century in Britain may create more interest in the study of how mass consumption and fashion played their part in influencing the course of history. One interesting conclusion from this work is that consumption, and the fashion that inevitably accompanies it, may have played a key role in the democratisation of society as we moved from the rigid hierarchical orthodoxy of the middle ages to the emerging democracy of the nineteenth and early twentieth centuries. In Elizabethan times the value of goods was heavily influenced by their "patina" — the sheen they acquired from constant handling over the years. This created what was referred to as a five-generation rule, which stood for the number of generations that were required for a family to be able to accumulate enough wealth to be fully accepted in polite society, or whatever passed for polite society at the time. But

---

[18] Schama, S., *Citizens: A Chronicle of the Great Revolution*, Alfred A. Knopf, Inc., New York, 1989.

[19] Ferriter, D., *The Transformation of Ireland, 1900–2000*, Profile Books, 2004.

somewhere in the sixteenth century goods became valuable not for their patina but for their novelty. All of this meant that new wealth could now compete equally with "old money", and goods became an important element of social change:

> Suddenly high standing individuals could find more status in things that were new than in things that were old — the new system of status allocation favoured initiative and accomplishment rather than mere standing, using product's new mobility and recognition of ability — the patina strategy had served the cause of relative rigidity, fixity and immobility.[20]

Consumer goods have always had the capacity to communicate cultural meaning; where we live, what we wear, what we eat and drink and the other goods and gadgets we possess all communicate stories about ourselves and individuals have always been conscious of this. The point of this brief foray into the history of consumption is to show that although not everyone could afford all the goods that they wanted the ones they did choose were carefully designed to convey appropriate stories about themselves. There was no behind-the-scenes manipulation, no "Mr Big" pulling the strings. Sisters and brothers have always been doing it for themselves.

But although the belief among many intellectuals that consumer culture is a form of oppression is still widespread, a more celebratory attitude towards consumers is now beginning to emerge. Consumption and in particular brand consumption are now being celebrated for allowing people more freedom to express themselves and more control over the business world.

Centre Stage: The Consumer in the Modern World

At the beginning of the twentieth century Oscar Wilde portrayed the lives of the upper classes in the most powerful and wealthiest country in the world at the time in a series of dazzling plays that

---

[20] McCracken, G., *Culture and Consumption*, Indiana University Press, 1988.

took London's West End by storm. The plays were peppered with witty epigrams which exemplified the characters' attitudes to life: "I admit I smoke; a man should always have an occupation of some kind".[21] Most of the main characters have no jobs as we would understand the term but live off inherited wealth or the dividends from investments of one kind or another. They take great care with their appearance, changing from one elaborate and stylish outfit to another and the remainder of their time is divided between entertaining, seducing and gossiping with each other. Wilde conceived life itself to be a work of art and although his portrayal of his characters was accurate it applied only to a very small section of society. At the beginning of the twenty-first century a majority of the people in western societies, admittedly in varying degrees, are slowly but surely attaining the capacity to deal with their own lives as a work of art and it could be argued that once some of the current younger generation inherit their parents' property they will be able to indulge themselves in the life of a character from a Wilde play.

Average wealth in Ireland has tripled in the last twenty years and the main consequence is a vast increase in the options open to the majority of the population. At the beginning of the twentieth century thousands of Irish people took the emigrant boat in destitute overcrowded conditions to seek a new life in New York. At the beginning of the twenty-first century thousands of Irish people flew in comfort to New York to do their Christmas shopping. In the Dublin suburb of Ranelagh thirty years ago there were no restaurants; today in Ranelagh there are twenty and you can choose between Mexican, Italian, Thai, Chinese, American, Spanish, French and of course Irish. Every exotic location under the sun is now within reach; Irish travellers can be in the Caribbean on a cheap flight in less time than it takes to drive from Dublin to West

---

[21] Hewetson, C., *The Wisdom of Oscar Wilde,* Philosophical Society Inc (NY), 1967.

Cork. The latest *haute couture* from Paris and Milan is still out of reach for most people but high-quality reproductions are readily available in Irish shopping centres across the country.

The two advertising campaigns that most catch the mood and spirit of these very changing times for Irish consumers are for L'Oreal and Phillipe Patek. L'Oreal's now famous copyline, "Because I'm worth it", is probably the most apposite reflection of the current zeitgeist. It is the ultimate battle-cry of the new individualism: "I have as much right to the best things in life as anyone else and I'm going to get them." It is also the ultimate expression of the democratic ideal and although some intellectual critics may bemoan the fact that most people would prefer to indulge their new freedom and wealth sunning themselves on a Caribbean beach, eating papayas and sipping rum instead of coming to grips with the philosophy of Ludwig Wittgenstein in a remote rainswept cottage in Killary Harbour, the essence of democracy is people taking control of their own lives and making their own choices.

The Phillipe Patek campaign also features a striking copyline: "Who are you going to be in the next twenty-four hours?" This line is also an accurate reflection of one of the most significant changes facilitated by the new culture of consumption — the ability to adopt multiple personalities depending on our moods, whims and desires. It is also an expression of a new-found freedom for many people who had previously been stereotyped by their economic and social circumstances.

It is probably not without significance that the two marketing communications campaigns that represent the most accurate reflection of the new consumer feature female models. Ever since Ibsen's Nora walked out of the Helmer household and her eponymous *Doll's House* in 1879 women have been marching to freedom and equality and by the twenty-first century the majority of women in Western society had a wide range of choice of who they wanted to be in the next twenty-four hours because they felt they were worth it. Consumer brands play a powerful role in fulfilling these objectives:

> If it is true that our most profound work as human beings is to construct ourselves, to appear on a stage of our choosing, then the activity of acquiring the costumes and props, buildings and stage sets and acting out our roles is not just a secondary one — we need brands and the spaces in which they and we appear seem to be melded together.[22]

This quotation comes from a lavishly illustrated and produced publication issued as part of an exhibition devoted to brands at the Victoria and Albert Museum in London in 2000. The very fact of the venerable V&A devoting its valuable space and time to "brands" was an indication of how seriously the whole subject was now being taken. The main theme of the publication and programme notes was that brands were now playing a central role in defining people's identity and constructing their social lives. There are many who will be alarmed by this development but it could be argued that there is nothing new here; some people have always defined themselves very carefully and deliberately by the clothes they wore, the food they eat, the goods they surrounded themselves with, even the places they went on holidays. Only two things have changed: in the past very few people could afford the luxury of doing this, and secondly, these goods were not referred to as brands. Even French philosophers were dragged into the debate and one of them made the point that we are all producers of meaning, displaying a concept of identity through the goods we consume so that brands are "tools for the construction of personhood". Leaving aside the infelicities of the phrase itself, it does represent a useful summary of the changing nature of the role of brands.

Some commentators go further and suggest that the consumption of brands has now taken over the central role that was once

---

[22] Betsky, A., "All the World's a Store: The Spaces of Shopping", in *Brand New*, Pavitt, J. (Ed.), V&A Publications, 2000.

played by job occupation. This assumes that everyone now enjoys the life of leisure that was enjoyed by Wilde's characters but as this is self-evidently not the case it seems hard to sustain this argument. Others have argued that brands have now taken over the role once played by religion and politics in people's lives; that people now "believe" in brands in the way that they once believed in the church and in political parties. Again this argument is difficult to sustain. There are one or two brands — Apple and Harley-Davidson spring to mind — which evoke extraordinary levels of loyalty and devotion among a committed minority, but the analogy with religion and politics has always struck me as being a bit far-fetched.

There are two reasons why the consumption of brands is now being used to a much greater extent than in the past to define people's identities. The first is that people have more freedom due to their improved economic circumstances. The second main change from the past is that we are now much more likely to "read" meaning into texts like brands because of the development of semiology and the subsequent writings of people like Roland Barthes. His ground-breaking *Mythologies*[23] taught us to see patterns of belief in everyday objects which had not previously been considered worthy of academic attention.

Consumer Culture: Liberation or Oppression?

In spite of a more enlightened view of the role of brands in defining personalities in the modern world, the issue of the manipulated consumer remains. Is consumer culture a form of oppression or liberation? This is still a frequently asked question and usually the answer depends on the writer's own values rather than on any objective truth: "discussions about consumption and consumerism are always value-laden".[24] Until recently most discussion of

---

[23] Barthes, R., *Mythologies,* Jonathon Kaye, 1972.

[24] Gabriel, W. and Lang, T., *The Unmanageable Consumer*, Sage Publications, London, 1995.

the subject viewed the consumer as being continuously manipulated by the forces of big business and succumbing mindlessly to the Machiavellian machinations of mass marketing. As we have noted earlier, a different tone entered the debate in recent years:

> More recently a more celebratory image of the consumer has predominated — instead of a victim the consumer has been depicted as a free-thinking individual who constructs a sense of self out of their consuming culture in ways that are regardless of such limitations of class gender or even geography.[25]

Another strand to this argument is that many of the barriers that inhibited people's freedom of action in the past have been dismantled. Until very recently "the self" was defined and constrained by birth, location, occupation and social class. The most obvious constraint was lack of wealth but there has also been a dismantling of class barriers, age barriers and many other hierarchies which are no more.

The best way to experience this is to visit any modern workplace. It is now much more difficult to spot who's the boss, who's in charge, who are the senior people. Dress has become much more democratic, deferential attitudes have all but disappeared and even office space has become more equal.

There has also been a gradual loss of expert authority in many areas. Professions which until recently exercised almost complete authority in their area of expertise are now subject to an unprecedented level of questioning and even rebellion. Teachers are coming under scrutiny from parents and even children, doctors are being contradicted by patients who have discovered alternative remedies on the internet and the once absolute authority of the clergy is in complete disarray. These societal changes mean that people are much more likely to be able to define their own identity

---

[25] Pavitt, J., "Branding the Individual", in *Brand New*, V&A Publications, 2000.

than have it defined for them. Brands are a primary source of defining one's identity. Well-defined brands are identified with well-defined stories about themselves which are constructed and disseminated by marketing communications. People can choose to define themselves by the stories they find most attractive:

> Branding has passed the cultural chasm. In the past brands scrved merely as forms of entertainment. In today's consumer culture branding provides an answer to our identity crises. Brands create purpose and give our lives meaning. They enable us to construct our social world. In other words in our search for place and purpose in life consumer culture is replacing tradition.[26]

These sentiments were widely shared at the end of the twentieth century when the hype surrounding brands was at its height. Although it probably did apply to a small range of consumer goods it would be a mistake to assume that self-identity was the only factor in buying behaviour; traditional reasons for purchasing goods like use value and exchange value are still dominant in most markets, but as Western societies experienced rapid economic growth towards the end of the twentieth century increasing individualism meant that more people were able to construct identi ties for themselves through the act of consumption:

> The subject of consumption is nothing if not an actor in search of an identity — asking a basic core identity, the post-modern subject constructs itself around the image it projects for others in consumer culture — "I am what you perceive me to be" — consumption enables people to change hats as often as the occasion demands.[27]

---

[26] Wipperfurth, A., *Brand Hijack*, Penguin Books, 2005.
[27] Pavitt, ibid.

These important societal changes have also been the subject of wide-ranging philosophical and sociological academic debate and a whole new discipline of consumer studies has emerged under the umbrella of cultural values. Zygmunt Bauman is one of the most prolific commentators in this area and he has highlighted the societal changes that have led to the increasing emphasis on consumerism. In commenting on the rise of neo-liberalism and the increase in individualism, he has placed consumption in a central role in modern society:

> Today's societies are integrated around consumption rather than production — freedom is modelled on freedom to choose how one satisfies individual desires and constructs one's identity via the medium of the consumer market.[28]

Bauman is not particularly sympathetic to this development but his antipathy is due to a belief that there is still a substantial underclass in most developed societies who are denied access to the fruits of the new consumption-driven era and the majority are too seduced by consumption to support any political movement devoted towards any fundamental change in the status quo. From a branding perspective the important issue here is the way that intellectuals who spend their time examining the nature of the society in which we live have put consumption in such a central role in the life of the majority of people in the Western world:

> The cement that links the social system, its institutions and the everyday experiences of individuals in the world today — consumption has become the primary means of experiencing an identity — the same central role which was played by work, by job occupation or profession in modern society

---

[28] Leighton, D., "Searching for Politics in an Uncertain World: Interview with Zygmunt Bauman", *Renewal (A Journal of Labour Politics)*, Volume X, No. 1, Wynford, 2002.

is now performed in contemporary society by consumer choice.[29]

One of the most detailed descriptions of the new consumer comes from Yiannis Gabriel and Tim Lang in their book, appropriately called *The Unmanageable Consumer*.[30] Here they put forward the view that the new consumer is more in control than in the past and is therefore not capable of being managed by business in the way that is often assumed by critics of the consumer society. This view is echoed by Wendy Gordon's depiction of the new consumer as "multi-headed". Gordon is particularly critical of traditional attitudes to consumers adopted by the business world, which assumed a degree of control that was probably never the case.

But in spite of some variations in the way consumers are described there is a reasonable level of consensus on two points: that twenty-first-century consumers are more in control of their own actions and are not being manipulated by either business, government, religion or any other outside forces; and secondly, that they are constantly changing — there are no fixed identities. It is possible that the former point has always had more validity than was assumed in the past especially by management theorists with their love of military language, "targets", "penetration", "reach" and "frequency", which gave them the illusion of total control.

The second point about continually changing identities is due to the influence of postmodernism on cultural commentators. The idea that postmodernism could help to explain anything may strike some people as naïve as it is such a notoriously difficult concept to grasp but there are many aspects of the post-modern which provide useful insights into the world of consumption. In fact, in spite of the excess intellectual baggage attached to the term it is almost impossible to ignore if we want to come to terms with the modern world.

---

[29] Leighton, D., ibid.

[30] Gabrielle, Y. and Lang, T., ibid.

There are a number of postmodernist strands of thought that are relevant in an attempt to understand the modern consumer:

- The end of totalising systems of thought, the end of certainty, the end of a single view of reality; instead the postmodernist offers complexity, ambiguity and disorder. Where there is no absolute orthodoxy people are free to construct their own so rather than looking for universal truths we should exercise our own judgement:

  > Gone are the days of sweeping cultural ideas and moral certainties; gone are powerful role models untouched by scandal and corruption; gone are the starring symbols; gone too are the great cultural accomplishments. In a world where heroes are cut down to size, perfection remains elusive, the dreaming surfaces of material goods, their pristine packaging and virginal existence inevitably attract our attention.[31]

- The belief that we are not self-created beings, people initially endowed with character and goals, but people who can choose who and what they want to be by their own decisions. One of the most famous women in advertising, Mary Wells, summed it up well in her autobiography: "I had to invent my life, an American tradition — no one invented a life and handed it to me — my identity my universe was mine to create".[32]

In addition to the main currents of contemporary philosophical thinking, the reality of modern life tends to conspire against fixed identities. The anonymity of working in vast urban spaces, living in vast open suburbs and shopping in vast air-conditioned shopping centres encourages the adoption of different styles, identities and personalities. A recent case study for Marks & Spenser lingerie in the UK quotes a respondent in a group discussion, who sums

---

[31] Ibid.

[32] Wells, N., *A Big Life in Advertising*, Alfred A. Knopf, 2000.

up the feeling: "Sometimes I shop and feel like a mum, other times I feel like a vamp."[33]

If the overwhelming weight of evidence suggests that the modern consumer is firmly in control there is one remaining area of doubt: the issue of choice or, as some commentators would have it, the illusion of choice. It has been suggested that much of what passes for choice is a chimera and that it is foolish to imagine we have any real choice when there is so much evidence of a homogenisation of goods around the world. The increasing concentration of power in the retail trade would tend to support this view and in spite of the size of the modern retail outlets, of the 2,000 varieties of apple that are known, only about five are ever on sale in most supermarkets:

> We're faced with a profusion of minor choices and a dearth of major choices, we can enter a supermarket and choose between twenty different brands of margarine but many of us have no choice but to enter that supermarket — were we to tell the corporations dominating some sectors that we were dissatisfied and wished to take our business elsewhere, they would ask which planet we had in mind.[34]

Although there is some validity in this argument I don't think that it contradicts the basic premise that the modern consumer has more choice than ever before and that they exert a reasonable measure of control over the whole process. People in most western countries have an infinitely more varied selection of foods, drinks, clothes, machines of all kinds and gadgets of every description than at any time in human history. The growth of the major retailers will ultimately be curtailed by a backlash against their size and predictability and there will probably be a steady trickle back to

---

33 Huntley, A. and Walker, N., "Nice Knickers Don't Sell Themselves", Advertising Works XIII WARC (UK), 2005.

34 Monbiot, G., *Capital State*, Macmillan, 2000.

neighbourhood butchers, bakers, candlestick-makers, greengrocers and fishmongers.

The Consumer of the Future

At the risk of drawing a crooked line from an unwarranted assumption to a foregone conclusion, which is one definition of forecasting, I think there are three possible developments of the new consumer. They are separate but not necessarily mutually exclusive.

The Ethical Consumer

This is a movement that has been around for some time as the proliferation of ethical investment funds will testify to but there is some evidence that it could become a much greater force across a much wider range of markets in the immediate future. Consider again the essence of brands and branding: they represent the stories that people associate with the products and services that they buy; the more powerful the brand the more defined and distinctive the story and people choose brands because they like the stories. It must follow therefore that if the story becomes tarnished in any way people will stop buying the brand. Today's consumer has enough disposable income to be able to switch brands if they don't like the stories they are hearing; and today's global communications, especially the internet, means that no story can be kept secret for very long.

The following are three examples of a shift in power from producer to consumer:

- *Nike*: The revelations about the conditions of employment in sub-contracted factories in the developing world forced the company to invest enormous sums of money to improve pay and conditions in spite of the fact that conditions were probably better than average for the areas in which the factories were located and they were the responsibility of the sub-contractor, not Nike. It was also significant that details of these conditions came to the attention of a wider public as a result of a book by a consumer activist and the subsequent outcry was created by viral messages across the internet. As a direct consequence of this consumer activism, Nike has now decided to publish their entire list of contract manufacturers on the internet. This means that in future anyone will be able to check out employment conditions in any of the 800 factories where Nike clothes and footwear are made.[35]

- **Shell**: When the Brent Spar drilling platform was at the end of its life, Shell decided to sink it into the ocean. Environmental group Greenpeace opposed the move and wanted Shell to bring it to shore and dismantle it. Greenpeace is also a brand and its story was more convincing to consumers around the world and was able to force Shell see things their way, in spite of the fact that many environmental experts felt that Shell's original decision was the more environmentally correct.

- **Edun**: The recent launch of the Edun fashion brand is another example of this trend. Created by Ali Hewson and Bono with New York clothing designer Rogan Gregory, the brand aims to create sustainable employment in Africa, South America and India. It will be run as a profit-making business using locally managed factories and it is hoped that others will replicate the model.

The growth of the "fair trade" movement is another straw in the wind and the following future scenario envisaged by the Danish writer Rolf Jensen may be more than just a speck on the horizon:

> To an increasing degree we're prepared to change brands if a product does not reflect our convictions. The political consumer is an up-and-coming factor in Scandinavia and the rest of Northern Europe. This is a consumer who while

---

[35] Shapinker, N., "Nike Ushers in a New Age of Corporate Responsibility", *Financial Times*, 20 April 2005.

> shopping for weekend groceries will vote with the shopping cart by buying ecology, animal welfare, bananas and coffee from small independent producers and wine from countries that refrain from testing nuclear devices in the Pacific.[36]

The basic premise of this forecast is that more consumers are likely in the future to want to buy goods and services from businesses that are known to be civilised places to work, that contribute to the local community in which they operate, that are environmentally aware and active, that do not engage in dubious financial practices which may be just within the letter of the law but are designed to avoid paying their full share of taxes — in summary, businesses that have a good story to tell about themselves.

This line of thought often draws a visceral response from economic and social columnists of the neo-conservative variety, who have been in the ascendant since the late 1980s. In the same way that they regard any interference with the miraculous and mysterious workings of the market as the equivalent of a mortal sin, they regard any business that deviates from the single-minded objective of maximising shareholder profits as being well on the way to perdition:

> Motivation apart, businessmen do not have the knowledge to advance the public interest directly and will serve their fellows best if they concentrate on maximising their shareholders' equity rather than promoting exports, combating global warming or solving political problems. Social responsibility is a loose cannon and is a menace to itself and others; people function best if they have specific responsibilities for which they are held accountable by means which are transparent, verifiable and respect the realities of human nature.[37]

---

[36] Jensen, R., *The Dream Society*, McGraw-Hill, 1999.

[37] Brittan, S., *Financial Times*, 1 February 1996

In an important contribution to this subject in *The Economist*, McKinsey boss Ian Davis[38] makes the point that businesses will have to take a more enlightened role on this issue in future and that the debate should not be polarised between those who agree with Milton Friedman's view that the business of business is business and that social issues have no place, and the advocates of corporate social responsibility, who place too much of a burden on businesses to solve the problems of the world. But he tends to go further than the traditional "business is business" view by arguing that social issues are central to business whether they like it or not and that business cannot effectively hide behind the view that it is up to governments to set the laws and all companies have to do is operate within these laws. In defence of the argument that social issues are central to business, he makes the valid point that if the confectionery industry had been more alert to the emergence of the obesity issue they could have saved themselves a lot of trouble. He makes three recommendations to businesses: first, they should introduce formal measures to predict and discuss emerging social trends; second, they should be more assiduous in managing their social contracts within the society in which they operate; and finally, they should be seen to play a more active role in shaping debates on social issues:

> More than two centuries ago Rousseau's social contract helped to seed the idea among political leaders that they must serve the public good lest their legitimacy be threatened — the CEOs of today's big corporations should take to opportunity to restate and reinforce their own social contracts in order to help secure for the long term the invested billions of their shareholders.[39]

---

[38] Davis, I., "The Biggest Contract", *The Economist*, 28 May 2005.
[39] Ibid.

Such an approach is obviously not without risk but if this advice was followed it seems likely that corporate reputations would be enhanced. Unless the world is heading for a major economic collapse there is every reason to believe that there will be a growing number of consumers in a growing number of markets who will choose brands with a high socially responsible quotient:

> Today, consumers are looking more closely at companies and brands, asking what they stand for and what they contribute. Particularly for high spending consumers, altruistic concerns are more prominent, and they are looking for evidence of shared values with brands. Status and ostentation are giving way to something deeper — shared values in an almost implicit assumption of good value and service. Trust, honesty and fairness are what consumers say they value in a brand. In essence today's consumers are more demanding of, expect more from and judge the organisations and brands with which they interact against a broader and deeper set of criteria.[40]

The No Logo Consumer

The prediction that the so-called brand excesses of the 1990s would give way to an anti-brand movement in the new century has been frequently made but as yet there is little evidence that it has made any impact. We frequently read about people at the cutting edge of the fashion business claiming to have cut off all of the labels that were attached to the clothes that they wear but one suspects that people in the social circle of those fashion leaders will be perfectly able to spot the brand even without the logo. The heroine of William Gibson's latest novel is a "coolhunter" who can instantly assess whether a new design or product will succeed or not. She tries to disguise the labels of her clothes with a degree of elaboration bordering on paranoia:

---

[40] Nelson, W. and Garvey, B., "Using Research to 'Futureproof' Strategies", The Future Foundation (UK), January 2005.

> A small boy's black Fruit of the Loom T-shirt, a thin grey v-necked pullover purchased by the half-dozen from a supplier to a New England prep school and a new and oversized pair of black 501's with every trademark carefully removed, even the buttons have been ground flat and featureless, by a puzzled Korean locksmith in the Village.[41]

This is all too knowing and one is left with the impression that her "personhood" is much more carefully constructed than the average person's and that far from being immune to brands she is merely trying to distance herself from anything that might be considered popular. People consume partly to suit themselves but we are all social animals and we naturally seek the approval of others. We use brands to construct identities that will be approved and the size of the logo is irrelevant to the process. It could even be argued that the size of the logo is in inverse proportion to the level of fashion knowledge in any particular social group.

The ultimate expression of the no logo movement is the Burning Man project which began in the mid-1990s on the West Coast of America as a few people having a bonfire, and grew to such proportions that it is now a week-long event in the Nevada desert, "a week-long communal gathering that alters participants' consumption meaning and practices through discourse, rules and practice".[42] During the week all commercial transactions are banned, as are brands, and participants are encouraged to exchange the goods that are needed for survival. Part art festival, part happening, part cathartic release from the pressures and tribulations of the everyday world, Burning Man represents a search for an alternative way of life to the growing and "totalising" influence of consumer markets. Markets and their accompanying shopping centres are contrasted with communities: where markets

---

[41] Gibson, W., *Pattern Recognition*, Berkley, New York, 2003.

[42] Kozinets, R.B., "Can Consumers Escape the Market? Emancipatory Illuminations from Vernon N", *Consumer Research*, Volume 29, 2002.

isolate and fragment people, communities bring them together to share; where markets cause people to become passive, communities encourage self-expression; "to simplify the contrast, ideal communities are about caring and sharing with insiders while ideal markets are about transacting with outsiders". In spite of the success of the Burning Man project there is no evidence to suggest that it has had much effect outside the relatively small group of people who partake or who are aware of it and outside of the week in which it takes place. An international "Buy Nothing Day" takes place every year but has made no impact on the public.

The Jaded Consumer

Although consumers with attitude dominate the media portrayal of the species there are some signs of consumers with *ennui* beginning to emerge. Bestsellers with titles like *The Paradox of Affluence* and *Luxury Fever* and descriptions of people suffering from "Affluenza" are indicative of a growing clamour of "If I'm so well off why am I not any happier?" Affluenza has been described as a fearful, contagious, verbally transmitted condition of overload, debt, anxiety and waste resulting from the dogged pursuit of more. (See Chapter 14 for a more detailed discussion of the "Affluence v Affluenza" debate.) There is even a more formal medical condition, "oniomania",[43] which is a diagnosed compulsive shopping disorder. It has been evident to many observers for some time that shopping or "retail therapy" was never going to be much of a substitution for more enduring values:

> I think we lost the old knowledge that happiness is over-rated — that in some way life is overrated. We have lost somehow a sense of mystery — about us, our meaning, our role. Our ancestors believed in two worlds and understood this to be the solitary, poor, nasty, brutish and short one. We are the first generation of man to actually expect to find

---

[43] http://frugalliving.about.com/cs/consumeraddiction

happiness here on earth and our search for it has caused such unhappiness.[44]

But there is also another sense of unease with our current state which is more directly related to the nature of brands and branding than to existential angst. This has to do with one of the most important benefits of brands: their ability to mark us out from other people in our immediate social group in a way that is desirable and makes us feel better about ourselves. The goods which are best suited to satisfying this need are often in finite supply; they are what economists call "positional" goods. These are goods whose satisfaction derives to some extent not only from the intrinsic satisfaction they give to the user but from the fact that they are in such short supply that they are only available to the few. The most obvious examples are original works of art that only one person can own, but there are other less expansive goods that fall into this category — e.g. some top-of-the-range cars, admittance to some private schools, tickets for certain shows or membership of certain golf clubs. Another characteristic of positional goods is that unlike other goods, their value can decrease as more people are able to afford them:

> Positional goods or status goods increase utility only at the expense of someone else consuming less of that good and the utility gains to one individual are cancelled out by the utility losses to another.[45]

There have been some suggestions that what has been referred to as "retail therapy" is beginning to lose its healing power and is being replaced by consumer fatigue. There may also be a backlash against the 1990s' "high noon" of consumerism although this is a

---

44 Noonan, P., "You'd Cry Too", *Forbes*, 14 September 1992.

45 Binswanger, N., "Why Does Growth Fail To Make Us Happier? Some Mechanisms Behind the Paradox of Happiness", Papers from Conference on "The Paradoxes of Happiness and Economics", March 2003, University of Milano-Bicocca.

forecast which is regularly trotted out but which rarely comes to pass.

Conclusions

It is impossible to predict how the times we live in will be characterised by future generations but there seems little doubt that some consideration will have to be given to the degree to which consumption of material goods and in particular the importance attached to the act of shopping played such a dominant role in people's lives in the late twentieth and early twenty-first centuries.

Although there may be some arguments about the degree of absolute control the ordinary citizen exerts over the process, there will be widespread agreement that they are the main players. They have more money than previous generations; they have access to infinitely more information than ever before; and they are more marketing-literate. If there is any manipulating to be done it will be carried out by the consumers themselves. A recent survey of consumer power in *The Economist* opened with the following statement:

> The claim that the customer is king always rang hollow, but now the digital marketplace has made it come true. Even buying a car, long considered to be one of the worst retail experiences anyone can have, is now being transformed; over 80% of Ford's customers in America have already researched their perspective purchase on the internet before they arrive at a showroom and most have come with a specification sheet showing the precise car they want from the dealer's stock and the price they are prepared to pay.[46]

Of the three potential developments among consumers discussed above, the ethical consumer is the most likely to have a major impact. In spite of, or perhaps because of, the free market fundamen-

---

[46] Markillie, P., "Crowned At Last: A Survey of Consumer Power", *The Economist*, 2 April 2005.

talists' argument that the only business of business is to maximise shareholder revenue, the most effective way to achieve that objective in the future will be to manage a business from a much more consciously ethical perspective. The no-logo consumer seems to be a non-runner. People are social animals and brands play too much of an important role in the socialisation process for them to disappear. But there will be a growing market for brands that are so discreetly designed that they don't look like brands, except to the people in the immediate circle of those attracted to "no logo"-type goods. The jaded consumer is a more likely prospect. As society becomes wealthier the paradox of affluence and the dilemma posed by the issue of positional goods will intensify. Brand management will need to become more flexible to cope with this issue and the concept of "special editions" of brands is likely to play a greater role:

> The logo mania of the late 90s is over now. There is something vaguely obscene — and not a little dumb — about spending hundreds of pounds on a designer handbag that everybody thinks is a fake from your local street market anyway. The word "luxury" has become so overused as to become completely meaningless.[47]

Whatever trends, fads or fashions emerge it now seems clear that consumers are in the driving seat and although critics of the consumer society are not going to disappear, their arguments will need to be more carefully thought out than most of them are at present if they are to have any effect:

> It has become fashionable among some commentators to condemn modern consumer culture, insisting that it sustains itself on the creation of false wants. Self-indulgence, one hears, erodes the bonds of civil society. The critics may be correct. Whatever the truth, they sound a lot like those

---

[47] Tungate, M., *Fashion Brands: Branding Style from Armani to Zara*, Kogan Page, 2004.

eighteenth-century moralists who fretted that ordinary people could not handle the temptations of the market-place. This perspective underestimates the capacity of men and women to comprehend their own political situation. It is true that goods can corrupt. But in certain circumstances they can be made to speak to power. The choice is ours to make.[48]

---

[48] Breen, T.H., *The Marketplace of Revolution: How Consumer Politics Shaped American Independence,* Oxford University Press, 2005.

13

THE FUTURE OF BRANDING

Despite changes in nomenclature and some overlap in the dates there is a reasonable level of agreement that the history of branding can be divided roughly into the following three stages:

- **Stage 1:** Rational/Functional Age — 1900–1950s

- **Stage 2:** Emotional Age — 1950–1990s

- **Stage 3:** Conceptual/Intellectual/Philosophical Age — 1990– ?

There is no reason why the third age of branding won't be around for some time but competition is unrelenting and some brands will always be trying to enter uncharted waters to gain a competitive advantage. Apart from the obvious desire to differentiate oneself from competitors there is now an additional need to break new ground: the increasing marketing sophistication and jaded media palettes of the public. Conducting qualitative research among any young target audience about new advertising campaigns is the equivalent of being confronted with a group of Quentin Tarantinos who are all experts in production techniques and filmic references. They are also no slouches when it comes to deconstructing marketing strategies. Attracting their attention and keeping them interested involves a constant search for new stimuli.

What follows is a run-through of some possible routes that may be worth investigating in the search for new brand communication strategies.

CULTURAL BRANDING

This is undoubtedly the most intriguing new direction and is the subject of one of the most important contributions to the study of branding in recent years, *How Brands Become Icons* by Professor Douglas Holt.[1] According to Holt the most successful brands in the future will be the ones that engage in what he refers to as "cultural branding". They will compete with other cultural products — TV programmes, films, music, sports, video games and books — and will therefore have to understand the underlying issues that pre-occupy the society in which they operate. He illustrates his thesis with an analysis of the advertising history of some iconic American brands and argues that without understanding the societal changes and cultural issues that were current at the time, it would be impossible to understand the reasons for the success of these brands. His acute observations on the evolution of VW advertising since the classic Bill Bernbach press ads of the 1960s, "Think Small" and "Lemon", is a convincing argument for his case:

> Iconic brands provide extraordinary identity value because
> they address the collective anxieties and desires of a nation
> — the foundational premise of the cultural branding model
> is that iconic brands perform national identity myths that
> resolve cultural contradictions.[2]

In order to create an iconic brand through cultural branding we have to study cultural history and examine how it has created the issues that underlie the social tensions and cultural discourses of the day.

Holt presents a four-point plan for starting the process of cultural branding: firstly, identify a cultural contradiction in society; secondly, act as a cultural activist; then create an original cultural

---

[1] Holt, D., *How Brands Become Icons*, Harvard Business School Press, 2003.
[2] Ibid.

expression from that contradiction; and finally develop an authentic populist voice to express a viewpoint.

America is a country rich in myths that sustain that society and provide an endless supply of material for cultural branding. The rugged individualism of the frontier and the communal experience of the melting pot have been plundered many times to create iconic American brands and because of the power of Hollywood many of these brands have been successfully exported around the world. Ireland does not share any of those myths and one of Seamus Heaney's best-known poems describes our dilemma:

> We have no prairies
> To slice a big sun at evening —
> Everywhere the eye concedes to
> Encroaching horizon,
>
> Is wooed into the cyclops' eye
> Of a tarn. Our unfenced country
> Is bog that keeps crusting
> Between the sights of the sun.[3]

Perhaps one of the most central issues of cultural discourse in Ireland has been emigration. It has been the subject of every conceivable type of artistic expression over the years — film, plays, poetry, sculpture, novels, not to mention some of the most memorable as well as maudlin music. A number of Irish brands have appropriated the theme from time to time so we do have some experience of cultural branding. The best example was the brilliantly executed ESB commercial, "Going Home" from the mid-1980s. In this commercial all the obvious themes of emigration were on display, the son "hero" returning home for a visit, being driven from the airport/harbour/station by Dad, casting a wry eye out of the car window at signs of progress in the old home town, all intercut with the anxious and proud mother bustling around the house, her ex-

---

[3] Heaney, S., *Door Into The Dark*, Faber and Faber, 1969.

clusive domain, making the last-minute preparations, patting the fresh bed linen, baking the brown bread, all courtesy of the advertiser. The soundtrack was an integral part of the whole: the haunting voice, the evocative lyrics:

> I think I'm goin' back to the things I learned so well / in my youth I think I'm returning to / those days when I was young enough to know the truth.[4]

The final subtle touch was the singer: our very own Mary Isobel Catherine Bernadette O'Brien, aka the incomparable Dusty Springfield, the London-born daughter of Irish emigrants.

Although emigration is still a factor in Irish life, the remarkable economic transformation of the last decade has removed some emotive power from the issue as we now grapple with problems that rapid prosperity brings in its wake. Irish society has been transformed in a very short space of time, leading one academic to comment that "Irish society has undergone two transformations in recent history: one in the 1890s with the creation of nationalist Ireland, and another in the 1990s with the creation of neo-liberal Ireland, also known as the Celtic Tiger".[5] As result there is no shortage of "cultural contradictions" in contemporary Irish society and therefore no excuses for not trying to make use of these changes to build stronger brands. These "cultural contradictions" are described in the final chapter.

Notable Examples of Cultural Branding
Camper

The shoe brand from Majorca advocates a Mediterranean way of life, exemplified by their slogan, "walk don't run". Although the shoes are designed with comfort and durability rather than fashion

---

4 Copy from ESB advertisement "Going Home", 1985.

5 Haahr, M. "The Art/Technology Interface: Innovation and Identity in Information-Age Ireland", *The Irish Review*. No.31, Spring-Summer 2004.

in mind they have become a high-fashion item and the brand now has over 80 stores worldwide. Their managing director is reported to have said, "Camper's ambition is to have not simply commercial success but to act as a cultural influence"[6] and the brand is built around the idea of slowing down, walking instead of frantically rushing everywhere and generally taking life a little easier.

Kit-Kat

The brand recently changed the format of its long-running "Have a break, have a Kit-Kat" campaign to a more overt reference to resolving a "cultural" contradiction. Instead of merely suggesting to people to take a break, they started to act as a cultural activist by suggesting that people were not taking enough breaks. In a key commercial for this campaign, a presenter talks straight to camera as he describes the life of a salmon:

> The Salmon. The Salmon spends its life relentlessly striving to get upstream. In ceaseless endeavour, it fights the currents of massive rivers, drags itself over rocks and shallow water, forces its way up huge waterfalls, never stops, never rests, just battles and battles its way upstream; finally, heroically, reaches its goal and is absolutely knackered, and it dies. Remember, you are not a salmon. Have a break, have a Kit-Kat.[7]

Power's Gold Label

The theme of this campaign is summed up in a phrase attributed to the photographer Henri Cartier-Bresson: "Intensity is more important than longevity." The brand is regarded as the quintessential Irish whiskey, with an uncompromising full-bodied taste, so it complements the message of living life to the full. The narrator in a recent theme commercial expressed the idea as follows:

---

[6] www.camper.com

[7] Copy from Kit Kat "Salmon" ad, 2004.

I will embrace each day. I will make more journeys. I will leave home without a map. I will arrive with less baggage. I will go to those places I have never been. I will take more chances. I will open my eyes. I will listen. I won't abandon my roots. I will never settle for less.[8]

FUSION BRANDING

If cultural branding represents a logical step forward from most of the components of the third age of branding, fusion branding is a return to basics. The author of a book on the subject, Nick Wreden,[9] believes not only that marketing communications will be of very little relevance for successful branding in the future but that the whole marketing concept will not be the critical factor. Instead he argues that operational excellence and in particular logistical superiority will be the main drivers of successful brands as the public force businesses into higher standards of service. Quality, service fulfilment and innovation over time will be essential and the supply chain will become a critical issue.

As always, societal changes are behind the logic of this analysis. People have more disposable money, but less disposable time. Because of this they are prepared to pay a little extra for quality products that save time. The growth of the ready-to-eat meal market is ample testament to that and the fact that the "risen people" will now pay to have their lettuce leaves washed for them rather than buy a head of lettuce and wash it themselves shows the extent of "time poverty" in the brave new world of prosperous Ireland.

A second area of change is in the level of service expectations which have risen dramatically after decades of an "ah, sure it'll do" attitude. In the 1970s and 1980s the Dublin-based supermarket group Superquinn raised people's expectation of service through

---

[8] Copy from Power "I Will" ad, 2003.

[9] Wreden, N., *Fusion Branding: How to Forge Your Brand for the Future*, Wiley. 2001.

their own high standards, continuous innovations and regular feedback from consumers, whose gripes were noted and acted upon and whose suggestions were implemented. All businesses must now do everything they can to improve service levels but service quality is a beast with a voracious appetite and is never satisfied. If you embark on the road to better service, you have to accept that your journey will never end and you will have to increase your speed progressively.

The third area of change is the internet and the telecommunications revolution in general which means you can never switch off, because there is always a customer somewhere who is switched on. The new technology is a double-edged sword; it enables businesses to provide a better, more immediate and more personal service to its customers but it enables customers to demand more at the same time. Amazon is a classic fusion brand, which has been built on the basis of personalised customer service and supply chain excellence rather than more traditional marketing communications.

The thinking behind fusion branding is that service levels rather than physical innovations will determine business success in the future. New product innovations will be replicated within such a short time period that the only sustainable difference will be service quality.

Tesco's well documented "every little helps" campaign is a classic case study in fusion branding. Between 1990 and 1999, Tesco's share of the UK grocery market increased from 9.1% to 15.4%,[10] overtaking Sainsbury's along the way in 1995 to become the brand leader. Sainsbury's main strength had been their unrivalled reputation for quality and the first stage in the new Tesco strategy in the early part of the 1990s was to concentrate on improving quality and upgrading stores and merchandise. Once

---

[10] Sharpe, A. and Bamford, J., "How 'Every Little Helps' was a Great Help to Tesco", *Advertising Works*, 11 WARC 2000.

management were confident that they could exceed or at least match the competition on quality they launched the "every little helps" campaign in 1993. Over 100 new initiatives were introduced, including baby-changing facilities, removal of sweets from checkouts, a new value range and Clubcard.

The following survey results show the extent to which the image of the Tesco brand improved across a range of attributes.

Table 8: Tesco's Brand Image Improvement, 1990–2000[11]

	1990 (% agreeing)	2000 (% agreeing)
Always introducing new ideas	28	31
Stocks a wide range of products	23	47
Has competitive low prices	23	36
Offers good value for money	21	37
Has friendly approachable staff	19	40
Has high quality products overall	17	40

A new book by Patrick Barwise and Sean Meehan of the London Business School takes the argument for fusion branding a little further by suggesting that consumers are rarely looking for something unique; in many markets they are more concerned with making sure everything works and will buy the brand that satisfies the basic requirements of the product or service sector in question if it performs a little better than the competition: "What customers really value is product and service quality, simplicity, convenience, reliability and reasonable value for money."[12] They challenge the conventional wisdom that it is impossible to differentiate the basics and that you have to either have some major branding initia-

---

[11] Ibid.

[12] Barwise, P. and Mehan, S., *Simply Better*, London University Press, 2004.

tive through a marketing communications breakthrough or change the rules of the market to gain a competitive advantage. They cite Toyota and Orange as examples of two businesses who manage the basics of their respective markets better than their competitors and who have out-performed them as a result. The essence of their argument, and that of fusion branding as a whole, is summarised by their conclusion from the Orange case study; the first priority should be to deliver the generic category benefits better than the competition. You don't have to be the category pioneer but you should aim to be the first with genuine product/ service improvements.

Notable Examples of Fusion Branding
Toyota

This brand has been one of the best-selling marques in the Irish market for over twenty years. The original success of the brand was due to the superior range of extras offered at competitive prices combined with an unrivalled reputation for reliability. As the other marques improved their range of extras and their reliability, Toyota began to capitalise on their superior engineering excellence with the slogan, "The Best Built Cars in the World". This campaign theme was introduced in Ireland in the early 1990s and has been running ever since, augmented by the continuous technical innovations that Toyota has introduced.

Superquinn

Although Tesco are usually cited as the fusion brand *par excellence* a case could be made for Superquinn especially in the 1980s and early 1990s when their founder and chief executive, Fergal Quinn, introduced a continuous series of service initiatives which made them the most admired company in Ireland at the time.

Many of these initiatives are described in Quinn's book *Crowning the Consumer*.[13]

Amazon

The three main characteristics of the best fusion brands are "immediacy", "personalisation", and "reach".[14] Amazon is one of the prime examples of all three — books can be ordered at any time, from anywhere and once you've made contact with them you are greeted by your first name from then on and given suggestions about new books that might be of interest to you on the basis of previous orders.

QUAKER BRANDING

If it didn't sound too much like the title of a Thomas Hardy novel, this section could be called "The Return of the Quaker". Now that the history of branding is attracting more attention we have become more aware of the remarkable number of brands introduced over a century ago, and still household names today, that were founded by individuals inspired more by the ethically based Quaker approach to business than the maximising shareholder value ethos that predominates in today's business environment. Hershey in the US, Cadbury in the UK, Jacobson (who founded Carlsberg) in Denmark and Bewley and Jacob in Ireland all started their businesses with the primary objective of the general betterment of society and in particular the alleviation of poverty in their immediate vicinity.

Although their entrepreneurial initiatives show no sign of being replicated in the twenty-first century, there are signs that the fundamentalist free market "take-no-prisoners while you maximise shareholder revenue" attitude that characterised the last

---

13 Quinn, F., *Crowning the Customer*, O'Brien Press, 1990.
14 Wreden, Ibid.

decades of the twentieth century may be coming to an end. Long-established brands are all owned now by publicly quoted companies who give unswerving allegiance to extracting the maximum profit from their businesses but many of the successful new enterprises take a more relaxed approach and allocate part of their profits, their expertise and their time to community projects and other good causes. Scandinavian brand commentators have been to the fore in propagating this movement in recent years.

> True, there is a compelling argument to be made that investors buy shares for financial gain, not for any other reason. But there's growing evidence that this dynamic is changing, that other concerns of investors and the demands of other stakeholders are taking a more active role in determining the value of a business in the world and that financial performance is increasingly dependent on multiple measures of trust and goodwill among stakeholders.[15]

It has also been pointed out that the command-and-control model of management which was a product of the industrial age is not going to work in the information or knowledge age where "the workers" have now completed Marx's historic objective by owning the means of production — creativity and relationship networks, as well as knowledge and expertise. But the real instigators of a possible move towards more ethical branding are the public at large who, while showing a declining level of interest in traditional political parties, are at the same time joining political interest groups in greater numbers than ever. From international groups like Greenpeace and Amnesty International to local groups like Coastwatch and Goal, people are finding more satisfactory political outlets in these organisations. Some commentators believe that there will be an accompanying market for convictions with people wanting to buy brands that are in some way associated with or actively

---

[15] Myers, D., "Whose Brand is it Anyway?" Chapter in *Beyond Branding*, Ind, N. (ed.), Kogan Page, 2003.

involved in ecology, the environment, human rights, or local community groups, and that it will therefore come as no surprise that:

> . . . companies will gradually enter the market for convictions; the curtain has definitely closed on the era when a company's sole objective was profitability, that type of game, the one with rational rules, is over, and a new game is beginning, with new rules and they are more complex, they still involve the imperative of profitability but on top of this comes a choice of convictions.[16]

In an essay in the book *Beyond Branding*,[17] Denzil Meyers describes four industrial-era practices which he believes will be damaging to businesses and brands who continue to adopt them in the new knowledge era:

- Disregard for finite raw materials and the environment in general;

- Employees seen as costs to be invested in as little as possible;

- Seeking to dominate markets by marketing communications;

- Fiscal sleight-of-hand to minimise tax.

A further impetus to a more Quaker-inspired approach to business is the move towards greater transparency and accountability.

Ireland's Minister of Finance during the economic boom of the mid- and late-1990s, Charlie McCreevy, once referred somewhat sarcastically to the Goddess OTA — the new demand for openness, transparency and accountability. Although he was voicing some doubts about the validity of these so-called virtues and no doubt questioning the motives of their proponents there seems little doubt that demands for ethical business practices will grow.

---

[16] Jensen, R., *The Dream Society*, McGraw Hill, 1999.
[17] Myers, Ibid.

Notable Examples of Quaker Branding

Body Shop

Body Shop is one of the best-known examples of ethical or Quaker branding. This brand was specifically set up to provide cosmetics that were made from raw materials which cause minimal damage to wildlife or the environment and the company has always supported small producer communities in underdeveloped countries which supply natural ingredients.

The core values of the brand are highly political and the company believe that the more successful the brand becomes, the more the world will change for the better.

Cafédirect

Cafédirect is a roast and ground coffee brand established in the UK in 1991 to provide better prices and a more stable trading relationship for coffee producers in mainly developing countries. Now a £100 million company and the third biggest brand in the UK roast and ground coffee market, it buys direct from 33 producer organisations in 11 countries, ensuring that over a quarter of a million growers receive a fair income. A percentage of gross profits, eight per cent in 2003, is given back to producer partners' organisations.[18]

Co-operative Bank

In the early 1990s Co-operative Bank occupied a very small space (two per cent market share) in the newly deregulated British financial services market. Faced with a declining market share, the bank decided to capitalise on its ethical heritage and invited its 30,000 customers to express their opinion on the issues that most concerned them. This led to a new investment policy which included a list of industries, countries, and companies that the bank

---

[18] Ahonen, T. and Moore, A., "Communities Dominate Brands", Future Text (UK), 2005.

would not invest in. They then ran advertisements explaining their investment policy which resulted in a rise in retail customer deposits from £1 billion in 1993 to £6 billion in 2003.[19]

POSITIONAL BRANDING

Like Quaker branding, this is a category that is likely to grow in the future but as yet there are not many detailed case histories. The title comes from an influential book[20] by the economist Fred Hirsch in which he discussed the paradox of affluence twenty years before it became a preoccupation of the chattering classes. He noted that as the average level of consumption rises an increasing proportion takes on a social role. Those of us involved in branding on a day-to-day basis would argue that all consumption involves a social role but Hirsch wasn't concerned with brands; the concept was never discussed outside marketing communications circles in the 1970s. He was trying to come to terms with the implications of a declining level of satisfaction with goods of all kinds as more people were able to afford them. The tourist market is the most obvious example; the phrase "tourists degrade tourism" has been used to describe the phenomenon where the more people who are attracted to an amenity, the less enjoyment there is for everyone as a result of congestion and overcrowding . From a brand perspective, the most telling point in the book is when the author quotes Keynes's distinction between "these needs which are absolute in the sense that we feel them whatever the situation of our fellow human beings may be, and those which are relative in the sense that we feel them only if their satisfaction lifts us above, makes us feel superior to our fellows".[21] This is a pretty astute observation today but the fact that it was made in 1930 is am-

---

[19] Edward, M. and Day, D., *Creating Fashion Brands*, Kogan Page, 2005.
[20] Hirsch, F., *Social Limits to Growth*, Routledge & Kegan Paul, 1977.
[21] Ibid.

ple testament to Keynes's genius. Positional brands make us "feel superior to our fellows".

Increasing wealth will mean increasing demand for positional goods and positional branding will become more important in future. Such brands include goods that are in finite supply (e.g. certain wine vintages); or goods that are unavailable in a particular market and can only be obtained by travelling abroad (e.g. anything with the Abercrombie & Fitch label); and goods that are so expensive that only a small minority of the population could afford them (e.g. Lotus Elise cars).

If we accept that the desire to "feel superior to our fellows" has always formed a part of human nature but that it is only in the relatively recent past that a majority of the population had the disposable income to use the purchase of goods for this purpose, it should follow that more people will be searching for more positional brands in future.

The market that has responded best to this need is an unlikely one: specialist publishers. They have published hardback and paperback editions for many years but more recently such publishers have begun to add a limited specially produced signed edition in special slipcases. If the hardback sells for between €20 and €30, the special can sell for up to €500. People willingly pay the amount; special editions are usually oversubscribed, partly because they want to own something that only a few people will have in their possession and partly because there is a very real chance of capital appreciation.

The drinks industry has dabbled in the area of positional goods and Irish Distillers' Middleton Reserve is an example. Car companies have also dipped their toe in the water with a number of limited edition models and vintage cars are a classic case of positional goods. Even the world's most powerful brand, Coca Cola, has commissioned the über-cool fashion designer Mathew Williamson to produce limited edition bottle designs. It is a strategic approach that we are likely to see more of as businesses wake up to the fact that more people can now afford to pay for goods that will enable them to feel superior to their contemporaries.

Notable Examples of Positional Branding
Ravida Sicilian

This is a brand of sea salt in the US market that sells for fifty times the price of ordinary sea salts. There are an increasing number of food brands whose main selling platform is exclusive distribution combined with a vast price premium over competitive brands. Claims of authenticity, purity and all kinds of "curative" properties will also be included in the brand promise but price and exclusivity are the most important selling attributes.

Puma

Puma has managed to differentiate itself from more powerful rivals Nike and Adidas by charging higher prices and creating regular limited additions. Only 888 pairs of its Shudoh Tang sneakers were ever made.[22]

Bathing Cape

This is a cult brand known to aficionados as "Bape" — Japanese t-shirts and baseball caps decorated with a simian face and retailing for around €80. The brand shuns endorsements and advertising and is only on limited distribution, thus enabling those "in the know" to retain an aura of cultural superiority.

TRICKSTER BRANDING

Increasing doubts are being expressed about the degree of influence that marketing departments actually have over the markets they purport to "control". In the process, one of the founding fa-

---

[22] Tungate, M., *Fashion Brands: Branding Style from Armani to Zara*, Kogan Page, 2004.

thers of marketing, Professor Philip Kottler, whose monumental textbook *Marketing Management* is now in its sixth edition and has been studied by generations of marketing students all over the world, has come in for the type of criticism only academics are able to deliver:

> Kottler's *Marketing Places* is a half-baked hack work of the lowest order, it exhibits not a shred, not a smidgen, not a scintilla of scholarship or academic rigour; it is a gruesome melange of tired and tested truisms, re-heated anecdotes, bogus recommendations, pseudo insights, specious check-lists and the sort of simplistic sloganeering that even Tom Peters would be disinclined to dispense.[23]

The backlash against traditional marketing theory is based on the view that it assumes too much power, and that the analysis, planning, implementation and control model that underlies much of marketing theory hopelessly exaggerates the power we actually have.

The most vociferous critic of the command-and-control view of marketing is Stephen Brown, a Business Professor at The University of Ulster, who is quoted above, and who has been a consistent thorn in the side of conventional marketing in a series of books during the last decade. Brown sees conventional marketing as an essentially positivist discipline, seeking the Holy Grail of universal laws and objective knowledge, desperate for scientific respectability, and in the process suffering from a severe dose of "physics envy". His most consistent theme is that this type of thinking is modernist, whereas the world has moved, for better or worse, into a post-modern era. Modernism was characterised by the primacy of reason, empiricism, science and universalism and dated from the Enlightenment to the early part of the twentieth century, when it faced a backlash from the growing post-modernist movement. Modern science was

---

[23] Brown, Stephen, *Post Modern Marketing II*, Thompson Business Press, 1998.

undermined in the twentieth century by developments in thermo-dynamics, quantum physics and chaos theory. All three develop-ments challenged the scientific certainties of an earlier era and sug-gested that the world is more unpredictable and less amenable to precise calculation than was previously envisaged. Brown argues that if the world of science is now so unpredictable, then surely the idea of attempting to introduce an element of mathematical purity into marketing is doomed to failure!

Brown believes so and this line of thinking eventually led him to the belief that the nineteenth century rather than the twentieth century was the hey-day of marketing. He rubbishes the notion that we could ever be "close to the consumer" and puts forward the alternative view that consumers basically don't know what they really want but that the last thing they do want is a "relationship" with a brand. All we can usefully do is to entertain people — hence his admiration for nineteenth-century marketing exemplified by the travelling snake-oil salesmen of the American West. No one really believed any of the sales pitch of the snake-oil medicine men but people were willing to suspend their disbelief for a bit of enter-tainment, a welcome amusing break from the ordinary and the fleeting possibility that there was a "miracle" cure for baldness. Brown elevates P.T. Barnum, of the famous Barnum and Bailey, as the "Everest, the Einstein, the Edison of consumer exploitation". Barnum's motto, or vision statement in today's language, was that "there's one born every minute".

Brown believes that modern marketing's greatest failure is a lack of entertainment. Consumers want to be entertained, teased, and are even prepared to be tricked. This brings us to the subject of the Trickster, a well known figure in psychological and anthro-pological literature, which is supposed to represent:

> . . . the part of ourselves that secretly desires the fantastic, representing our wishes for exaggeration, seduction and es-cape from the mundanities and tragedies of everyday life — the Trickster is the spirit of disorder, and enemy of bounda-

ries, law and order everywhere — the Trickster represents protest and the pleasures of illogic and chaos.[24]

It has been claimed that the concept of the trickster is as much a part of humanity as the concept of God. It is the spirit that allows us to break out of the conformity imposed upon us by the constraints of family, job and predominant culture, or our own personalities. The trickster within us exists to question, to poke fun at authority and generally play with existing conventions. A well-known example was the role of the court jester in medieval times, who could say things in the hearing of royalty that others could not — a function which some of today's rulers could well re-introduce.

If the intellectual underpinning of the trickster brand is the universal nature of the concept since the beginning of time, on the one hand, and the nature of our new post-modern era on the other, there is also a more practical and pressing reason for a renewed interest in the subject: the increasing difficulty of attracting the attention of a very media- and marketing-literate consumer in an era of declining audiences for the mass media. Although the trickster may be an ambiguous, dangerous and often foolish figure, the jester, the clown and the magician always manage to attract attention. They also fulfil another important task in modern communications; they entertain. We will probably be seeing a lot more of them.

Notable Examples of Trickster Branding

Ryanair

Ryanair could be considered a classic Trickster brand. It ignores all the accepted best practice rules and conventions of marketing, especially the current obsession with "consumer-centricity". Instead of being "passionate about the consumer" the company seems to go out of its way to antagonise them. But it's a very subtle

---

[24] Cooper, P., "The Trickster: Creativity in Modern Advertising and Branding", Market Research Annual Conference, 2000.

strategy, because it exemplifies the core positioning of the brand: a low-cost, no-frills airline. The chief executive, Micheal O'Leary, also epitomises the Trickster figure with his aviator-showman stereotype persona.

Budweiser

The Budweiser "Frogs" campaign from the early 1990s was a classic example of the subversive nature of trickster advertising. In literature the trickster often takes on half-human, half-animal form. The rationale for the trickster is based on being allowed to say things that in normal circumstances would not be tolerated. The cynical dialogue indulged in by the "frogs" would not have been tolerated by humans in a beer commercial.

Diesel

Founded by a young man from rural Sicily, Renzo Rosso, who "ran up a pair of jeans on his mother's sewing machine and went on to build a global brand".[25] Diesel is a self-proclaimed anti-fashion brand whose advertising relies on irony to make acerbic comment on western society.

PURITAN BRANDING

In times of economic prosperity and consumption excess there is inevitably a backlash; enter the new puritans or the more wittily designated "Neo-Croms". To some extent they have always been with us; there have always been critics of the consumer society, but the rise of global brands and the relentless focus on brands in the mass media has created an opportunity for brands that make a virtue out of downplaying their brand credentials. As usual, there is an element of one-upmanship going on here. Once previously exclusive brands become affordable by the mass market, they lose their

---

[25] Tungate, ibid.

cachet. Fashion has been described as "gentility running away from vulgarity and afraid of being overtaken" and a recent example of this phenomenon was the problems encountered by the long established iconic British fashion brand Burberry because it suddenly became part of the uniform of a young underclass known as "chavs". Chavs are generally derided as intellectually challenged, jobless, tasteless and slightly sinister and are easily identified by their predilection for trainers, baseball caps and masses of cheap gold jewellery. Their surprise adoption of the famous Burberry plaid as a uniform *de jour* risked frightening their traditional upmarket customers when the practice became widespread in 2004. Luckily for Burberry, chavs are fickle followers of fashion and having moved on to a new fad the upmarket label can return to dignified normality.

Widespread acceptance by a mass audience of something once enjoyed exclusively by the cognoscenti always creates problems. Instead of a feeling of pride that their taste is being recognised by more people they are likely to experience a sense of disappointment. Familiarity breeds contempt. A good example of this phenomenon is the disdain felt by lovers of baroque music for Albinoni's *Adagio in G minor* because of its recent rise in popularity among a much wider audience. The cognoscenti in any field will always want to be ahead of the pack and the fact that increasing prosperity, leisure time and education is widening membership of "the pack" means there will be more opportunities for astute brand owners to market niche brands to discerning audiences. If these niche brands can somehow be positioned as being non-conspicuous, environmentally friendly and authentic, they will be even more successful. The final icing on the cake would be to somehow ensure that the brand is "cool", an incredibly difficult task:

> Cool is any form of self-expression that stimulates another
> person to wonder "what if" and motivates the other person

319

to go through the process of adopting the witnessed form of self-expression and re-appropriating it as their own style.[26]

It could be argued that puritan branding is no different than positional branding and there are undoubtedly similarities but there is a crucial distinction; the neo-croms are more environmentally concerned and are motivated by an anti-fashion, anti-consumption ethic which in turn makes them automatically suspicious of well-known brand names. They are easily and frequently satirised:

> Buying big limousines and power boats was crass but it was virtuous to practise the perfectionism of small things — for example devoting fanatical attention to the purchase of exactly the right kind of pasta strainer, a distinctive doorknob or an ingeniously designed corkscrew. Similarly it is now far too vulgar to be seen buying champagne. It is, however, a sign of good taste if you are prepared to spend huge amounts of money on a bag of potatoes or a lump of pig-meat. Ideally, of course, these should be cooked in an oven fired with carefully selected pieces of heritage coal lovingly hand-mined from a rare seam near a hamlet in South Wales and transported by horse and cart to the city. Yes, it costs a fortune but you wouldn't believe how much it enhances your food's flavour, texture and goodness.[27]

Notable Examples of Puritan Branding

Muji

This well-known Japanese label has some claim to be the original puritan brand. Now 25 years old, its original name was Mujirushi (no brand) Ryohin (quality goods). It has now spread to Europe with 15 shops in the UK and a small one in Dublin. There are a wide variety of products in the Muji range and their stores have been de-

---

[26] Gaskins, G., "The Science of Cool", *The Advertiser*, November 2003.

[27] Tomkins, R., *Financial Times*, 11 November 2005.

scribed as "Woolworths meets Marks and Spencer meets John Lewis".[28] Colours are relentlessly neutral but they employ world-famous designers and their products represent a pared-down minimalist aesthetic that is particularly attractive to the neo-croms.

American Apparel

A Los Angeles-based brand producing high-quality fitted modern t-shirts, jerseys and sweatshirts which contain no marks, logos or insignia or anything which would identify them as an American Apparel product. The brand also trades heavily on the fact that it is based in a downtown area of a major American city and has not contracted out production to sweatshops in Third World countries. This brand has recorded huge growth in sales in recent years but its controversial advertising and catalogues may have as much to do with the brand's success as its no-logo stance: "To look at an American Apparel catalogue or ad is to look at the closest thing there is to amateur porn without it actually being amateur porn."[29]

Farmers' Markets

These are a favourite haunt of the neo-croms. Having started some time ago from humble backgrounds with modest ambitions they are now mushrooming all over the place and there are estimated to be fifteen in Dublin alone selling a wide range of unbranded food, clothes and other products. They are of course "unbranded" only in the conventional sense; they are not made by big businesses and don't have widely recognisable brand names. But they are brands, often with very professional "stories". Neo-croms become attached to their favourite suppliers at these markets in exactly the same way that shoppers in mainstream supermarkets do.

---

[28] Rattray, F., "Your life in their Hands", *Observer*, 18 September 2005.
[29] Saver, A., "American Apparel: All Sweaty", Brandchannel.com.

Conclusions

Brand success in the future will almost certainly necessitate being prepared to follow one or more of the five potential strategies outlined above. It should also be made clear they are not mutually exclusive strategies. Many brands could adopt more than one approach and to some extent it could be argued that brands that do not have a strong element of "fusion" about them will eventually fail. Public tolerance for any shortcomings in operational and logistical excellence is low and even if this approach is not the core of a brand's positioning, it would still be expected to score highly on this dimension. The same will also probably be true for the Quaker approach.

In fact one could envisage a "super-brand" of the future as being socially responsible (Quaker), operationally first rate (Fusion), in limited supply (Positional), environmentally friendly and understated (Puritan) communicating its values in an anarchic and outrageous humourous way (Trickster), that provides cultural solutions for the society in which it operates (Cultural).

14

SIX CULTURAL CONTRADICTIONS IN TWENTY-FIRST-CENTURY IRELAND

The previous chapter described six possible directions for branding in the twenty-first century. The first and probably the most important is cultural branding, where marketing communications are based on cultural contradictions in the society in which the brand operates. A good example would be the widely discussed "cash rich, time poor" issue which is being experienced by significant sections of the population in many Western societies. A variety of brands, in particular food brands, have been positioned as potential solutions to this "contradiction".

Irish society has probably undergone more profound changes in the last decade than any in living memory and offers a rich source of potential material for resolving "cultural contradictions". A number of them are identified and outlined in this chapter.

(1) Freedom vs Restraint

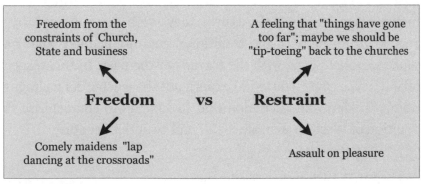

Sexual intercourse, which famously began in Britain in 1963, took a little longer to reach Irish shores but by the 1990s both church and state had been forcibly ejected from a large number of Irish homes, prompting suggestions that it began in Ireland in 1993, although this ignored the famous outcry in the 1960s by a frustrated politician that there was "no sex in Ireland before *The Late Late Show*". One of the most dramatic illustrations of our changing sexual mores was the percentage of live births outside marriage, which in 1988 was well below the European average — 12 per cent compared to 18 per cent — but by the end of the 1990s was marginally ahead, having more than doubled to 28 per cent compared to the European average of 26 per cent; and by 2005 the figure had reached 34 per cent.[1] The succession of sexual scandals involving senior clerical figures at the time weakened the authority of the once all-powerful Catholic Church and the revelations of financial impropriety and unambiguous corruption at senior levels of the political, civil service and business establishments put a further strain on all forms of authority in Irish society.

The sudden change from one of the most socially conservative societies in Europe to a much more liberated society was bound to create tensions. The most obvious fault-line was between young and old and on a wide range of issues the main divide in market research surveys carried out during the 1990s was not between urban and rural, or between the social classes but between the under- and over-forties. But to some extent everyone felt the pressure, because although the transformation of the economic fortunes of the country were largely progressive, they were accompanied by a breakdown in many of the traditional comfort blankets that had helped people to cope with the travails of the past. In this respect, Ireland in the 1990s started to experience the existential feelings of anomie, anxiety and alienation that had begun to characterise the condition of Western man since the mid-twentieth century:

---

[1] CSO Report, "Vital Statistics", Quarter One 2005.

> To be modern is to find ourselves in an environment that promises us adventure, power, joy, growth, transformation of ourselves and the world, and at the same time, that threatens to destroy everything we have, everything we know, everything we are.[2]

There are, perhaps inevitably, signs of a backlash and as people try to come to terms with the pace of change they begin to wonder if the baby has been thrown out with the bathwater. Few people are prepared to question the desirability of the new Ireland, few people are under any illusions about the real nature of Irish society in the past, but a few heads are beginning to appear above the parapet, notably the Ombudswoman, Emily O'Reilly, who articulated the feelings of many in a widely reported speech at the Céifin annual conference in November 2004:

> Why are we still whingeing? Why after that gargantuan transformation of public and private life in a direction that many of the country's most thoughtful and concerned citizens wished for, is there still an enormous disquiet about the nature of our Irish society and the sort of people we have become. It would be good if we recognised the new religions of sex and drink and shopping for what they are and tiptoed back to the churches. It may not even be necessary to believe; it may be sufficient just to remind ourselves of some of the universal truths about charity and decency and how to live a good life, all of which are contained in the teachings of the major religions.[3]

Another aspect of the backlash is the increasing pressure on politicians to curb some of the excesses — binge drinking, speeding, obesity — through legislation. We are by no means alone in this development, which has been dubbed the "assault on pleasure" in the UK.

---

[2] Mazarr, M., *Global Trends: 2005*, Macmillan Press, 1999.

[3] O' Reilly, E., "Imagining the Future: An Irish Perspective", Annual Céifin Conference, 2004.

Any brand considering using this "cultural contradiction" would need to tread warily, because although it is an issue bubbling under the surface of many people's minds, it can be very emotional and confusing. A number of food brands have tentatively played with the notion of "the taste you thought had gone forever", but the problem for most of the food we buy nowadays is that it bears little resemblance to the taste of the past. Contrasting the present with a romanticised idyllic rustic past is a standard ploy of brand owners in other markets, especially the UK and US, but the wounds of our past are still too raw for the strategy to work in this market. But as long as this issue is on people's minds, it will remain a potentially powerful way to gain attention if it can be introduced in a credible way. Probably the most fruitful route would be to assess whether our products or services can be positioned as providing some kind of balance between the present and some of the good things from the past; sometimes it is only when we are freed from tradition that we can appreciate the advantages of integrity, authenticity and continuity.

(2) Individualism vs Community

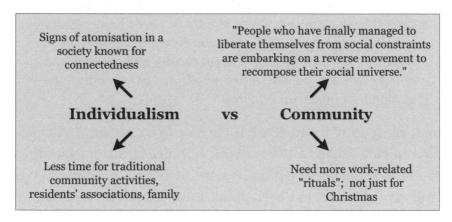

The rise of individualism has been one of the most significant developments in the Western world in the last half century but it was to some extent dependent on a rise in living standards, so like some of the other trappings of modernity it was a little late arriving in Ireland. When it did arrive in the 1990s it created a certain amount of tension in a society that had always been characterised by close family and community ties:

> The emergence of informational capitalism and Ireland's semi-peripheral integration into it brings to the fore a cultural discourse prioritising individualism, entrepreneurship, flexibility, innovation, mobility and competitiveness both as personal attributes to be cultivated by the individual and as dominant social values. These displace earlier discourses prioritising national identity, family, self-sacrifice and nationalism.[4]

A dramatic illustration of the change was the phenomenon in the main cities of commuters who were now sharing two of the three main meals of the day with work colleagues and only one with their families, with breakfast being brought into work or bought along the way to avoid early morning traffic congestion, and lunch consumed at the desk. Inevitably, family and community ties weakened as work colleagues became the new "family". Work-related rituals became a monthly, even weekly, event and office parties were no longer confined to Christmas.

The decline of involvement in local community activities has been well-documented in the US by Professor Robert Putnam, whose *Bowling Alone*[5] thesis pointed out the dangers to a healthy society caused by fewer people having the time or inclination to participate. But man is a social animal and if traditional outlets are denied then new outlets will emerge: "people who have finally managed to liberate themselves from social constraints are embarking on a reverse movement to recompose their social uni-

---

[4] Kirby, P., Gibbons, L., Cronin, M., "Introduction: The Reinvention of Ireland: A Critical Perspective" in *Reinventing Ireland*, Kirby, P., Gibbons, L., Cronin, M. (Eds.), Pluto Press, 2002.

[5] Puttnam, R., *Bowling Alone*, Simon & Schuster, New York, 2000.

verse".[6] The evidence of this "recomposition" is all around us, from the extraordinary mushrooming of informal reading clubs to groups of male golfers taking a week off together in Spain. The growth of tribal groups based on shared interests has been greatly facilitated by the internet which has the capacity to bring together people from all over the world based on even the most obscure and esoteric subjects.

At the same time, given the importance society attaches to family life, we are continually being urged to find the time to reconnect with family life. There are many categories of goods and services, from mobile phones to motor cars and from ready-to-eat meals to fast food restaurants, which can be positioned to provide answers to this "cultural contradiction".

Another area of potential backlash against the prevailing mood of individualism is the fact that although it is natural to want to maximise economic success, it is often the case in modern society that this can only be achieved at the expense of others and this goes against the old Irish spirit of *meitheal*, which has been defined as "a system of co-operative seasonal farm work involving reciprocal exchanges of labour and farm animals".[7] It is unlikely that a few decades of economic prosperity could wipe out an ideal that is deeply embedded in the Irish psyche and it has been argued that in spite of the current dominance of Hobbesian philosophy human beings have always acted altruistically: "Some instinctive degree of co-operation, empathy and altruism is part of human nature, built into our genetic code just as fear, anger or hair colour."[8]

---

[6] Cova, B. and C., "The Tribalisation of Society and its Impact on the Conduct of Marketing", *European Journal of Marketing*, January 2001.

[7] Millar, K.A., *Emigrants or Exiles*, Oxford University Press, 1985.

[8] Mazarr, ibid.

(3) Globalisation vs *Dinnseanchas*

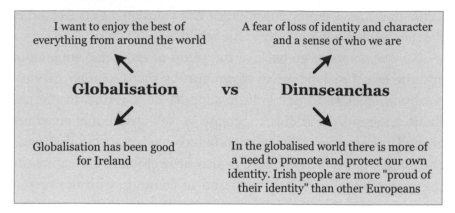

This is another "cultural contradiction" which is to be found in many European countries but is particularly acute in Ireland. There was always an intensely strong emotional loyalty to local counties, villages and even townlands in this country and Irish playwrights, Brian Friel in particular, have often used this attachment to dramatic effect. In Friel's *Philadelphia Here I Come!* this conflict is played out between the public and the private side of the central character, Gar, whose emotional attachment to the village of Ballybeg is in conflict his desire to escape its stultifying influence. In twenty-first-century Ireland there is a feeling that life is moving too fast, that we may be jettisoning too quickly tried and trusted ways of life that have served us well in the past. The classic illustration of this contradiction is the giant shopping centres that are positioned in strategic locations around Dublin like an invading army waiting to attack. "All the shops are the same ones that you see all over the world and you could be anywhere", the critics moan, and undoubtedly they have a point. But we have a real dilemma in trying to resolve this contradiction because we are acutely aware of the fact that of all the countries in the world we have probably benefited most from globalisation. Foreign firms and capital inflows have been largely responsible for the Irish economic boom. Foreign enterprises now dominate Irish manufacturing, accounting for almost

80 per cent of total production and 91 per cent of total exports.[9] The influential A.T. Kearney consultancy has calculated that Ireland is the most globalised economy in the world.[10]

No one wants to go back to the years of economic stagnation and the heartbreaking waves of emigration that was their inevitable by-product and there is little support for a return to the pathetic attempts of trying to create a self-sustaining economy around a protective tariff wall that failed so miserably in the 1930s and 1940s. Nevertheless, there is also little stomach for capitulating completely to a global mush and in common with the rest of Europe, especially the smaller countries, there are signs of an increasing attachment to local forms of identity. Hence the "contradiction", which is accentuated in Ireland by the strong "*dinnseanchas*" tradition which involves an intense attachment to the lore of the local:

> The ancient Irish form of *dinnseanchas* — by which a place's significance is communicated and sustained through the Gaelic place name and the myth, folklore and history associated with the place.[11]

It is now widely acknowledged that instead of diminishing people's attachment to nation states, globalisation may be having the opposite effect:

> The more evident our common needs become the more brutal becomes the human insistence on the claims of difference. The centripetal forces — of need, labour and science — which are pulling us together as a species are counter-

---

[9] Tansey, P., "Economic Briefing: 2004/2005", McConnells Advertising Publication, 2004.

[10] Fagan, G.H. "Globalised Ireland, or Contemporary Transformations of National Identity?" in *The End of Irish History?*, Coulter, C and Coleman, S. (eds.), Manchester University Press, 2003.

[11] John, B., *Reading the Ground: The Poetry of Thomas Kinsella*, Cura Press, 1996.

balanced by centrifugal forces, the claims of tribe, race, sect, region and nation pulling us apart.[12]

This "contradiction" does not mean that an appeal based on a "buy Irish" platform would be successful; Irish people will still want to buy the best from all over the world, but they will also want to attach themselves to goods and services that represent both excellence and Irishness. The GAA is the most notable beneficiary of this development. If you had predicted in the summer of 1995 that within a decade young people all over the country would be parading around towns, shopping centres, beaches, pubs and clubs wearing their county GAA shirts you would have been laughed at; but that is precisely what was happening by 2005. The extraordinary rise in the popularity, not to mention fashionability, of *gaelscoileanna* (there are even 6,000 references to them on Google) is further testament to the "human insistence on claims of difference":

> In an Irish context the increasing popularity of the Irish language during the 1990s can be identified as an affirmation of local identity in response to economic globalisation but also as an initiative to draw on the Irish linguistic and cultural past to situate people in the present.[13]

These developments have not gone unnoticed by the commercial world and a number of major advertisers including Guinness, AIB, Bank of Ireland and Vodafone, have been vying with each other in recent years to portray Gaelic football and hurling players as heroic warriors. The level of heroism has now become a little demented, but the advertising industry was never one to hide its hyperbolic light under a bushel. The most interesting brand involvement in this area is Club Energise's sponsorship of the Gaelic

---

[12] Ignatieff, M., quoted in *New World's Fissures*, Demos Publications (UK), 1994.

[13] Haahr, M., "The Art/Technology Interface: Innovation and Identity in Information-Age Ireland", *The Irish Review*, No. 31, Spring/Summer 2004, Cork University Press.

Players' Association. This was a slightly controversial move because there was an element of conflict between the players and the games' administrators and businesses are always loath to be associated with any form of controversy; but it has paid off handsomely for the Irish newcomer which has achieved a 20 per cent market share within three years, mainly at the expense of the multinational brand leader, Lucozade.

Of all of the "cultural contradictions" in modern Ireland, this probably represents the most interesting to exploit.

(4) Affluence vs Affluenza

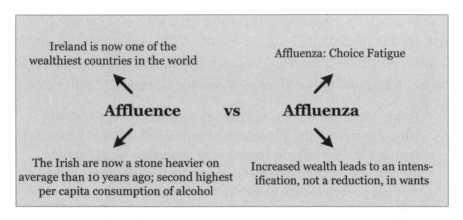

When an economy grows as fast in a very short space of time as the Irish economy has, it is almost inevitable that infrastructural developments will not be able to keep pace. It is therefore no coincidence that the major political debates in Ireland at present are about the real and perceived inadequacies of the transport system, the health service and educational standards. A number of the early chroniclers of Ireland's economic boom have also pointed out that the country moved to the right during the 1990s and that attitudes towards taxation have become "visceral"[14] and a recent

---

[14] O'Connell, M., *Changed Utterly: Ireland and the New Irish Psyche*, The Liffey Press, 2001.

survey comparing attitudes and values in different European countries showed that an astonishing 75 per cent of Irish adults believe that people who cheat on their tax returns were justified in doing so.[15] These tangible issues are well known and widely discussed. However, increased prosperity also led to the emergence of more abstract ailments already familiar in America and therefore equipped with the catchy titles that country does so well — "affluenza". This is a condition which has now spread to the rest of the developed world and has been defined as "a painful, contagious, virally transmitted condition of overload, debt, anxiety and waste resulting from the dogged pursuit of more".[16] It is a "condition" that nobody had any sympathy for when it arrived unannounced in Ireland in the late 1990s. It was also considered impolite to mention the fact that increased choice, increased wealth and increased material possessions came nowhere near to solving the eternal problems of the human race and that increased wealth would be more likely to lead to an intensification rather than a reduction of want. Of course, anyone who was still listening to the Catholic Church, or any church for that matter, would hardly be surprised to learn this fact.

Although this has became a very real "cultural contradiction" in Irish society, it is not immediately obvious how it can be exploited by brand owners. However, as with a number of these contradictions, the answer probably lies in some form of better balance and Aristotle's *Nicomachean Ethics*, which introduces his famous doctrine of "the golden mean", is a good starting point for predicting likely trends in the immediate future. This doctrine starts from the premise that we all want to be as happy as possible but that "unbridled self-indulgence and self-assertion will bring us into perpetual conflict with other people and in any case it is bad

---

[15] Loek, H., Luijkx, R., van Zundert, M., "Atlas of European Values Study", 2005.

[16] Hamilton, C. and Denniss, R., *Affluenza: When too Much is Never Enough*, Allen & Unwin (Sydney), 2005.

for our character. The golden mean is a virtue — a midway point between two extremes each of which is a vice; the aim is to be a balanced personality".[17] Products and services which can be legitimately positioned as helping to provide balance in people's lives could be very successful in future.

(5) Control vs Chaos

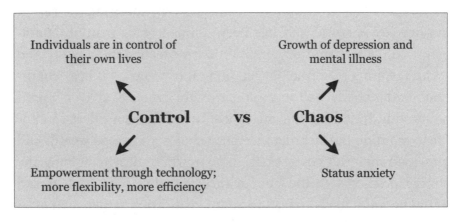

There are genuine practical benefits from the new electronic communication devices. They facilitate more flexible working arrangements which is an important benefit now that over half of all married women are working either full-time or part-time in the workforce. They also facilitate the setting up of small businesses which will probably have to play a greater role in the economy of the future; and by contributing to the "death of distance" they enable businesses in Ireland to compete better in world markets. From this perspective Ireland has benefited from the ITC revolution and this, combined with our excellent communication skills, has made the country an attractive location for overseas business investment. But as always there is a sting in the tail. The new technological marvels, especially the electronic devices, laptops, Blackberries and mobile phones, that enable us to keep in touch

---

[17] Magee, B., *The Story of Philosophy*, Dorling Kindersley, 1998.

24/7/365, are also capable of driving us crazy, sometimes literally. Although we are technically in control, all too often we feel at the mercy of random events and the fact that we are now equipped with a range of gadgets makes the subsequent let-down all the more disillusioning.

Comments about the "time poor, cash rich" society and the "doing better, feeling worse" syndrome are indicative of the disillusionment and a leading commentator on this issue, Professor Anthony Clare, has said that "what does emerge loud and clear and is reflected in the people I see clinically is that the often competing demands of work and home are very difficult to manage in today's Ireland".[18]

One of the effects of the rise in the levels of stress is the increasing numbers of people being treated for depression and seeking counselling and psychotherapy, which are now becoming acceptable and valuable forms of treatment. In a recent survey in the UK, appropriately titled "The Age of Therapy",[19] it was estimated that one in five adults had personally experienced some form of counselling. There are no comparable figures for Ireland but anecdotal evidence suggests that we may not be all that far behind.

Another cause of stress in modern Ireland is what has been referred to as "status anxiety", a phenomenon best expressed in Gore Vidal's famous assertion that "whenever a friend succeeds, a little something in me dies". Although Ireland's economic success has, with some exceptions, lifted all boats, it has lifted some very much more than others and therefore created as much frustration as satisfaction.

This "contradiction" should provide businesses in the telecoms and financial services sectors some fruitful avenues for brand positioning.

---

[18] Clare, Dr A., *Sunday Independent*, 2 July 2000.

[19] "The Age of Therapy", The Future Foundation (London), 2004.

(6) Conformity vs Creativity

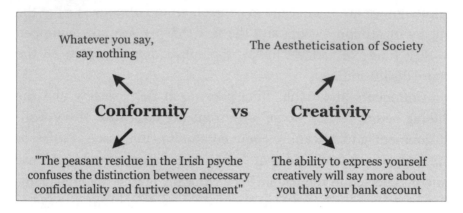

If the downside of the move to a more individualistic society is materialism and a lack of civic spirit, the upside is greater self-confidence and a willingness to express our thoughts and feelings more openly. Ever since the famine Irish society has been characterised by an unhealthy degree of furtiveness. This was neatly summarised by Professor Joe Lee in his study of the Irish twentieth-century experience: "The peasant residue in the Irish psyche confuses the distinction between necessary confidentiality and furtive concealment."[20]

However, a degree of economic prosperity, whatever unpleasant side effects it may bring in its train, works wonders for self-confidence. An early sign of this was the marked improvement in the standard of architecture in cities and towns all over the country, accompanied by an increase in visual literacy by a generation weaned on a diet of TV imagery. In spite of constant references to a "dumbing-down" of society a more convincing case could be made for the opposite argument. As more people reach the higher levels of Maslow's famous hierarchy, the urge to see one's own story in print, to hear one's own music and song being aired and to

[20] Lee, J., *Ireland 1912-1985: Politics and Society*, Cambridge University Press, 1989.

be the curator of one's own life becomes stronger and there has been an outpouring of artistic expression in Ireland during the last few decades.

There was always a strong musical tradition in the country but it was the arrival of two unlikely and completely dissimilar individuals in Dublin in the late 1950s that first sparked a new creative revival. Bill Haley's explosive concerts in the Theatre Royal liberated an entire generation bored to distraction by the endless replays of the civil war among a tired clique of ageing politicians and stifled by the grim authoritarianism of an all-powerful Catholic Church. Rock 'n' roll came to the rescue and suddenly everyone between the age of 15 and 20 wanted to be in a band. Around the same time, a brooding figure from Cork arrived in Dublin determined to show that the bands did not have to be a pale imitation of what was happening anywhere else in the world. Seán Ó Riada resurrected an ancient musical tradition and wove it into a modern shape and the results, from the Chieftains to U2, from Thin Lizzy to The Corrs, did more to raise national self-confidence and make Ireland famous around the world than the actions of all of the country's politicians put together.

There was also a huge increase in literary output with Irish poets, novelists and playwrights succeeding on the world stage culminating in Seamus Heaney's Nobel Prize in 1995. In spite of some wry comments about Ireland's standing army of poets, the ubiquity of well-known published writers in cities and towns all over the country encouraged widespread artistic expression.

New technology also played a part. Printers can now print books cheaply in small print runs. Alternatively you can publish electronically using either your own website or one of the many blog sites. Computer-aided creativity is now not just the preserve of the big film studios and soon it will be possible to make high-quality films in your own home. Music will also benefit from new technology. Up to now, if you wanted to record a work of orchestral music you had to gather a group of musicians together; now you can "play" a computer to programme all the other instruments while you play your own.

There are many opportunities for brands to capitalise on this trend, which is probably more of a prediction than a contradiction.

INDEX